THE WAY
FORWARD

THE WAY FORWARD

Renewing the American Idea

Paul Ryan

TWELVE

New York   Boston

Twelve
Hachette Book Group
1290 Avenue of the Americas
New York, NY 10104

www.HachetteBookGroup.com

Printed in the United States of America

RRD-C

Originally published in hardcover by Hachette Book Group.

First trade edition: August 2015

10 9 8 7 6 5 4 3 2 1

Twelve is an imprint of Grand Central Publishing.
The Twelve name and logo are trademarks of Hachette Book Group, Inc.

The Hachette Speakers Bureau provides a wide range of authors for speaking events. To find out more, go to www.hachettespeakersbureau.com or call (866) 376-6591.

The publisher is not responsible for websites (or their content)
that are not owned by the publisher.

Library of Congress Cataloging-in-Publication Data

Ryan, Paul, 1970–
The way forward : renewing the American idea / Paul Ryan.
    pages cm
  Includes bibliographical references and index.
  ISBN 978-1-4555-5756-1 (hardback) — ISBN 978-1-4789-2776-1 (audio book) —
ISBN 978-1-4789-2777-8 (audio download)   1. United States—Politics and
government—2009–   2. Conservatism—United States.   3. Republican Party
(U.S. : 1854–)   4. Presidents—United States—Election—2012.   I. Title.
  E907.R93 2014
  320.97309'05—dc23

2014020847

ISBN 978-1-4555-5757-8 (pbk.)

For Janna, Liza, Charlie, and Sam

and

In Memory of Paul M. Ryan and Prudence M. Little

Contents

Introduction

I should probably explain at the outset that I never expected to write a book—and that's just one in a long list of experiences I never imagined I'd have.

I didn't expect to work in Washington, D.C., for very long, or to find that work so compelling that I'd come to view public policy as a worthy vocation.

I never thought I'd run for Congress, and when I embarked on my first campaign—at just twenty-eight years old—I didn't think I would likely win.

And I certainly never thought that I'd become the GOP vice presidential nominee.

And yet it's these unexpected moments that have provided the best opportunities to work on the issues I care about: economic growth, saving Medicare and Social Security, fixing our broken health-care system, and passing on to the next generation a nation that is secure and debt-free.

These are the kinds of challenges that ideally would bring out the best in both parties. After all, such concerns aren't the exclusive domain of liberals or conservatives—and there's common ground to be found. Yet nearly two years have passed since our last presidential election, and we still find ourselves moving in the wrong direction. We've doubled down on a lot of the programs and policies that got us off course in the first place.

And the true price of this state of affairs is the erosion of the American Idea—a way of life made possible by our commitment to the principles of freedom and equality and rooted in our respect for every person's natural rights.

When we speak about America as being exceptional, this is—in part—what we mean. And when people talk about our country being on the wrong track, this is what's at stake.

Of course, these days it's not talk about our problems that is in short supply. What's missing is fresh thinking, good solutions, and real leadership.

In this moment, we're framing up America for the twenty-first century. The questions before us are: How do we preserve the American Idea for the next generation? How do we ensure this experiment in liberty endures? And finding the answers to those questions starts with an honest debate about the different paths before us—and the choices we have to make.

One path—the course that liberal progressivism is offering—is a government-centered approach. Along this path, the federal government continues to expand, attempting to meet our every need with outdated policies that put the state at the center of our lives. It leads to a future in which America's best century is the last century. It's a future in which the American Idea is in serious jeopardy.

The second path puts society, not government, at the center of American life. Through a restoration of our founding principles, it expands freedom and fosters risk-taking, ingenuity, and creativity. Instead of growing government, it grows the economy—offering greater opportunity and prosperity for all. Along this path, government provides the necessary support rather than taking on the commanding role.

Mapping this path has been the focus of much of my work in Congress. Of course, my hope wasn't that I'd be writing about these ideas; I thought I'd be helping implement them as part of a Romney administration.

But it didn't take long for me to realize that while we may have lost an election, the cause continues. And those of us who are privileged to serve in public office have a duty to offer our fellow citizens a real and meaningful choice about the way forward. This book is my contribution to that conversation.

* * *

When I sat down to write, I had two questions in front of me. The first was, *How did we get here?* That question guides part I of this book.

It traces my own journey, which runs through Janesville, Wisconsin, where I grew up and first learned about the American Idea. And it discusses how, as a country, we slid further away from that idea, first because Republicans failed to stay true to our principles, and then because of the liberal progressive agenda that President Obama has pursued.

While part I of this book includes my recollections of people and events over the years, this is not an exhaustive memoir; where those things exist it is simply to explain my thinking—and what was happening from my viewpoint at the time. It is also not intended to be a comprehensive history. The events and conversations discussed are described as I remember them, and if I have made misstatements, it is not a product of ill intent but simply the limits of memory contending with the passage of time.

In writing this book, the other question I considered was, *Where do we go from here?* Part II of this book answers that question, first by looking at what liberal progressivism is offering and the vision that conservatism can deliver.

I believe the conservative vision can appeal to the majority of our fellow citizens. It offers a way of life that consists of a dynamic economy, a thriving civil society, and a government that protects our rights while offering a real safety net for those in need without overpowering the private economy and the private lives of citizens. And while the best vehicle for conservative thought and policies is the Republican Party, the GOP faces serious challenges that, in recent years, have led to critical losses at the polls.

Part II tackles this issue as well, describing the Republican Party's current vulnerabilities. Among them, the caricature of the party that the Left has promoted—and the ways in which the GOP itself has played into that caricature instead of disproving it.

In these pages, I attempt to offer some ideas about how the party can overcome this challenge and others—and reach out to Americans from every walk of life.

While it's true that our country's current problems are urgent and real, I don't view them as insurmountable. When I visit our big cities and our small-town communities, I see our untapped potential—and the signs of a great American comeback in the making. And I know if we make the right decision—if we choose the path that restores our founding principles and puts society, not government, at the center of American life—then we can renew the American Idea.

The time is right, the need is urgent, and I know we can find the way forward.

Paul Ryan
May 2014

PART ONE

How We Got Here

CHAPTER 1

A Tale of Two Cities

When the day finally came, I changed out of my suit, threw on a camouflage hat and shirt, and slipped out the back. In hindsight, I probably could have done without the camo. It was broad daylight, and I was surrounded by neighbors I'd known my whole life—and media trackers who had spent three weeks reporting my every move. Any one of them could easily have spotted me.

It was August 2012, and the press was eager for any indication that Mitt Romney had picked his running mate. Reporters from ABC and NBC camped out in my front yard, trying to figure out if I was missing so they could report that an announcement was coming.

Frankly, my wife, Janna, and I thought that anyone looking for breaking news on our lawn in Janesville that summer was going to be disappointed. In the days leading up to the Wisconsin primary on April 3, Mitt Romney and I had crisscrossed the state campaigning. We grabbed food at Culver's in Johnson Creek. I introduced him to my cousin at Schreiner's Restaurant in Fond du Lac. We visited with phone bank volunteers in Fitchburg. Along the way, we got to know one another. We talked about faith—my Catholicism, his Mormonism. We shared stories about our kids. We had long discussions about economics and what his initial legislative push would look like if he were elected president. We discussed what his first budget proposal would include and which tax and entitlement reforms he would advance to help get the economy growing and our debt under control.

By the time we'd wrapped up our trip, I thought Mitt Romney would make an outstanding president, but I did not think I'd be his choice for a running mate.

For starters, word had it that the "short list" was pretty long and included a lot of first-rate names: Chris Christie, Tim Pawlenty, Kelly Ayotte, Marco Rubio, Condoleezza Rice, Rob Portman, and John Thune.

Then, there was the matter of my work as chairman of the House Budget Committee. I was—and am—proud of the budget proposals we produced, but they contained the kind of specifics that can be easily mischaracterized in the rough-and-tumble, sound-bite atmosphere of a presidential campaign. There were also the changes I'd proposed to shore up Social Security and Medicare. If Mitt added me to the ticket, he would own them and have to defend them, too. I wasn't sure that was something he or his strategists would want to do.

So I was a bit surprised when, several weeks after our Wisconsin trip, Mitt called.

"We've got a list of people we're considering for the VP position on the ticket," Mitt explained. "I'm calling because I am hoping that you and Janna will consider going through the vetting process with us."

"It's really an honor to be considered," I said. "I'd have to talk with Janna about it, but we're definitely interested."

"Great," said Mitt. "You two talk. In the meantime, Beth Myers from our team will send over the form that you need to fill out."

The form turned out to be a very, very long questionnaire. The day it arrived, Janna and I spent a Sunday afternoon poring through it all. We flipped through page after page of inquiries into taxes, finances, policy positions, and drug use. There were dozens of questions. When all was said and done, it would take one month of work and five full notebooks to answer all of them.

I turned to Janna and said, "You realize that if we do this and Mitt asks us to join the ticket, we have to say yes. The way I see it, we're pretty much making the decision now, so we have to be right with it."

Janna nodded. "That's right. I don't think there's any turning back once we fill this out," she said. "If we send this back to them, we'll have to be all in, but I doubt we're going to get picked. You're the guy with all the spending cuts and policy specifics, and *that* guy never gets picked."

We spent a long time talking things through. For us, the whole decision really came down to two questions: What could a Romney presidency mean for the country? And what would this decision mean for our family?

For years, I'd been working on issues I really cared about—retirement security, health-care reform, and a debt-free future. I'd long hoped the policy proposals my colleagues and I had been advancing in the House might be championed by the GOP nominee—a goal that had new urgency given a sluggish economic recovery and high unemployment rate. Joining the ticket exceeded even those aspirations; it could make our proposals some of the guiding documents in a Republican presidency. When Janna and I looked at the decision that way, it seemed like an amazing opportunity.

The campaign would also change our family life. Almost every week, I left our home in Janesville and boarded a plane for Washington, D.C., while Janna and the kids started their routine of school, sports practices, and homework. At night, I'd talk on the phone with them before crashing on a cot in my office. Typically, I'd be back in the district in time for the weekend, but if things were busy and the House stayed in session, I might have only a twenty-four-hour window to spend with Janna, Liza, Charlie, and Sam. As we discussed how this decision could affect our children, I remembered something George W. Bush once told me: *Life in the White House is actually pretty nice for a family.* Compared to Congress, we'd actually see each other more. Living in the vice president's residence would mean we'd be under the same roof seven days a week.

So we filled out the questionnaire, and then we tried not to get our hopes up. Our family calendar was a testament to just how slim we thought the chances were that I'd be spending the rest of the year visiting battleground states. The dates were filled with reelection rallies, a family backpacking trip, and an annual bow-hunting outing with my brother-in-law, Mark.

There were even plans for a consolation prize: a wood pellet smoker I'd seen at the Janesville Ace Hardware store earlier in the summer. I told Janna I had my eye on that smoker. "Okay," she said, smiling. "Then let's make a deal. *When* Mitt Romney does not pick you to be his running mate, I'll let you buy it." That was how we thought about it: We were sure being bumped off the short list was a matter of *when*, not *if*. In my mind, I was already making plans for weekends spent hunting and smoking venison bratwurst and summer sausage.

Then, early on a Sunday morning in late July, I got an e-mail from Beth Myers, the senior aide who had been Mitt's chief of staff when he was governor of Massachusetts and was now running the search process for him. She asked to speak with me later in the day. I was pretty sure I knew what was coming. I drove home from a taping for *Face the Nation* and picked up Janna and the kids for church. "We're getting closure," I told her. "I'm getting the thanks-but-no-thanks call today."

When Beth and I connected later, I was prepared to accept the news gracefully. Instead, she said, "It's become a very, very short list. We need you to fill out another questionnaire. And we need it back by the end of the day." The last one had taken a lawyer, an accountant, and several weeks to put together. Would I be able to finish this one that quickly? Yes, she assured me. This one would be easy.

When I got the e-mail, there were a lot of odd questions: What's your neck size? What's your shirt size? Would you rather travel from one town to the next late at night or make the trip early the next day? What do you eat for breakfast?

I showed the questionnaire to Janna. She looked at me and said, "Holy cow. This could actually happen."

Not long after we returned the form, Mitt called and invited me to a meeting at Beth's house in Brookline, Massachusetts, a suburb outside of Boston. My good friend and chief of staff, Andy Speth, drove me down to Chicago a couple of days later and checked me into a hotel at O'Hare under his name. The next morning I took the first flight into Hartford, Connecticut, where Beth's nineteen-year-old son, Curt, picked me up and then drove me to the Myers family home. I actually spent the last stretch of the drive under a blanket in the backseat of the car. I was told not to emerge until we pulled into the garage and closed the door.

The day before, I had asked Beth if any other potential running mates had been invited to a similar meeting, if this was a final interview of sorts. She replied, "Nope, you're the only one—unless, of course, you screw this up."

Once I got inside the house, Beth welcomed me with a nice lunch while we waited for Mitt. Then, when he arrived, Beth left, and Mitt and I sat together at her dining room table. He thanked me for making the trip.

"It's important to me that you understand why I'm running for president," Mitt said. "I'm deeply worried about the country. I look at all of our challenges and I see President Barack Obama taking us in the wrong direction. I'm afraid that if we don't change course now, we're going to put all of these burdens—the debt, the deficit, a stagnant economy—on our kids and grandkids. We could lose the country."

"That's what motivates me, too," I said. "And it's why the last few years have been really frustrating. For a while, I had hope that we might be able to get something bipartisan done at least on the fiscal side of things. I feel a great sense of urgency about that, but it's going to take more than a Republican majority in the House. We need a president who will work with us and make the debt and the economy a priority."

Mitt nodded. "Well, that's why I'm running. The question I've got in front of me right now is who is in the best position to help me—not just to win this election but to govern if we win. I've read the things you've written, what you've said. My team made sure I had all the information I needed to think about this decision from every angle."

"Speaking from the other side of the process," I said, "I assure you it's definitely been thorough."

"Look, my own view is that it comes down to this: You know how Congress works, and you've shown that you know how to get things done there. I want to fix our economic problems and turn the country around, but I'm going to need help. I know how to manage large organizations. I know business and I understand economics. You know Congress and the budget and how to navigate Washington, D.C. We complement each other. So I'm asking for your help with this. Will you join me on the ticket?"

I shook his hand and said, "Let's get this done."

*   *   *

Within a week, I was slipping out the back door of our house in Janesville in my hunting camo. The campaign's insistence that everything be kept under wraps meant the number of people who knew what I was up to could be tallied on two hands. My kids didn't even know the news yet. The whole thing felt surreal.

The house that we live in now is on the same block and about a hundred yards from where I grew up. So, as I snuck across our backyard, I made my way into the woods where I had spent afternoons and weekends playing as a kid. After more than a week in uncharted waters, it felt good to be in a familiar spot. I could see the place where my friends and I had played capture the flag. I crawled over part of the tree fort that I had built with my buddy Tom Thorpe. Out ahead of me was my childhood home. It was the first moment I'd really had to myself since the meeting with Mitt.

There, in the quiet of the woods where I grew up, the reality of what was about to happen hit me. I thought about our kids. Janna and I had made a conscious decision to join the ticket, but they had not. They didn't even know what was coming. Would they be ready? Would this change be good for them?

I also thought about the gravity of the moment and what the election could mean for our country—both if we won and if we lost. I said a silent prayer that I'd be up to the challenge, that I'd be worthy of the faith so many people had placed in me, that I'd make the most of this chance. Then I called Andy Speth and told him I was ready to go.

Minutes later, Andy's wife, Katy, appeared on the street a few yards away, driving the Speth family Chevy Express van. I jogged out of the woods, alongside my parents' old house, down the driveway where I learned how to ride a bike, and jumped in. Andy, Janna, Liza, Charlie, and Sam were waiting there, huddled in the backseat with the blinds closed. Together, we drove through the streets of Janesville, past the homes of friends and neighbors and family members. We didn't stop until we reached a small airport in Waukegan, Illinois.

Back at our house, my sister-in-law, Dana, did her best to make it look like another regular night at the Ryans' was well under way. She turned on all the lights, let our dogs out into the backyard and brought them back in again, and kept the volume up on the TV. Then, at bedtime, she shut the place down.

Later Dana told us how she watched from our living room as Alex Moe, a nice young woman who had been our NBC tracker for several weeks, made her way to the front door of our house. She knocked, hoping for comment on the campaign's announcement that their VP pick would officially join Mitt on the deck of the USS *Wisconsin* the following day. No one answered, but Alex didn't go away completely empty-handed; our neighbor Marcia Nelesen came over and offered her a beer.

By midnight, the crawl on MSNBC announced "NBC News: Sources say Rep. Paul Ryan is Romney's vice presidential pick." Everyone kept reporting, "We hear it's Ryan," and Alex tried to explain to Chuck Todd that there was nothing going on at our house. As Chuck sat behind the anchor desk back at MSNBC headquarters, Alex stood on our front lawn and said, "We do believe Congressman Ryan and his wife and his three children are inside." Meanwhile, our plane had already touched down in Elizabeth City, North Carolina.

The flight down was an emotional trip. Big secrets among kids often become rumors among neighbors in a small town, ricocheting back and forth and up and down the street. We'd decided it would be best to wait and tell Liza, Charlie, and Sam when we were on the plane. By the time we were in the air, our kids thought that Janna and I had lost our minds. In the span of an afternoon, they had been rushed out the back door of our house only to spend three hours waiting in the Speths' living room. Then they sat huddled in the backseat of a van as they watched their dad come running out of the woods. There were a lot of questions.

All along, Janna and I had been worried about how our children would take the news. Waiting to tell them had seemed like a good idea—not just for the sake of secrecy, but also for their peace of mind. We thought it would be easier to digest everything as it was happening instead of trying to envision it in the abstract. But as the moment to tell them finally arrived, Janna and I thought that maybe we'd made a mistake. We'd had time to get comfortable with the idea of a campaign and what it could mean. Maybe all of this was too much to spring on them at once.

Liza, then ten, had already started to put the pieces together. Naturally gregarious and adventurous, she was eager to get the details about our impromptu trip. At eight years old, Charlie was a little more quiet and shy. He and our youngest, normally happy-go-lucky seven-year-old Sam, were openly confused and a little unsettled by the day's events.

As we prepared to take off, the questions kept coming. *What is this plane? Where are we going?*

When we got in the air, Janna and I gathered them around.

"You know how I've been talking with Mitt Romney?" I asked. "Well, he's asked me to join him on the ticket for vice president. We're flying down to make the announcement."

"Oh my gosh!" said Liza. "We're going there right now?"

"Yeah," I said. "We're flying to North Carolina now, and then we're going to drive to Virginia tomorrow, where we'll do a big rally to make the announcement. Isn't that great?"

Liza nodded enthusiastically.

"When is the election?" Sam asked.

"It's going to be in November," I replied.

Then Charlie put it all together. "Wait a second," he said. "Dad, does this mean we have to leave Janesville?"

Janna and I looked at each other and exchanged a nervous glance. "Well, if we win, yeah. It does," I explained. "We'd have to leave for four or eight years."

And then came the tears. It wasn't totally unexpected, but for me as a dad, it was hard.

Charlie's first concerns were about switching schools. "What about Saint John's? What about my friends?" he asked. "I can't leave Janesville. Dad, we don't *want* to leave Janesville."

Sam started to get upset, too. "We're leaving our house? Why are we leaving our house? What about my friend Carter? What about my teacher?"

Janna and I tried comforting them with assurances that friends could visit and there would be great teachers at a new school. Janna put her arm around Charlie. "This is a big deal for Dad, for all of us," she said. "Our family is going to get to do something that can help the country and all of our friends back home."

It was no use. The mood on the plane had shifted from excitement to a sense of loss and worry.

"Guys, I know this is hard," I said. "If we win, you're right—a lot of things are going to change, and some of those changes will be difficult. But some of them are going to be for the better. We'll all be together under the same roof during the week. We can eat dinner together every night."

Finally, in a desperate effort to console them, I added, "Plus, if we win, the place we get to live in has a pool."

That stopped Sam in his tracks. "We get to move to a place with a pool?"

"Yes."

"Wow," Sam said, mulling it over. "Well, that's pretty cool. I could probably move if it meant we were going to have a pool."

Sam was quick to come around, and Liza was old enough to see the bigger picture. For Charlie, it took about a month longer.

I knew how he felt. Having lived in Janesville for thirty-eight of my forty-two years, part of me didn't want to leave, either. Janesville was more than just my home or where I grew up. Our town shaped my values and my worldview. It taught me about the importance of family and the meaning of community. It was where I witnessed firsthand the kinds of life stories that are possible only in our country, and where I came to understand that with our rights and opportunities comes a responsibility to pass along a better country to our kids and grandkids. For me, Janesville was—and is—the embodiment of the American Idea.

* * *

The American Idea is a way of life made possible by our commitment to the principles of freedom and equality—and rooted in our respect for every person's natural rights. It's the kind of life Janesville's first residents were seeking when they settled our town in 1835—not long before one of my ancestors, an Irish peasant named James Ryan, arrived on the scene.

In 1851, six years into the Irish potato famine, James got on a ship bound for America. Like hundreds of thousands of his fellow countrymen and -women, James made his way across the Atlantic Ocean. Signs posted throughout the boat tried to prepare them for the challenges they would face when starting over in the New World. A good friend of mine who's into Irish history recently sent me a copy of one such sign. It reads:

> Advice to Irish Emigrants: In the United States, labor is there the first condition of life, and industry is the lot of all men. Wealth is not idolized; but there is no degradation connected with labor; on the contrary, it is honorable, and held in general estimation.
>
> In the remote parts of America, an industrious youth may follow any occupation without being looked down upon or sustain loss of character, and he may rationally expect to raise himself in the world by his labor.

In America, a man's success must altogether rest with himself—it will depend on his industry, sobriety, diligence and virtue.

For a man like James Ryan, this would have been welcome news. Having suffered through years of setbacks brought on by famine and fever in his homeland, he was ready to prove himself and make his mark.

My great-great-grandfather purportedly arrived in Boston and then worked the railroad westward until he earned enough money to buy a farm. As luck would have it, he reached his goal just as he arrived in south central Wisconsin. It was summertime, and in the rolling hills, green grass, cornfields, and faces of his fellow Irish, he saw great possibilities.

According to family lore, James thought, *This kind of looks like Ireland.* Of course, then came the winter and I imagine he must have said, "Oh crap!" But he made a go of it, and my family has been in Janesville ever since, five generations now.

Over the years, the Ryan family got bigger…and bigger. My brother Tobin and I once stayed up late into the night and tried to count up all the cousins we have in town. We stopped at sixty-seven. There are eight Ryan households within six blocks of where I live now. My aunt Dinty and uncle Don (who is actually my first cousin once removed, but we call him our "uncle" because it's shorter and because he's an avuncular sort of guy) live across the street. My cousin Pat is right next door. My brother Tobin is two blocks away.

My family's story is no different from the history of so many in Janesville. The Campbells, the Cullens, the Kennedys, the O'Learys, the Fitzgeralds, the Sheridans, the Murphys, and the Fagans—the list goes on and on, and most of their family trees look a lot like mine: plenty of branches and deep roots in our town.

The early Ryans played a modest role in Janesville's growth. My great-grandfather P. W. Ryan and his wife, Mariah Murphy, started an earth-moving business that my cousin, Adam, still runs today. However, it was a pen company founded by local resident George Parker that first put our town on the map.

Parker Pens were sold across the country and around the world. The company also had strong ties to the United States military. During World War I, American soldiers used George's "trench pen" out in the field. At the end of World War II, General Douglas MacArthur signed the Japanese surrender papers with a Parker Duofold pen. Two of General Dwight Eisenhower's "Parker 51s" authorized the German Armistice. Later, a beaming Eisenhower would pose for photographers, holding two Parker pens in a "V" for victory.

By 1918, George and his sons had turned their family business into an international powerhouse with over $1 million in sales. For decades, their factory was one of our town's largest employers. But by far, it was General Motors that had the greatest impact on Janesville's economy.

During World War I, Billy Durant, the cofounder of GM, was looking for a way to get into the tractor business so he could better compete with Henry Ford. He bought the Samson Tractor Company in Stockton, California, merged it with the Janesville Machine Company, and set up shop in town. The plant churned out the Samson Model M tractor and the smaller "Iron Horse."

When the war ended, so did the tractor boom, but the auto industry was on the rise. Durant liquidated Samson Tractor and converted the Janesville plant into a factory that could produce cars. On Valentine's Day in 1923, the first Chevrolet built there rolled off the lines. By April 1967, the Janesville GM plant had built 6 million cars and trucks. By 1978, the plant employed 7,100 people directly and countless more indirectly. Up and down the streets, storefronts popped up around the plant. They housed manufacturers that supplied auto parts, restaurants that fed the GM workers, and the small businesses where everyone shopped.

By the 1970s, over forty-six thousand people lived in Janesville, including me and my parents and three siblings. My father, Paul Murray Ryan, was fourth-generation Janesville, the youngest of two kids born to Stanley and Edith McCarty Ryan. He spent his early childhood in the historic Fourth Ward, where descendants of the original Irish immigrants lived. They told stories about humble beginnings and meager livings scratched out in places where people looked down upon the Irish.

A soft-spoken and kind man, my father followed in his own father's footsteps and studied the law. To pay for tuition and books, my dad worked at the local GM plant. I can still remember the pale white, bumpy scar that ran across his finger in the spot where the doctor had reattached the tip after it was accidentally cut off on the job. He didn't seem to think much of that scar, but for me it was a reminder that anything worth achieving required sacrifice.

Not long after he finished law school, my father met my mom. My dad was immediately captivated by the smart, beautiful, and capable Elizabeth "Betty" Hutter. In 1956, a time when comparatively few women pursued the hard sciences, my mom earned a degree in medical technology. After graduation, she took a job in Milwaukee with a doctor who was doing research in blood genetics. She helped him gather data and conduct experiments.

One weekend, my mom traveled to Janesville for a wedding. Her boyfriend at the time was out of the country on business. Eager to be a good host, the father of the bride asked his friend, a small-town lawyer, to escort her to the party following the rehearsal dinner. The lawyer was my dad, and they were married less than a year later.

My parents lived in my dad's hometown. Years earlier, my

grandfather had died at age fifty-seven. My father was just three months away from graduating from law school, and once he finished his studies, he had dedicated his career to the family law practice.

By the time I was born in 1970 at Mercy Hospital on a cold January day, the Ryan household was already a pretty busy place. My older sister, Janet, was nine years old. It was no secret that she was hoping my mom would have a girl; for far too long, she had been outnumbered by our brothers Stan, then eight, and Tobin, five. When I showed up, Janet was less than pleased. My parents, on the other hand, were delighted. My mom used to call me their "bonus" child, an extra and unexpected arrival that rounded out her brood to an even four.

We lived in an area known as Courthouse Hill at 216 South Garfield Avenue. Along our block, modest Colonial-style homes with facades of brick and siding sat in well-kept rows. Doctors, lawyers, and business owners lived on the same streets as pipefitters, GM workers, and teachers.

The appeal of Janesville has always been that it's a tight-knit community where people can support their families, make their own opportunities, and know the dignity of a solid day's work. Growing up, no one ever really talked about money or class. It was generally assumed that everyone fell into one of two categories: "middle class" or "would be soon."

People really didn't care much about what you did for a living or how much money you made; they were much more interested in what kind of person you were. What bonded Janesville was a shared set of values. We were encouraged to meet our potential. There was an emphasis on personal responsibility and accountability. And as a kid, if you did something wrong, somebody would make sure your mom heard about it. I know that from experience.

Wisconsin winters are freezing cold with temperatures that

regularly dip below zero and big storms that bring deep snowfalls. After school, I could always find a few kids willing to bundle up in mittens, hats, and multiple layers and walk around the neighborhood. We'd build huge snow forts and throw snowballs at each other. If the day dragged on a little too long, someone would inevitably get the idea that we should try to hit passing cars with our icy weaponry. For the most part, people just kept on going, but every once in a while, we'd hit a car and the driver would slam on the brakes. The minute we saw the bright red glow of taillights, we'd hightail it out of there, stopping only when our lungs hurt from sucking down too much cold air. Then we'd look around and, seeing no adults, figure we'd made a clean escape. And nearly every time, I'd come home to an angry Betty Ryan who had just gotten off the phone with a neighbor who tipped her off, reminding me that my mom had eyes and ears everywhere.

It made it hard to pull childhood pranks, but all the kids in the neighborhood were better off with everyone keeping an eye on us. Consequences were part of how people showed they loved you; they cared what kind of lessons you learned, because they cared about what kind of person you were going to be. This all might sound a little too *Leave It to Beaver*, and I am sure being a kid meant all of the adult concerns and hardships around me didn't completely register. But for me, Janesville was—and is—a kind, close-knit community where people looked out for one another.

Of course, even without the watchful eyes of neighbors, I wouldn't have been able to get in much trouble; the nuns at St. Mary School would make sure of that. The school was part of the second oldest Catholic parish in Janesville, Nativity of Mary, which was established in 1876. It was housed in a large, red brick building with two doors at one corner and, above them, banners carved out of stone. One banner read FOR GOD, the other FOR COUNTRY. Every morning, my friends and I would file in beneath those words on our way to class. There were about thirty kids per grade, spanning kindergarten through middle school.

My brother Tobin was five years ahead of me at St. Mary, and to my delight, he and his friends didn't seem to mind much when I tagged along. When I was eight, they let me be the "manager" of their basketball team. It mostly involved chasing down stray rebounds, but I got to go to every practice and every game.

Between Monday and Friday, the nuns at St. Mary taught us our multiplication tables, our vocabulary words, and our prayers. On Sundays in the fall, I spent my mornings there as an altar boy, but my afternoons were reserved for green and gold.

The Packers games were something I looked forward to all week. Our family was like all others—we would put on Packers gear and huddle around the TV to talk strategy and watch the game. At larger gatherings, there were cookouts at halftime with sizable spreads of cheese, bratwurst, Pabst Blue Ribbon, and Miller. A lot of guys who warmed themselves around the grill had been on the Packer season-ticket waiting list for most of their lives.

Like most kids in Janesville, I was raised on the Packers, Badgers, Bucks, and Brewers. But we got WGN, the television station that broadcast from Chicago, so I also ended up watching the Cubs games. It pains me to admit it, but even now I find myself rooting for the perennial losers from the North Side.

While I liked watching sports, what I enjoyed most was being outside. I liked to fish, hike, and play in the woods. And, like most kids, I spent the entire school year looking forward to summer.

We didn't take fancy or expensive vacations; instead, we'd pack up the car for a couple of weeks in July or August and hit the road. My mom loved the outdoors, and she would always plan a trip to the national forests in Colorado. We'd spend a week backpacking, rafting, mountain climbing, and fishing. My siblings and I learned a lot about self-sufficiency on those excursions into the wilderness.

Tobin likes to tell the story about the time we trekked up an especially challenging Colorado mountain during a summer snowstorm. When we finally got up top, the view was something right out of a postcard—a vast openness with a lake and sheep-filled meadow below. I was around seven years old, and apparently I just started singing "America the Beautiful," spontaneously and off-key. Tobin always got a big kick out of that.

But what I remember best about those trips was my mom's can-do spirit. My dad wasn't a huge fan of camping or the outdoors, so he wasn't exactly disappointed when work commitments kept him from our Colorado excursions. Even without backup, my mom never gave a second thought to packing up the kids and hitting the trail. My dad would drop us off at the edge of the woods—four kids, rations for a few nights, and camping gear—and my mom would throw on her backpack and say, "Off we go!" Then she'd lead us down the trail and into the backcountry of Colorado.

Now that I'm a parent, I can see that my mom was trying to instill in us a sense of resilience and self-reliance by teaching us how to find our way through the wilderness, catch and cook our own food, and start a fire. But what was even more powerful was her example. I spent my childhood thinking nothing could stop her, and her love of nature and adventure was infectious.

For my dad, traveling was a way to teach us about the world beyond Janesville—and to satisfy his amusing and all-consuming interest in coin collecting. He liked to take us wherever the annual summer show of the American Numismatic Association (ANA) was being held. During the trip, we'd stop off to see a local attraction or visit a big city. I got to see a lot of the country that way.

In 1982, when the ANA met in Boston, my parents planned out a road trip that took us through Michigan. My aunt Ellen was an administrative assistant with the Oscar Mayer Company in Madison, Wisconsin, and she had gotten my older brother Stan a summer job at the company's office in Livonia, Michigan, outside of Detroit. The plan was to visit Stan and then see a little bit of the Motor City before we got on our way.

Whenever we took our road trips, my dad really wanted us to experience places that were different from where we lived—even if all we had time to do was look out the car window. I can still remember him driving us slowly through towns and cities, saying, "Okay, everybody, *absorb*." It was his way of marking the moment when we should quiet down, look around, and soak it all in.

We spent only an afternoon in Detroit, but I absorbed quite a bit. I was just twelve years old, and coming from a small town, just being in a big city was pretty exciting for me. I remember staring up at Hudson's Department Store, which stretched twenty-nine floors into the sky. My dad talked a little bit about Detroit's history as he drove. He explained that it was the birthplace of the American auto industry, a fact that hit home with me since there was a GM factory in our town.

By the time we visited Detroit, the glory days of its postwar peak in population and prosperity had already passed. The middle class had pulled up stakes and moved elsewhere while gangs, crime, and the drug trade had moved in.

All that mattered a lot if you lived in Detroit, but for a tourist who kept on the beaten path, those forces simmered out of view. In many ways, to the casual observer Detroit was still the dynamic city that had been part of FDR's arsenal of democracy, turning auto factories into wartime facilities that cranked out the tanks, airplane parts and engines, and vehicles that American soldiers used during World War II.

Of course, in the 1980s, those same factories were struggling to keep pace with significant challenges from the Far East. At the beginning of the decade, Japan became the world's top auto producer, sending Detroit into a flurry of restructuring and innovation.

The increased competition also placed intense pressures on workers, who shouldered the burden of boosting productivity.

Yet, in 1982, a visitor could still imagine Detroit in its heyday. It looked like a city that had seen better times but could still get its act together and turn things around.

My family visited Detroit during a brief ten-year window in which the city's revenue exceeded its debt. Spending some time with its budget in the black had helped slow the city's slide into total despair. But when I returned twenty-six years later, this time to represent my hometown as a member of Congress at a meeting with GM executives, Detroit could not have looked more different.

* * *

By mid-September 2008, the auto industry had been in real trouble for years, and the economic dislocation that rocked the Motor City was rippling through our community. In an effort to cut costs, GM put the Janesville plant on its list of locations slated to close. We stood to lose 1,512 jobs. Leaders in Wisconsin were working to find an alternative solution. As part of the ongoing talks, I joined a bipartisan delegation that traveled to Detroit to ask company officials to spare our plant.

On the very same day our group met with the GM brass, Lehman Brothers announced it needed a buyer or would face certain collapse. Across the country, the economic crisis took most Americans by surprise, but what I saw in Detroit was decades in the making.

Block after block, we drove by vacant buildings scarred by graffiti. Our car passed entire neighborhoods of boarded-up houses and smashed windows. Apartment buildings and storefronts had rotted out or burned down, leaving skeletons of rusted metal and charred wood. A year later, *Time* magazine would put Detroit on its cover, comparing the devastation in the city to a natural disaster.

In 1950, Detroit was America's fourth-largest city. By 2009, it had dropped to eleventh place. As I write, it has slipped to number eighteen. In the course of a decade—between 2000 and 2010—a quarter of Detroit's citizens packed up and moved out. To put that in perspective, a PBS *NewsHour* investigation determined that it was as if one person had left the city every twenty-two minutes during those years.

The decline of Detroit is a sixty-year story of how a city that was once the envy of the world slowly eroded before our very eyes, in part because of bad economic policy—a cycle of spending, borrowing, and taxing until the bottom fell out. It's a story worth understanding, because it's a warning of what's to come if we don't reform our broken institutions at the national level.

When Detroit declared bankruptcy in 2013, the *Detroit Free Press* dug through thousands of pages of archival files to try and figure out what went wrong. The resulting special report reads like a fiscal autopsy showing so many pressing problems that it's hard to pinpoint the exact cause of death.

First, it's clear that the size and scope of the city government grew beyond the community's ability to pay for it. In the 1950s, when business was booming and the population was more than 1.8 million, the city needed a robust workforce to fund municipal services. In the years that followed, however, the population steadily declined—20 percent between 1970 and 1980, another 7.5 percent between 1990 and 2000, and fully 25 percent between 2000 and 2010. Cuts to the government workforce just didn't keep pace.

What it cost to keep paying those salaries was only the tip of the iceberg. Many city government positions came with generous retirement and health-care benefits, the result of concessions made to public-sector unions over the years. Coupled with a workforce that didn't shrink with the declining population, those packages saddled Detroit with massive legacy costs. By 2012, the city had almost twice as many retired workers as it did active ones. Carrying the promises made to those workers became a heavy burden that the city could not afford. The *Detroit Free Press* analysis found that the city's "spending on retiree health care soared 46 percent from 2000 to 2012, even as its general fund revenue fell 20 percent."

And then there were decisions that just defy common sense. For example, when the city's pension funds yielded earnings that exceeded expectations, that money wasn't reinvested or saved for a rainy day. Instead, city leaders paid bonuses to current and retired workers. Among retirees, these were known as "thirteenth checks," a fringe benefit that would show up in the mail after the regular twelve checks for the year had been paid. Estimates show that if the city had kept those excess earnings in its coffers between 1985 and 2008, it would be over $1.9 billion richer today.

Of course, while all of these statistics point to poor management, they aren't fatal in and of themselves. The real problem was that when the bill came due, city leaders either passed it on to Detroiters in the form of higher taxes or simply passed the buck altogether.

Bettie Buss used to work as a budget staffer for the city. When the *Detroit Free Press* interviewed her, she summed up the mindset of its leaders this way: "The whole culture [was] how do we get what we want and not pay for it until tomorrow and tomorrow and tomorrow?" The answer was to borrow money and raise taxes.

In 1962, the city imposed a new income tax. In 1971, it added a new utility tax. In 1999, it introduced a wagering tax on casinos. Current taxes kept rising, and for the most part, the government bureaucracy kept growing.

The problem was that all those taxes made Detroit a much more expensive place to work, invest, or live. Companies and families fled, and as that happened, the intertwined networks of support that make neighborhoods strong began to weaken. Then property values—and property-tax revenues—started to fall.

It was a perfect storm that wiped out city revenues. In 1960, the city took in money from only three sources: state-shared revenue, property taxes, and service fees. Its revenues totaled $2 billion. In 2012, even with its new revenue streams, it raised just $1.1 billion for the year.

With little will to cut expenses and a big budget gap, city leaders increasingly turned to borrowing to stay afloat. In 1986, Detroit saw its bond rating raised; Standard and Poor's deemed it "investment-grade." That set off a flurry of borrowing activity that several mayoral administrations used to cover operating costs.

By 2013, all of the spending, borrowing, and mismanagement had caught up with the city. It had racked up a huge deficit and was carrying $17 billion in debt. Spread across the remaining population, every man, woman, and child owed $25,000.

Much of the city's debt was due to unfunded pension liabilities, which an accounting firm hired by the city's emergency manager put around $3.5 billion. That figure represents decades of promises that the government made to workers and now had no way to keep.

Detroit, of course, is not the only city guilty of spending more than it takes in. But it is the most egregious example of an alarming trend in which elected leaders keep on borrowing and racking up debt instead of making tough choices and reining in government spending. The *Detroit Free Press* responded to the sorry state of affairs this way:

> It's hard to know why Detroit's leaders allowed the city to sink, a little further each year. For some generations, it was surely denial. No American city has fallen so far, so fast. In the early days, it's easy to understand why Detroit leaders saw decline as an aberration. But at some point, the fact that this was Detroit's new normal should have sunk in. It shouldn't have come to this.

If you're a Detroit resident, you're probably nodding your head. In 2012, Detroit had the highest income-tax rate and the highest property-tax rate in Michigan. With tax rates like those, you'd expect a city with top-notch services, safe streets, and good public schools. Instead, many citizens are living in a scene reminiscent of NBC's post-apocalyptic drama *Revolution*.

At night, some areas of town are pitch-black because around 40 percent of the streetlights don't work. Trash litters the streets. In a place once called the City of Homeowners, there are now 78,000 abandoned structures and 66,000 abandoned lots. The city simply can't afford to knock down all the empty buildings and homes.

For Detroit firefighters, those buildings aren't just eyesores; they're fuel. There are 12,000 fires annually in the city, and in nearly 1,000 cases, arson is the cause. In February 2013, the Detroit Fire Department announced that it would no longer use its hydraulic aerial ladders unless the situation was immediately life threatening. They were worried about the safety of their firefighters, because inspections were long overdue on the city's nineteen hook-and-ladder trucks.

The violent crime rate in Detroit is five times the national average. In fact, the murder rate has reached a forty-year high. The statistics can be hard to comprehend without context, so consider this observation made by Joe Duncan, president of the Detroit Police Officers Association: Between 2001 and 2012, we lost nearly 2,000 Americans on the battlefields of Afghanistan. During that same period, more than 4,000 Americans were murdered on the streets of Detroit.

The city's budget crisis means it can't hire more police officers. It's actually been reducing the force's ranks, since officers who retire are not replaced. Understaffed and overwhelmed, the Detroit Police Department solves less than 10 percent of reported crimes. If you call for help, it takes them an average of fifty-eight minutes to respond.

Almost 60 percent of Detroit's children live in poverty, and seven in ten don't have a two-parent home. To say the public school system is failing doesn't even begin to describe what's going on. In 2009, the city shocked the nation—and nearly everyone in education—when it posted the worst results in the thirty-year history of the National Assessment of Educational Progress test. Of the results, one education expert said, "They are barely above what one would expect simply by chance, as if the kids simply guessed the answers."

The 2011 results weren't much better. Detroit's fourth graders came in dead last in reading and math. Its eighth graders took last place in math and second to last in reading. In 2012, Michigan began requiring all high school juniors to take the ACT. That spring, only 1.6 percent of eleventh graders—eighty students in the whole city—earned a score that would qualify them as "college ready."

Today, around seven hundred thousand people live in Detroit. The median household income has declined by one-third, and in 2011, half of the city's households made less than $25,000 a year. The unemployment rate now stands at over 18 percent. That's much improved over its peak of 24.9 percent four years ago, but it's probably not much comfort for those still looking for a job.

Increasingly, Detroiters have had to turn to federal and state programs just to get by. In 2011, 41 percent of Detroit households received food assistance. Almost 83 percent of Detroit students qualify for free or reduced-price lunch.

In 2013, the state of Michigan took over the city, and Governor Rick Snyder declared a financial emergency. That July, the city filed for Chapter 9, marking the largest municipal bankruptcy in American history.

But the great tragedy of Detroit can't be found in court filings or on spreadsheets. The great tragedy is how far away that city has gotten from the American Idea—the way of life that offers our citizens opportunity, prosperity, and a chance to rise to their potential.

*　*　*

There are a lot of differences between Detroit and Janesville: our economies, our histories, and our size. But, for our purposes, the most important distinction is the different ideas about government—its proper role, its proper scope, and its approach to sustaining the American Idea—that you find in each place.

This distinction really begins with a simple question. When we look at America, what's the first thing we see: government or society? For me, the answer is society.

Life isn't just defined by what we can do as individuals, but also by what we can do together. Society functions through institutions that operate in the space between the individual and the state. They include the family and extend to what academics call "civil society"—our religious organizations, our charitable groups, and the markets that compose our free economy.

In a society-centered vision, government exists to protect the space where all of these great things occur. That's what America's constitutional republic has long set out as the role of the state. It is the role that government is supposed to play in the American Idea.

This adds up to a very important role for government, but it is a supporting one. Government is not the ultimate or supreme social institution; rather, it is the enabler of other institutions. It exists to keep us safe, to enforce uniform laws, to enable free and open exchange, to ensure fair competition in the marketplace, to promote economic growth, and to provide some basic protections to the vulnerable from the worst risks of modern life.

But when government doesn't live up to these responsibilities—or oversteps its proper boundaries—all kinds of problems emerge. Instead of facilitating our way of life, it hollows out that vital space where the things we find most meaningful and rewarding occur.

On this point, what has happened in Detroit is instructive. Government grew too large, spent too much, and failed to fulfill its most basic tasks. In turn, it eroded the space for the community—and its way of life. The society's energy and resources have been sapped. Families are struggling. Educational and professional opportunities are in short supply. The buildings are barely standing, and more important, they're empty—literally bereft of the thriving, dynamic community that once filled their walls.

Detroit has been hollowed out by a vision that puts government, not society, at the center of the picture. And it's a reminder of what's at risk when government overextends itself in this way: our private lives, our connections, our civic institutions, and our opportunities. When government takes a leading role instead of a supporting one, it makes it difficult—and, in some cases, impossible—to sustain the space where we actually live our lives.

Janesville isn't immune to these problems. Over the last six years, we've felt the impact of bad policies and tough times. We have experienced the kind of economic dislocation that the Great Recession and weak recovery have inflicted on much of America. GM had planned to shutter its Janesville plant in 2010, but when the financial crisis sent auto sales tumbling, it decided to move up the closure by more than a year. In December 2008, over one thousand of our neighbors and friends lost their jobs. Some $220 million of payroll vanished from a town of sixty thousand people almost overnight.

Suddenly, we were facing the tough decisions and hard times that the people of Detroit know all too well. Those who lost their jobs had three choices: They could move away from the place they called home, they could try to reinvent themselves by going back to school, or they could take a job that paid much less and didn't match their skills.

I'll never forget visiting my hunting buddy and barber, Gail, in late 2008. His wife had just gotten the news that she was being laid off from her job at the plant. They had two young boys, and they counted on her paycheck and benefits to make ends meet.

"Paul," he said, the corners of his eyes creased with worry, "I'm just not sure what we're going to do."

Gail's family couldn't afford to lose his wife's salary, and she couldn't find a new job in Janesville that would pay her a similar wage. Out of not-so-great options, Gail's wife took a company transfer and started working at the GM plant down in Kansas City. Every week, she would drive there and report for work—nearly five hundred miles and over eight hours each way. Every weekend, she'd come back home and try to make up for lost time, catching up with Gail and their kids. Eventually the strain of that arrangement took its toll. Both economically and emotionally, they couldn't keep up. Their home was foreclosed upon and their marriage ended in divorce.

The economic crisis eliminated jobs, wiped out savings accounts, and broke up families. In our town, its first casualty was the GM plant, but it soon crept into the restaurants where workers ate, the stores where they bought their kids' clothes, and the smaller manufacturers that had supplied the factory with parts and machinery. Our neighbor John was one of more than 840 workers who lost their jobs at Lear, a company that made seats for the SUVs that were built at the GM plant. Fortunately, John and his family were able to figure out a way for him to go back to school. They sacrificed a lot to pay their monthly bills. Through hard work and good fortune, John got back on his feet. Today, he's a biology teacher at one of our local middle schools. He was able to reinvent himself and become financially and personally fulfilled.

It's been harder for my friend John Fredricks, who used to be a team coordinator at the plant. When someone called in sick or went on break, John would fill in for them on the production line. He knew how to weld, drill, assemble parts, and double-check work to make sure it met quality standards. He'd show up in the morning and sit in the foreman's office, waiting to get his marching orders for the day. Once his assignment came down from the floor manager, he'd take his spot on the line with enthusiasm.

John made a good living, but once the plant closed, jobs were hard to find—even for a guy as skilled, versatile, and dependable as he is. Today, he works at the local Kwik Trip, a gas station and convenience store. It pays a lot less, and he's capable of much more, but John just can't find an opportunity that matches his background and skills.

The aftershock of the plant closing rippled through our community. The struggle isn't immediately apparent the way it is in a place like Detroit. Nowadays, if you drive around the quiet streets of Janesville at five p.m. on a weeknight, things don't look much different from how they did when I was a kid. The streetlights still work, the lawns are neatly trimmed, and the neighborhood kids play in their driveways until dinnertime. We don't have blocks of vacant buildings or idle fire trucks. But inside a lot of homes, the effects of the downturn are there. For some families the worst is over, but most will tell you that they're still trying to recover, that they haven't come close to making up the ground they lost.

Perhaps Janesville's saving grace is that while we're grappling with the effects of national policies and practices that put government at the center and have slowed the recovery down, that mindset hasn't crept into every corner of our community. The fundamental strengths present in the Janesville of my youth have been worn down, but they're still there. Janesville has always been a place where society is at the center of the vision—a place where people could pursue their happiness, realize their dreams, and provide for their kids. Yes, there were hardships—pain and heartbreak—but the bonds of community helped folks get back on their feet. That's the kind of life the American Idea is supposed to make available to all. And yet, in communities across our country, that way of life is now in jeopardy.

The process of renewing the American Idea starts with making the shift from a government-centered vision to a society-centered one. Such a shift would build upon the good work going on in Janesville and Detroit.

When I was growing up, my hometown was the kind of community where everyone pitched in. For grown-ups, the day didn't end at quitting time and the week didn't close out on Friday. People got involved, and their efforts held everyone together. There was no shortage of fraternal organizations and charitable associations to join: the Elks, the Kiwanis Club, the Eagles Club, the Moose Lodge, the Masons, the Knights of Columbus, the Independent Order of Odd Fellows, the Art League, the American Association of University Women, the VFW, the American Legion, and the YMCA. Men and women who worked at the GM plant were proud brothers and sisters of the UAW Local 95. Our parishes and houses of worship formed a network of compassion and care.

Together, the men and women who belonged to these organizations sponsored college scholarships, community betterment projects, and fund-raising drives for worthy causes in faraway places. When times were tough or tragedy struck, casseroles would show up at a front door and school carpools would add an extra stop. People would keep you in their prayers.

That instinct to get involved and help out is still part of our town's character. For example, in recent years, those with business experience—our bankers, entrepreneurs, investors, and accountants—have tried to figure out how to bring good-paying jobs back to our community. After work and on weekends, they put together PowerPoint presentations and investment proposals to encourage companies to relocate to our town. They're trying to help people like John and Gail rebuild their lives in Janesville.

Political scientists like to say that those kinds of efforts are part of "civil society," but in Janesville we just think of it as our community. And while our plant has closed and good jobs are scarce, our community is still going strong.

The importance of civil society is something Janesville and Detroit have in common—as I found during a visit in 2012 to the Cornerstone School.

Cornerstone has been teaching students in Detroit for twenty years. The school stands in a light brown brick building on Grove Avenue. The *Detroit News* keeps an interactive map that catalogs major crimes, and the area around Cornerstone is studded with little dots. Yellow for a shooting, red for a homicide. Click on the dots and you'll see stories of tragedies that shouldn't happen in America, let alone within walking distance of a school: a thirty-nine-year-old man who was shot but refused to provide information about his assailant. A cabdriver found murdered in his car—the second such crime in a week. A fifteen-year-old seriously injured in a drive-by. When the kids of Cornerstone head home at the end of the day, these are the neighborhoods they return to.

But when I walked through the doors of the school two years ago, it felt a lot like Janesville to me. Clark Durant, one of the eighty-five civic leaders who helped found the school, welcomed me. Clark is a tall guy in his midsixties with wire-rimmed glasses and white hair that's thinned out a bit up top. He's worked as a lawyer and for an investment firm. Ronald Reagan appointed him to lead the Legal Services Corporation, and he rescued the bankrupt Ann Arbor Railroad. But what he's most interested in, the thing he talks most passionately about, is education. When Clark gets going, he doesn't just gesture enthusiastically; he uses his whole body and the space all around him to make his point. He has an infectious enthusiasm about the subject that really draws people in.

As Clark walked me around Cornerstone, he told me that the inspiration for its founding was a speech that the Catholic archbishop Adam Maida delivered in 1990 before the Detroit Economic Club. In it, the archbishop referenced the Bible's Book of Revelation, calling upon those present "to make all things new" again. He asked his listeners to help Detroit's students by immersing them in a Christ-centered culture of shared values and unconditional love.

Today, 95 percent of Cornerstone's students graduate high school, and 91 percent go on to college. On the day I visited, I got to talking with a tenth grader named Alexis. She told me her favorite subject was economics, and I was shocked to learn she was already reading books I didn't encounter until college. I also met Camille, a seventh grader who scored in the top 3 percent of the nation in math.

Cornerstone is about more than academic achievement, though. It's a community of committed administrators and faculty, concerned Detroiters, dedicated parents, and talented kids. When I visited Cornerstone, I saw young minds yearning to learn, to reach their potential and be successful. And, perhaps more important, I saw adults eager to help them.

The students enrolled and adults involved in the Cornerstone School are more than champions of the American Idea—they are proof that it is alive and well. Despite the tough times that have ravaged their city, these citizens are doing their best to promote opportunity—and they are doing it as a community. These men and women are a reminder that the problem is not our people or their potential. The problem is bad policies and failed leadership.

For decades, elected and appointed officials in Detroit have made entire careers out of borrowing and spending and passing the buck. And that's not including the people who went far beyond shirking responsibility. Some of them actually committed crimes, causing even more harm to the people of their city.

Last October, Mayor Kwame Kilpatrick was sentenced to twenty-eight years in prison, having been convicted of dozens of charges, including racketeering and extortion. During Kilpatrick's administration, at least eighteen other public officials were found guilty of corrupt activity, as well. They are just the most recent in a long line of Detroit officials who have broken the public's trust, often by participating in schemes that stole millions of dollars from taxpayers and the city's coffers.

Honesty and integrity are the bare minimum of what we should expect from our leaders, and a lot of Detroit's problems stem from an absence of both. But we also expect our leaders to make the tough decisions and to solve problems. By those measures as well, officials in the Motor City have fallen woefully short.

Of course, Detroit is one city. You could even argue it's an aberration. But when I look at Detroit, I see a warning about what our country might face if we do not rethink how we are governing ourselves: a place full of good people with lots of potential lost amid the wreckage of bad policies and failed leadership. A place where bankruptcy has eroded security, liberty, prosperity, and economic mobility.

The problem is that as a country we're pursuing a lot of the same policies that got Detroit into trouble. We're spending too much and living off borrowed money. We're growing government at an unsustainable rate, often at the expense of civil society and individual freedom. And we're putting government, not society, at the center of the vision that guides our priorities and policies. If we keep it up, we risk following in the path that has left Detroit ravaged. That's not the kind of legacy any of us wants to pass on to our children and their kids.

Most of America is facing what Janesville now faces: uncertainty, insecurity, and the sense that something has gone wrong. If we fail to take these sentiments seriously and to think anew about how to revive economic opportunity and social cohesion in our country, we could in time come to face something more like what Detroit is facing: a disastrous collapse of self-government that makes it hard to see a path back to prosperity. Turning America around is not a matter of going back to the past. It is a matter of recapturing the way Americans have always thought about the future—that mix of responsibility, hope, and ambition that has allowed each generation of Americans to leave its children and grandchildren a better country. The fall of Detroit, and the unease in Janesville, should be warning flags that force us all to confront our failure to take the future seriously.

It should be impossible to ignore these warnings. But these days, I notice a lot of politicians are trying to do just that. They prefer to practice the politics of division instead of doing the real work of advancing solutions. When the pie is shrinking, when businesses are closing, and when workers are losing their jobs, the temptation to exploit fear and envy always returns. But all that does is sap our country of the unity we need to turn things around.

Life in America should not be a zero-sum game. If someone else is succeeding, it doesn't have to mean that you are losing out. And if it feels that way, then the leadership of this country is failing you.

That's why this book is focused not on the small squabbles that tend to dominate our public discourse these days, but on the big challenges we're facing. Because I still believe we can overcome them.

How do we do that? What's the best way to get America back on track? How do we heal Janesville, Detroit, and all of the other communities that have been struggling in recent years? How do we save the American Idea?

Those answers can be found in the story of how we got here.

CHAPTER 2

Sink or Swim

When I finally made my way back to Janesville, a little over two weeks had passed since the sprint across my backyard to join the Romney campaign. Along the way, we'd traded in the Speth family van for a motorcade of police cars and black SUVs. Everywhere our team went, screaming sirens and a pack of Secret Service agents and journalists announced our arrival.

Together, our caravan drove up to my alma mater, Craig High School, past the fields where I'd played soccer and run track. I hopped out, traveling through the halls where I'd gone to class and into the gym where I grew up watching and playing basketball. It was overwhelming to walk out onto that court, with Janna and our kids, as Mitt Romney's running mate.

The place was packed. Huge hand-painted banners proclaimed WISCONSIN PROUD and rooted BRING IT HOME PAUL! Dozens of people had their Packers Cheeseheads on. A group of kids wore T-shirts emblazoned with TEAM JANNA. People waved signs that read, WISCONSIN BELIEVES.

It seemed as if every face I saw in the crowd was a reminder of an important chapter in my life. I saw people who had volunteered on my first campaign; my priest, Father Randy; and dozens of Ryans—cousins and uncles and aunts. My brother Tobin introduced me. My mom stood in the bleachers cheering us on.

By the time I got to the stage, I was pretty choked up, but I managed to get a few words out. "It's good to be home," I said.

The rally was a celebration of our Janesville community. Having experienced the GM plant closing and the devastation left in its wake, our town understood the recession in a deeply personal way. As people stood and cheered, it was as if they were saying, *This thing hasn't beaten us. We're still here.*

The scene inspired me to go a little off script and share stories about friends, community leaders, and family members who had taken risks, worked hard, and were starting to get back on their feet. Just a few weeks earlier, President Obama had attributed that kind of success to government. Speaking to a crowd in Roanoke, Virginia, he said, "If you've got a business, you didn't build that. Somebody else made that happen."

The quote's substance and context have been heavily debated, but its basic message was simple: Don't pretend you have earned what you have; it could never have happened without government.

In one sense, it's an obvious point. Our society sustains the preconditions for prosperity. But it is also a profound misunderstanding, because those preconditions don't make success happen, and it is hard to imagine a worse attitude in an elected government leader than to suggest that people owe what they have to the state. The words seemed to confirm a general sense that the president was out of touch, that he didn't understand what people worked for, or what it took for people to take a risk and build a business, especially in bad economic times. What's more, he didn't appreciate that under his administration, government too often was getting in the way of success, not making it easier to attain.

That afternoon, it felt good to give the credit where it was due: to the people who'd earned it through their own decisions and hard work. But, looking back, I'm surprised I got the words out. The whole experience was incredibly moving. I kept looking around my high school gym and asking myself the same question: How did *I* get *here?*

* * *

Growing up, I didn't know much about politics. My parents were pretty apolitical. They voted, but they didn't attend rallies or donate to candidates or volunteer on campaigns. We didn't really talk about politics or politicians. It just wasn't a big part of our lives.

The one exception was Ronald Reagan. I knew about him mostly because my dad thought his story was so inspiring. He loved the idea that Ronald "Dutch" Reagan, an Irish guy who grew up on the shores of the Rock River just downstream from where we lived, had overcome a childhood of modest means and adversity and become president of the United States. I remember my dad would often see Reagan on the news and nod quietly, approvingly. We loved President Reagan, but not because he was a Republican. We loved him because he was one of us.

I can still vividly remember the day when John Hinckley tried to assassinate the president. I was eleven years old and we had just stood up to say a prayer in my classroom at St. Mary School. Our principal, Sister Evelyn, came on the loudspeaker and announced that the president had been shot. They excused us for the day, and we all went home. Given my dad's admiration for the president, that moment really resonated with me.

To me, President Reagan just seemed like a good man. Yet I didn't aspire to run for office. I wanted to be a doctor like my grandfather, my mother's dad.

I thought the world of my grandfather. He was a cardiologist in my mom's hometown, Fond du Lac, Wisconsin, and he loved his job. I remember going to a restaurant with him and running into one of his patients. They called their family over and excitedly introduced my grandfather to all of them.

"I was in rough shape, you know? It was a mess in here," the guy said, pointing toward his chest. Then he put his arm around my grandfather and said, "This guy saved my life."

My grandfather helped people, and any kid would have admired that. My greatest aspiration was to be like him. Meanwhile, my biggest concern in those days was probably whether my parents would ever let me go hunting. Of course, when you're young, it can come as an awful surprise just how quickly things can change—how youthful concerns and dreams can abruptly give way to grown-up problems and responsibilities. That's how it was for me.

It was the summer of 1986, and I had just wrapped up my sophomore year in high school. I was working the Quarter Pounder grill at McDonald's, and the night before I'd been out late cleaning up and closing the restaurant. The house was quiet when I came in. My mom was visiting my sister in Denver with my aunt Ellen. My dad and my brother Tobin, home from Notre Dame for the school break, had both gone to bed. My plan was to sleep in a bit the next day and then go mow the lawn.

In the morning, I awoke to the phone ringing. Tobin had left early to grab breakfast with a favorite high school teacher, so I assumed I was the only person in the house. When I answered the phone, my dad's assistant was on the other end.

"Do you know where your dad is?" she asked. "He's got clients waiting in the office."

I said I didn't know, but I'd go check. I went into his bedroom and found him. It was obvious I wouldn't be able to save him. His heart had stopped and he was gone. He was just fifty-five years old.

I was in shock, but instinct took over. I called 911 and then listened as the ambulance roared down our street and into our driveway. The paramedics rushed into the room, and as soon as they saw my dad on the bed they stopped, set down their equipment, and then just looked at me. They suggested we call a funeral home, so I mentioned Neil Schneider, a funeral director whom I had worked for my sophomore year, when I'd washed his hearses before school.

Neil called my uncle Don and my uncle Tom, who came right over. In the meantime, Tobin came home and I told him the news. We couldn't reach my mom. She had already started the eighteen-hour road trip back from Colorado, and no one I knew had a cell phone in those days. Telling her would have to wait until the next day, when she and my aunt finally made it home.

Tobin and I called our brother, Stan, in upstate New York, and our sister, Janet, in Denver. They flew into Chicago that night, and we picked them up at O'Hare. The next day, my mom pulled up, excited at the unexpected sight of all of her kids waiting in the driveway. Her birthday had been a few days before, and she thought everyone had flown in as a surprise. We brought her inside and broke the news as gently as we could.

My father's death was sudden, but looking back there were signs that it was coming. My dad was an Irish guy through and through. He was proud of his ancestry, but he was always worried about his perceived "weakness" for the drink. On the birth of my brother Stan, he was able to go cold turkey for over twenty years. But later in his life he returned to drink as an escape.

I was thirteen years old when this began. Most nights after work, my dad would look for the Canadian Club before he sat down with the paper. At first, it was just to unwind after a long day. But soon the glass remained in his hand well into the evening—through the nightly news, during dinner, and up until the time he went to bed.

There wasn't an easy or a succinct explanation for why my dad slipped into addiction, but I still tried to make sense of *why*. His health was failing in his final years, and I know he was stressed about that. He was worried about having a heart attack—that was how his own dad had died. My father was also suffering from glaucoma, an ocular disease that was hard to treat in those days. His eyesight was deteriorating rapidly, and he was afraid of going blind.

I always thought it was surprising that my dad turned to whiskey to deal with the stress brought on by his health problems. He certainly knew his family history meant he was vulnerable to addiction, and he was aware enough to recognize it and fight it when it came for him. During my early teenage years, he even went so far as to check himself into an in-patient program at the University of Wisconsin–Madison hospital for a couple of weeks.

My mom visited my dad while he was staying in the Madison facility, but she didn't want us kids to see him there. I remember her saying to Tobin and me, "He's trying to beat the curse that got his dad." It's a deep regret that I could not have been part of a solution.

While he certainly tried to fight it, my dad's addiction eventually won out. Over time, it made him more distant, irritable, and stressed. Before I lost him to a heart attack, whiskey had washed away some of the best parts of the man I knew.

Since his drinking had come on slowly, all the ways I adapted occurred almost imperceptibly. My mom and I got a lot closer, and I began to feel more protective of her. I also grew more independent— out of necessity. It helped me cope. But when my dad died and the slow process of grieving began to unfold, I finally felt the full weight of the loss and all the events that led up to it.

One night I needed to get out of the house, so I went on a long run. When I reached my high school, I lay down on the field where I practiced soccer and looked up at the night sky. The shock had worn off and the sadness had sunk in. But it was more than that. I was feeling sorry for myself. I was in a complete state of self-pity.

My father had died. My mom was alone. My siblings were grown and gone. And I remember thinking, *What am I going to do?*

I decided right then and there that I needed to step up. The way

I thought about it was "sink or swim," and I decided I was going to swim like hell. I wouldn't wallow. I wouldn't let the sadness and self-pity pull me down.

The implications of that decision hit me later in the week. After the funeral, there was a reception at our house. One of my dad's best friends, Ray Lewis, came over and put his hand on my shoulder. He was a man I trusted and knew well.

Ray said to me, "You have to be a man. You have to be there for your mom. You can't be a drain on her. You can't be a stress on her mind. Don't be a problem kid. You have to help your mom through this."

Ray basically told me to grow up. And I did. I grew up really fast.

*   *   *

My first test came quickly as I tried to help my mom out at home. Not long before my dad passed away, my grandmother had moved in with our family. Years earlier she had started showing signs of dementia, so we brought her down from Madison to live with us. Though she felt lost at times, my mom and I tried our best to do all the little things that would make her feel safe and loved.

My mom was fifty-two when my dad died. She needed to get a job, but things had changed a lot since she'd graduated in the 1950s with her science degree. She couldn't just go back into medical research; there had been too many advances to pick up where she'd left off. Besides, science wasn't her only passion; she'd always had a knack for artistic pursuits.

For most of my life, our family had been her work. She had tons of energy and was always involved in my life. She encouraged me to pursue hobbies that made me happy, like sports, and she never missed one of my games. But right before my dad died, my mom had started to dabble in interior design a bit, taking a class here and there at the University of Wisconsin. In the months after his death, she pursued her interest in earnest.

Losing my dad knocked my mom off her axis. She was stunned, sad, and overwhelmed. She had to create a whole new life and support me, so she threw herself into school.

Becoming an interior designer is much harder than you might realize. You have to know building codes, construction standards, contracts, and art history. My mom started taking two or three classes each semester to get the background she needed. Every weekday about the time I'd leave for school, she would get on a bus and ride forty miles each way to the campus in Madison. At night and on weekends, she studied hard to prepare for the licensing examination administered by the National Council for Interior Design Qualification. Eventually, she acquired her own small business and a studio space in Madison from a retiring interior designer, and later she hired several employees. I watched as Mom slowly transformed from a widow in grief to a small businesswoman whose happiness wasn't just in the past.

Two things hit us at once that year—first my dad's death, and then my grandmother's decline. They could have pulled our family apart, but they actually made my mom and me even closer. On weeknights, she would get back from Madison right around the time I returned home from sports practice. Together with my grandmother, we'd sit down to a late dinner. By then, my grandmother wasn't speaking very often, but she would sit with my mom and me as we caught each other up on our days.

With my dad's death, our relationship changed. My mom would tell me about her stresses at school and her worries about finances. She started treating me like an adult, and I took the trust and faith she placed in me seriously, because it meant a lot to me.

I remember one winter I was driving Stan's car home from the library. He had a rear-wheel-drive Toyota, and for fun I started doing fishtails in the middle of the road. A cop saw me and pulled me over. Like most teenagers confronted by the law, I started trying to talk my way out of it. I told the cop that the car was a stick shift and I didn't really know how to drive it. He didn't buy it.

"Where do you live?" he asked.

"Just over there," I said, pointing in the direction of my house. "On Garfield Avenue."

He told me to drive home slowly. He was going to follow me so he could talk to my parents.

When we got into the house, the cop described the scene and his suspicions to my mom. She listened and then turned to me.

"Is this true?" she asked.

I gave her the same line I had given the cop about not knowing how to drive Stan's car. My mom thought about it for a minute and then turned to the police officer.

"I want to thank you for coming here and telling me about this personally. And I appreciate your concern and that you made sure Paul got home safely. But I know my son. If he said he didn't do it on purpose, then I believe him."

That night I didn't sleep a wink. I felt so guilty. My mom had stuck up for me and I hadn't been honest with her. So, the next morning, I confessed. With everything we had been through, we had gotten a lot closer than most of my friends were with their parents. I knew the relationship I had with my mom was rare, and I didn't want to cause her any trouble or jeopardize that.

Those years of adversity taught me a lot about the importance of family. They also introduced me to Social Security. When my dad died, my Social Security survivor benefits gave me a financial backstop. I can still remember how it felt to open a bank account and put my benefits in a college fund. That money helped me pay for school.

Our family was also grateful for the help we got from my grandma's Social Security. It allowed us to hire a very kind woman who provided home care on weekdays while my mom and I were at school. Social Security helped us get the care that my grandmother needed, just as it's there for my mom today.

Those were my first personal experiences with the federal government, and it made a positive difference in our lives. The safety net assistance we got from Social Security was helpful and timely.

Those years also gave me a deeper appreciation for our community and friends. People in Janesville were there for us, eager to offer assistance and support. While a couple of women who had also lost their husbands helped my mom adjust to her new life, my dad's friends Hank Levihn and Bob Agard looked out for me. One of the things they made sure I didn't miss out on was the rite of passage in Wisconsin known as deer camp.

For as long as I can remember, I really wanted to hunt. It's a huge part of life in our state. The GM workers coordinated their leave time around hunting season, and when I was a kid, deer hunting was one of the few legitimate excuses for an absence from school.

My father was a tried and true Wisconsinite in every respect but this. He had no interest in hunting, and for some reason I never understood, he hated guns. Around the age of ten, I started bugging him about going hunting, but he thought it was too dangerous and I was too young.

To prove I could handle the responsibility, I got shooting lessons from a local outdoor writer, Duncan Pledger. Then I took and passed the state's hunter safety education course. I came back, certificate in hand, and pleaded, "Please, can I go hunting? Can I buy my own shotgun now?"

My mother had been rooting for me, quietly lobbying my dad behind the scenes. When I was twelve, he finally agreed that I could have a shotgun. I saved up some money, and Bob Agard arranged for me to buy a Browning BPS 20-gauge. My dad arranged for Hank to take me out with him and his son, my buddy Dave. Hank taught me to hunt for grouse, pheasant, and ducks.

After I lost my dad, Hank and Bob made a special point of bringing me on their hunting trips. Bob even made room for me with his family at deer camp that year and every year afterward. Together, those two men provided a fatherly presence, a good example, and much-needed advice. They stepped in and helped fill the void left by my father's death. And by bringing me hunting, they were doing much more than supporting a hobby. They were teaching me patience, focus, and discipline. Hunting gave me a special appreciation for the outdoors and became a refuge during tough periods in my life.

Yet, even with all the help and support of friends, our situation still felt overwhelming at times. But I'd decided not to sink; I was determined to swim. I started taking life more seriously, and one big step was obvious. I knew that I would have to beat the curse of poor health that had taken my father and his dad, so I started exercising regularly. Then, during my junior year, I became more committed to my studies and my school activities. I ran for class president with my cousin Adam as my VP, and we won. Senior year, it was Adam's turn to run at the top of the ticket, so I ran for a position as a nonvoting school board rep representing the high school.

When I'd started high school, I wanted to be a doctor like my grandfather. But my less-than-stellar performance in chemistry and physics quickly extinguished that dream. In its place emerged an interest in economic policy, which actually made sense given my family. Both of my brothers majored in economics in college, so I must have had a genetic predisposition to the dismal science. Eventually, I became interested not just in economic theory but also how that theory could be applied to real life. I started to become more aware of politics by following the policy debates that were prominent in the news.

My political philosophy was still forming, but I had a general sense that I was a conservative by the time I turned eighteen. In 1988, my dad's old law partner, George Steil Sr., served as the county chair for the Bush ticket, and he got me and my buddy Tim Kronquist involved. Tim and I did a lot of the legwork in our district that fall, putting up signs and handing out literature.

I also read just about everything I could get my hands on, starting with what was on my parents' bookshelf at home. My dad had been a huge fan of Winston Churchill, so we had all of his books and several biographies about him. I read *Free to Choose* by Milton and Rose Friedman. When she went back to school, my mom got a subscription to the *Wall Street Journal*. She was becoming more self-sufficient, and she wanted to be better informed about business, the economy, and current events. I'd often grab the newspaper when she was done and dive into the editorial page.

When I wasn't studying, reading, playing sports, or volunteering, I was working. It had always been important to my parents that I understood the value of a hard-earned dollar. If I needed something like clothes or schoolbooks, my parents would foot the bill. But if I wanted something like a stereo or a shotgun, I was expected to make my own money and pay at least half.

Over the years, I did all kinds of odd jobs so I could get things on my own. I painted houses, landscaped, mowed lawns, and washed hearses at the local funeral home. I worked in sales for the Oscar Mayer Company (and, for the record, I drove the Wienermobile only once). I spent two summers at Camp Manito-wish YMCA in northern Wisconsin—one washing dishes, the other as a counselor.

One of my best jobs was the summer I spent driving all over Wisconsin repairing signs with a friend whose family was so close to my own that we often refer to each other as cousins. His dad owned a silk-screening business that printed the decals that go on gas pumps and made branded wraps for the sides of trucks. Earlier that year he had been up for the Grande Cheese Company account, but to get the business he also needed to make big signs for all the dairy farmers who were part of Grande's supply chain. It wasn't really his expertise, and soon the signs got water in them and began to warp and crack. So my friend and I spent three months taking down the signs, bringing them back to the workshop where we repaired and resealed them, and then returning and putting them back up.

We spent a lot of time visiting with the dairy farmers while we worked. Most were happy to show us around their farms and introduce us to the "bossies"—that was the term they used for their cows. The nickname likely has its roots in the Latin phrase *bos*, which means *cow* or *ox*. But the term also made one thing very clear: On a dairy farm, it's really the cows that are in charge. I came away from the experience believing that being a dairy farmer is one of the hardest jobs on the planet.

*   *   *

By the time I arrived on the campus of Ohio's Miami University in 1988, I knew I wanted to study economics, and I was looking forward to being on my own. In high school, I'd had to shoulder a lot of responsibility unexpectedly. Now I could cut loose a little bit, and I did.

In the spring of freshman year, I pledged the Delta Tau Delta fraternity. The guys I lived with in the fraternity house eventually went in many different directions: from the Navy SEALs to the Army, medicine, teaching, business, and law. But there was little evidence then of the men we'd become. In fact, our weekends might have left the casual observer with the impression that all we did was party and play sports. While there was no shortage of either activity, I mostly liked the fraternity because I was part of a community, and I made a lot of friends who I'm still close with today.

The guys in our house spent a lot of time playing pranks. One night we got into a bottle rocket war with the fraternity across the street, the Sigma Nus. As we launched one particularly good shot, our rocket flew into an open window. Inside the Sigma Nu house, it skittered across the floor and through an open closet door, where it quickly ignited a few gallons of kerosene that the Sigma

Nus were storing so they could light outdoor torches at an upcoming party. We had about five seconds to celebrate our perfect shot before we saw the flames in the upper corner of their house. That ended the rocket war. No one was injured and the firefighters arrived before any real damage was done to the property. We were lucky the whole story didn't wind up in the police blotter. Lesson of the day: Don't get into a bottle rocket war with your windows open!

When not warring with rival fraternities, we partied with them. All in all, I probably had a pretty typical college experience, and my drinking, though heavy on occasion, was mostly under control. But what I remember about those years is that I couldn't shake the feeling that life should be about more than gratifying my own self-indulgence. That kind of nagged at me. More than once, I woke up with a hangover, looked in the mirror, and thought, *Is this how I want to live my life? Is this really the kind of guy I want to be?* And, of course, given the Ryans' history, I also thought, *This does not exactly work out well in my family.*

Of course, in a fraternity there's no shortage of company when you're reflecting upon a Saturday night of excess. Each Sunday, a few of the guys would atone for their evenings by crawling out of bed and into a pew at church. It didn't take away the headache, but it did seem to help them find a bit of the deeper meaning that can go missing in college life.

Unfortunately, I didn't have faith to balance me out then. I wasn't going to church. I'd been raised Catholic and gone to parochial school, where the nuns made sure I learned the basics. I could list the holy days of obligation and detail the Gospels. I could recite the Act of Contrition on command and knew the Apostle's Creed by heart. But of course, saying the words and feeling the meaning behind them are two very different things. Losing my dad was brutal for my whole family, and I can't say that the experience inclined my heart much toward faith.

In high school, I had tried to resolve the dissonance I felt by reading about different beliefs. I learned about all kinds of organized religions. I studied the writings of existentialists and atheists. But no matter the faith or philosophical position, my spiritual journey always brought me back to that same place where most everyone has been at one time or another: I believed in God, but I was mad at God. It wasn't until my midtwenties that—with the help of C. S. Lewis, Thomas Aquinas, the Gospel, and a few faithful friends—I would finally work that through.

So I'd come to college a lapsed Catholic—baptized, but non-practicing. I was certainly struggling a bit internally, but all of college's distractions made it easy not to focus on anything unsettling for too long. In between weekends spent messing around, I threw myself into my coursework during the week.

As I got into my major, I took classes with a professor by the name of Richard Hart. I enjoyed his macroeconomics courses a lot, and he could see the path I was on intellectually and politically. He recommended books and columnists he thought I might find interesting. At his suggestion, I read works by "the Austrians," Friedrich Hayek and Ludwig von Mises. Then, one day he handed me a copy of *National Review* magazine.

When I flipped through that first issue, a whole new world opened up to me. The magazine became a place where I could see what I was learning in the classroom applied to real problems in real time. By the time I started my junior year of college in 1990, I decided I wanted to see that process up close, and I applied to do a semester in Washington, D.C., at American University. I figured it was my one shot to live in the nation's capital and see how the political world really works.

As part of the program, I interned for my home-state senator, Bob Kasten, two days a week. When the spring semester was over, he offered me a paid summer internship on the Senate's Small Business Committee. It sounded interesting, and I decided to stay.

My stipend was pretty small, so I waited tables on the side and shared a one-bedroom apartment with three other guys. Space was tight—and the money tighter—but I had a great time. I learned a lot about the legislative process and how a Senate committee works. When the summer was over, I packed up and headed back to Ohio for senior year.

My first week back at school, I got a call from Cesar Conda, the senator's staff director at the committee. He said one of the guys on staff was leaving to go to grad school in May. If I wanted the job, they could hire me—for about half of his salary. Cesar needed an answer within two weeks, so he could budget accordingly.

I was torn. It was a great opportunity, but it wasn't really my plan. Ultimately, I aspired to go to grad school at the University of Chicago, get an advanced degree in economics, and then move back home to Wisconsin. More immediately, I figured I would rack up some life experiences—and my idea of "life experience" didn't involve a nine-to-five job in a suit and a tie. I wanted to go to Colorado after graduation and spend a few years with no responsibilities, just enjoying the outdoors. My grand plan was to climb mountains and wait tables in the summer, and then ski in the winter and try to get a job with the ski patrol to pay my way.

In my young life, I'd gone from my mom's house, where I had a lot of responsibilities, to a fraternity house, where I had close to none. I figured it couldn't hurt to take a couple of years and acclimate. What better place to adjust than the mountains of Colorado? Instead of jumping right into the working world, I would get there eventually and keep this life of few responsibilities going a little longer.

I called my mom and told her about the choice I was trying to make. My mom loved the outdoors, and she always encouraged us to find adventure in the Rockies. Our call, however, surprised me. She said, "If you go out to Colorado, you'll end up a ski bum. One year will turn into three, three will become six, and before you know it, you'll be thirty years old. You'll have missed this window in your life. Call Cesar back and take the job."

My mom wasn't big on politics. In fact, she thought anything beyond volunteering for a candidate or a congressional office was ridiculous, and she wasn't too keen on Washington, D.C. But if the choice was between working in public policy and waking up every day to go skiing, she knew which "hobby" she wanted to support. And underneath her encouragement I could sense her apprehension: *You've swum this far—don't start treading water now!*

In May, I moved back to D.C. and started my job with the committee. It didn't pay much, but I was learning a lot. Senator Kasten was a pro-growth, supply-side conservative who was very good at the mechanics of campaigns and the intricacy of policy work. He was a wonk, which is to say he was my kind of guy.

My schedule was pretty busy. During the week, I worked all day on the committee. On the weekends, I was a fitness trainer at a gym. And most nights I waited tables at Tortilla Coast, a Tex-Mex restaurant on Capitol Hill, so I could make rent. The place was known for offering cheap eats to cash-starved staffers, so there weren't a lot of menu items that could bump up the bill—or my tip. To upsell customers, I pushed any item that featured shrimp and got good at asking, "Would you like Sunset Sauce with that?" It was a tablespoon of queso, but it cost a couple of bucks. And if I'd been able to sell a lot of Sunset Sauce, when I closed out my shift, I could grab a Pacifico beer and visit with the motherly El Salvadoran women who took to calling me "Pablito" and cooked in the back.

When I'd arrived at my job on the committee, Bob Kasten was in the midst of a reelection campaign, and by summer, the race was pretty tight. I'd only been working there for just over three months, but I could sense people were concerned, so I asked what I could do to help. They said I could head home and take over the field operation in western Wisconsin.

I was not their best bet. I knew very little about campaigns. Up to then, my experience in retail politics was limited. I'd handed out literature for the '88 Bush campaign. I had gone door-to-door for local congressional candidate (and current House Speaker) John Boehner in college. But I didn't have the kind of field experience one would typically look for in campaign staff. Nevertheless, I liked Bob Kasten and I wanted to help. So I took a leave from his congressional staff, got in my truck, and went back home.

For the next three and a half months, I slept on the floor of the Republican County Headquarters in Eau Claire and showered in the basement bathroom of the nearby home of a Kasten supporter. I recruited and organized volunteers, put together literature drops, and planned bus tours. It was a crash course in Campaigning 101.

In the end, it wasn't enough to put Kasten over the top. He lost his seat to Russ Feingold, and I was out of a job. It was too late in the year to apply for grad school, so I traded in my job as a Senate staffer for life as a full-time waiter and fitness trainer on Capitol Hill. I'd spent six months in D.C., and I was starting to wonder if I would have been better off becoming a mountain man. I didn't know it yet, but I was about to get a call that would change everything.

* * *

After the 1992 elections, the Republicans were in the wilderness. Bob Kasten wasn't the only casualty that year. Bill Clinton won the presidency by defeating George Bush, and the Democrats kept control of the Senate and the House.

In an effort to help compensate for the conservative movement's diminished status, a think tank called Empower America was formed. The organization was meant to serve as a shadow government of sorts for the GOP and a campaign-in-waiting for the man who was likely to be our party's 1996 nominee: Jack Kemp.

Not long before Empower America got going, Kemp had come

into Tortilla Coast with a member of his staff. I had read his book, *An American Renaissance*, a couple of years before, and it had a deep impact on me. Turning those pages, I remember feeling like someone had perfectly and succinctly described my own political views and philosophy. So, out of respect, when I waited on him I didn't try to sell him on the Sunset Sauce.

Afterward, I told Cesar Conda that Jack Kemp had come by the restaurant. I mentioned how much I admired him and that I thought it would be cool to work for him someday. As luck would have it, not long after, Kemp started calling around and looking for staff to work at Empower America, specifically a young person who understood economics and could travel a lot. Bob Kasten and Cesar Conda both recommended me.

I made it to the second round of the hiring process and got an interview with Kemp. He'd been a quarterback for thirteen years, most famously with the Buffalo Bills, and he looked like one. Kemp was a compact, strong guy with a ruddy complexion and a shock of white hair. After some quick niceties, we got down to brass tacks.

He asked me, "What do you think is better—a tax credit or a tax-rate reduction? Should we reduce tax rates or should we give people tax credits?"

I knew what he was up to. Kemp was famous for convincing President Reagan of the merits of supply-side economics. As a member of Congress, he had authored the Reagan tax cuts, and his pro-growth ideas helped create the economic expansion of the 1980s and 1990s. Jack Kemp didn't just join the Reagan Revolution; he was the chief architect of some of its greatest victories.

In asking certain questions, he was trying to see if I was "on the model," which was the term we used for supply-siders in those days. I was. "A reduction in tax rates," I replied, "because growth occurs at the margin."

The questioning continued. He asked me about monetary and

economic policy. By the time the interview was over, I thought I'd done well, but I knew that might not be enough. I was only twenty-three years old, and my competition for the job included a long list of people with decades of experience and advanced degrees. I was relieved when I got a call from Empower America's policy director, Pete Wehner, who asked me to come in and meet with Bill Bennett, another member of the organization's leadership team.

Jack may have been a quarterback, but Bill is built like an offensive tackle. He's a big, imposing guy with strong opinions and a quick wit. In the 1980s, he'd served as President Reagan's secretary of education and later spent a year as the first director of national drug control policy under the first President Bush. By 1993, Bennett's writings had made him a leading figure in the decade's debates over virtue, culture, and morality.

He opened our meeting by saying, "Jack does economics. I do sex, drugs, and rock 'n' roll." We talked a little bit about his work on cultural issues. He asked about my family and where I grew up. Then we talked about football. He's a hopeless Buffalo Bills fan; in all my years of knowing him, I have yet to convince him to root for the Green Bay Packers.

Pete Wehner called and offered me the job later that week. He said, "We're taking a big risk on you. You're a lot younger and less experienced than anyone else we're looking at. But we think you have potential."

While I still considered public policy a career detour, Empower America was too good to pass up. Its ranks included the top talent in the conservative movement. In addition to Bill and Jack, there was Jeane Kirkpatrick, Reagan's ambassador to the United Nations, who cofounded Empower America and led its foreign policy initiatives. Former Minnesota congressman Vin Weber was the organization's president; Kevin Stach was the communications director; future White House speechwriters Mike Gerson and Marc Thiessen were in the communications shop; and David Kuo, who would also go on to be an author and a presidential aide, was the deputy director of policy. It was an impressive operation, and I figured it would be rude to take the job only to leave the next fall for grad school. I decided to stay for a couple of years and then get back to my plan.

As it turned out, Empower America was my grad school. I just didn't know it yet.

Jack liked to call politics the "battle of ideas." At Empower America, we fought that battle on two fronts. On the one hand, we tried to derail the Clinton administration's policy proposals on taxes, budgetary matters, and health care. We were also involved in the era's intraparty fight over the soul of the conservative movement and the GOP.

The agenda was simple: Empower Americans in every possible way. Lower taxes so they could keep more of their paychecks. Give parents more choices about where their kids went to school. And—this was closest to Jack's heart—help the poor by reforming welfare so they could move up the ladder and out of poverty. I was gaining a deeper appreciation for the American Idea; having seen it firsthand growing up in Janesville, I was now learning about how we preserve it through public policy.

I wrote memos in the policy shop and spent days at a time out on the road. Jack and Bill had schedules full of meetings and speeches across the country. They needed a policy staffer with a notebook full of good data at his fingertips. I was a young, single guy without a family or much in the way of personal responsibilities. I had plenty of time to burn, so the job of staffing them on trips often fell to me.

I was surprised to find that Bill Bennett and I had a lot in common. We both loved the outdoors and had climbed many of the same mountains in Colorado. Soon, we were climbing together. I remember one time we ascended Castle Peak in Colorado's Elk

Mountains. While we were crossing a large boulder field, the path was steep and the ground kept shifting underneath our feet.

Bill looked over at me and said, "Hey, just stand right in front of me. I'll grab you if I fall."

I remember thinking that if I let Bill Bennett fall to his death on that mountain I'd be forever known as "that kid who ruined the Republican Party." I also knew that if he went, he'd take me with him—and I wasn't quite ready to give my life for the cause just yet.

Bill had an important message that economics guys like me needed to hear: Culture matters. In 1992, he wrote:

> Individuals and families need support, their values need nourishment, in the common culture, in the public arena. Our common culture is not something manufactured by the upper stratum of society in the elegant salons of Washington, New York, or Cambridge. Rather, it embodies truths that most Americans can recognize and examine for themselves. These truths are passed down from generation to generation, transmitted in the family, in the classroom, and in our churches and synagogues.

Bill understood that all the tax cuts in the world don't matter much if you don't get the culture right. Delivering that message didn't always make him popular, but it made him important for our party and our country.

In many ways, Bill was a perfect complement to Jack's agenda and worldview. Many of my trips with Jack were to economics-related meetings and conferences. Widely assumed to be a presidential candidate, Jack was a rock star. He was recognized everywhere he went. People didn't carry cameras around then; they didn't have them at the ready like we do on our cell phones today. That turned out to be fine, because most people didn't need a picture. They just wanted to be able to say they had shaken hands with the man.

What I enjoyed most about traveling with Jack was that so many people from all walks of life absolutely loved him. He visited places that hadn't seen a national Republican leader in years, if ever. He would tour poverty-stricken areas and inner-city communities. He brought the message of conservatism to people who had never heard it before. He was always excited to tell his story, to share his ideas, and to talk about how conservative principles could make a difference in people's lives.

Whether we were in a halfway house or the ballroom of a five-star hotel, the reaction was always the same: People were drawn to Jack because they knew he cared. There was an infectious enthusiasm about him. It was amazing to watch him go into an urban housing project, challenge the Left's political monopoly, and make the case for free enterprise.

Seeing Jack in action and listening to him share his ideas was inspiring. It made me see the work of public service and public policy in a new light. Jack used to call himself a "bleeding-heart conservative." His was an inclusive, participatory kind of conservatism. It was a political belief that spoke to every American.

Jack knew the battle of ideas could be a tough business and it could make a big difference in people's lives. It was the same sense of service to others that my grandfather brought to his work as a doctor helping the sick. For Jack, poverty was a temporary state, not a chronic condition. And his policy prescription was to grow the economy so that every person had a solid start, a fair shot, and a real chance.

Jack Kemp taught me a good deal about economics. He believed in the possibilities of free people, in the power of free enterprise, and in the ability of strong communities to overcome poverty and despair. Looking back, I can see now that it was his enthusiasm for his beliefs that truly pulled me into politics. The sense of drift faded, and in its place, a sense of purpose formed. Jack's excitement for ideas and the way they could improve people's lives made me see public policy not as a hobby, but as a vocation.

My time at Empower America really was a turning point. While I still assumed grad school was out there in the future, I began thinking more and more that public policy was providing me the sort of fulfillment I was looking for. At the time, I could not see myself being any happier doing anything else. I took great satisfaction in working for Bill Bennett and Jack Kemp and being a foot soldier in the battle of ideas.

*　*　*

By January 1995, a confluence of forces—conservative candidates and their well-run campaigns, the Contract with America, the fallout from the Clinton health-care effort, the work of Empower America and other groups—had delivered big victories. For the first time in forty years, Republicans had control of the House. In the Senate, they reclaimed the majority after being out of power for eight long years.

At Empower America, the triumph was somewhat tempered by the news that both Bill and Jack had decided they wouldn't run for president in 1996. Then, as the new session of Congress got under way, I started getting calls.

The Republican midterm sweep in 1994 was a stunning defeat for Bill Clinton. In order to get reelected in 1996, he began "triangulating," positioning himself between the far left of his party and public perceptions about ours. That gave Republicans a lot of room in negotiations and enabled us to get things done. It also made the 104th Congress an exciting place to be.

I liked the idea of working for one of the hard-charging reformers who had just been elected. With Jack and Bill's encouragement,

I took a job with Congressman Sam Brownback as his legislative director.

I liked Sam a lot right from the start. He had grown up on a family farm and most recently served as the Kansas director of agriculture. Today the governor of Kansas, Sam has always been an earnest guy, clearly not the type who came to Congress just to go along to get along. He was determined to get things done, and he was not a man easily deterred.

Sam led a group called the New Federalists with Tom Coburn, Joe Scarborough, and John Shadegg, and he joined John Kasich's budget committee. I handled all of the budget issues and helped Sam write bills designed to get the federal budget under control. I worked on amendments to reform the immigration system by keeping families intact, which ended up passing and ultimately became law. And, of course, Republicans achieved a long-sought goal when the president signed welfare reform.

In June 1996, we were all surprised when Bob Dole resigned from the Senate to campaign full-time for president. Sam decided to make a go of it and run for Dole's seat. While his chief of staff went to Kansas to run that effort, I kept the congressional office going, and when I could, I volunteered my time to help the campaign. Sam had a tough primary before he could even get to the general, and I learned a lot about electoral politics from that race.

But for me, the most important aspect of that campaign wasn't political; it was personal. Sam is a deeply religious man. A self-described "seeker," he once told *Rolling Stone* magazine, "Every spiritual path has its own scent, and I want to inhale them all."

Sam was raised a Methodist, but by the time I met him, he had become an evangelical Christian. During the Senate campaign, he was thinking about converting again, this time to Catholicism.

Occasionally, I would head out to the state and drive him from one event to the next. He started asking me a lot of questions about my faith. I had already begun to become reacquainted with the church I'd grown up in, but having a non-Catholic asking me serious questions about church doctrine was an important responsibility. I took that seriously, and our talks became the catalyst for a deepening of my faith. At Sam's urging, I dove a little more into the writings of C. S. Lewis. By my midtwenties, I started attending Mass again. Sam kept searching and eventually converted to Catholicism himself.

Here, I guess an author is supposed to describe his Road to Damascus moment—the instant when everything became clear and he was forever changed. But the truth is that there wasn't one event or moment of drama that brought me back to the Catholic Church; it happened gradually. My father's death made God feel distant, but that feeling faded over time. Good things started happening. My mom fell in love and got remarried. I was meeting people and having experiences that meant a lot to me. My anger had subsided and I was happy. I guess you could say that while some people turn to faith in times of hardship, I returned to it, at least in part, out of gratitude.

Around that time, I also started to stay away from hard liquor. I remember going home for a family dinner, and my uncle Don, who is one of my favorite people, was there. He's my godfather and one of only two surviving Ryans from his generation. Because of that, Uncle Don is an important figure for the guys my age, and we all listen closely when he gives advice. Often, he wraps those life lessons in a story or a joke. At this particular dinner, he got the attention of a few of us guys in our twenties. With his classic wit and a twinkle in his eye, he leaned in and said, "You know why God invented whiskey, don't you?" He waited a beat, and then delivered the punch line: "To prevent the Irish from running the world. And it's worked so far."

It was a joke I'd heard before, but the next part was new.

Changing tone and becoming more serious, he looked at us and said, "And don't think it hasn't gotten our family as well. Steer clear and beware."

I'd never had a serious problem with drinking, but I had spent my life very conscious of my family history. It helped getting a gentle reminder from my uncle Don: *This happens in our family—don't let it happen to you.*

* * *

When Sam Brownback won his election, I went with him to the Senate and helped set up his office there. Soon after, I got an unexpected phone call from Mark Neumann, a Janesville guy who represented my home district in the House. He told me he was thinking about challenging Senator Russ Feingold in the next election. He asked if I could assemble the old Kasten team so he could get some ideas about how to run the race.

A week or so later, a bunch of us got together with Neumann in a conference room at the National Republican Congressional Committee. We talked for about an hour and a half, and as the meeting was breaking up, Mark asked me to walk with him so we could chat a bit more.

As we stood out on the corner of C and First Streets behind the Cannon House Office Building, he said, "Listen, I'm going to run for this Senate seat. I'd like you to come back to Wisconsin and manage my campaign."

I was surprised. I thanked him. "That's a great offer," I said. "But I'm not really a politics guy; I'm a policy guy."

He said, "I thought you might say that. In that case, you should run for my seat."

I don't think I did a very good job of hiding my surprise. "Run for your seat? That's crazy," I told him. "I'm twenty-seven years old!"

He laughed. "It's not that crazy. You understand the policies, right?"

"Yeah, I understand them about as well as a twenty-seven-year-old guy who's been here for a couple of years can."

"And you know how Congress works. You understand the job you'd have to do for your constituents?"

"Mark," I said, "I don't think I'm ready for something like that."

"You may be young, but you could do this. Why not?" He waved as he walked away and said, "Sleep on it and come see me in a few days."

So I waited and thought on it and then went to see him.

He asked, "What's your downside?"

I explained again that I was pretty young and I probably wouldn't win.

He said, "You know, if I listened to all the people who told me what I couldn't do, I'd never get anything done. What do you believe in? What do you care about?"

I talked with him about my work with Kemp. I explained that I liked being able to help advance good ideas. "But I've already decided that I'm going to grad school," I told him. "I miss Wisconsin. That's where I want to end up."

Neumann said, "Why go to grad school then? Run for this seat. If you win, you can keep fighting for the things you believe in *and* you can live in Janesville."

When he put it like that, it didn't sound all that absurd anymore. I started to do some soul searching. I talked to my family and friends.

I called Jack Kemp and asked, "Does this sound crazy to you?"

"Absolutely not," he said. "You should do it. I'll write the first check."

I called Bill Bennett. "Does this pass the laugh test?" I asked.

He said, "Yeah, sure it does." He offered to write the second check.

I talked it over with Sam, who offered this: "If you run, don't forget that you're doing this to make a difference in people's lives. Because there are going to be days when you come home and sit on the couch after talking to eight people who all just gave you bad news. And you're going to start wondering, *Why on earth did I get myself into this?* That's when you have to remember that you're in this to make a difference. That's how you soldier on when the going gets tough." Those words not only guided me through my first campaign, but through every race I've ever run.

Finally, I talked to my mom. She said, "Really?! You would want to do *that?*"

* * *

Ultimately I came to the conclusion that I loved public service and public policy—and I missed Wisconsin. I'd always felt like the path I was on was just a temporary moment between college and grad school. Then I ended up in places and met people who made a huge difference in how I saw the world. I realized that if you were a guy like me whose father, grandfather, and great-grandfather had all died before they reached sixty years old, if you felt as if time might be short and you wanted to make a difference, then public service might be the best way to go.

Five years after I first arrived in D.C., I finally realized that I hadn't taken a detour; I'd found the path. Going to graduate school made logical sense, but jumping into the battle of ideas felt right.

So I thought, *You know what? I'll give this a shot. I'll get in the arena. I'll just see if I can get the nomination. That would be amazing. And I don't want to go to my deathbed with regrets.*

Mark Neumann offered to give me a job in his district office so I could get set up and move back, but I wanted to be my own guy. I packed up and went home on my own terms. I worked for a bit with my cousins over at Ryan, Inc., the excavating firm they ran and one of several places I'd held odd jobs as a kid. But mostly, I committed myself to the campaign.

My mom was the first person to join Ryan for Congress. Officially she was my scheduler, but she did much more than that. She opened every door that needed opening. If you were in charge of a Rotary meeting or holding any kind of breakfast event, she'd convince you I had an idea you needed to hear. She spent her weekends walking with me through fairgrounds, attending pancake breakfasts, and going to parades.

My brother Tobin and his wife, Oakleigh, took leaves of absence from their jobs in London to come home and work on the campaign. Tobin became my political director, and Oakleigh recruited and organized a small army of volunteers. Their six-month-old daughter, Murray, spent every day with us at headquarters. We took turns playing with her in a corner of the office we'd cordoned off and turned into a makeshift day care. Meanwhile, my mom's white poodle, Major, circled laps around the tables and greeted people enthusiastically at the door.

Joining my family at headquarters was my only friend who knew anything about politics: my buddy from sixth-grade basketball camp, Andy Speth. In 1997, he was working for a Wisconsin state senator. He became my campaign press secretary, and since 1999, he's been my chief of staff.

George Steil, my dad's old law partner, was my campaign cochairman along with Steve King, a former Wisconsin GOP party chairman who was from a nearby town. My aunt Ellen came down from Madison to answer the phones. I had tons of cousins and friends who offered to pitch in. We were a ragtag operation, and it was very much a family affair.

When we started, I had very modest funds in my savings account. I lent most of that money to the campaign so we could buy a laptop and rent a vacant storefront in downtown Janesville on Milwaukee Street. We had no idea how to raise money and were lucky when a good friend, Mary Stitt, agreed to take us on as a charity case. By the time we were done, our team had raised $1.2 million for our effort, a pretty significant sum for a 1998 congressional race.

There were nine people rumored to be entering the GOP primary. All were older and had a lot more experience than I had. I knew that in order to measure up to their resumes, I'd have to work twice as hard.

My age was widely considered a disadvantage. I realized early on that the only way to win was to make sure people knew me for my ideas, not just my birth date. While most of the potential Republican candidates were waiting to be courted, I was busy convincing the grassroots activists that they should support me. By the time the primary rolled around, all of the serious contenders had dropped out or decided against getting in. My sole primary opponent was a guy named Michael Logan, who declined to debate but said he'd be willing to settle matters with a drag race. I passed on that offer.

We put a lot of work into clearing the primary field, but we were also helped by the fact that several would-be contenders didn't think the general election was winnable for a Republican candidate. If you look at Wisconsin, the First Congressional District sits in the bottom, southeast corner of the state, its eastern border bumping up against the waters of Lake Michigan. On the far east of the district lie two major population centers: Racine and Kenosha with nearly 80,000 people and just over 100,000 people, respectively. Janesville sits all the way on the other side, and in between is a lot of green space that used to be almost exclusively dairy land. As factories replaced the farms, the area became more industrial, offering lots of good-paying, blue-collar jobs.

Politically, Wisconsin's First District had traditionally leaned more toward the Democrats. Mark Neumann, a Republican, had won the previous two elections, but the races had been extremely close. Before him, Les Aspin, a Democrat who left to serve as President Clinton's defense secretary, had held the seat for twenty-two years, followed by Democrat Peter Barca.

Given that history, it was not surprising that when I got the GOP nomination, I was down by double digits in the polls. Early on, Tobin, Oakleigh, Andy, and I met with the rest of our small staff and spent a day sketching out our campaign plan on a whiteboard. I ran as the Paycheck Protection candidate, and all of our proposals were designed to help the citizens of the First District keep more of what they earned instead of sending it off to Washington, D.C. I ran as an economic conservative and I didn't shy away from being clear about what I believed. I was for limited government, lower taxes, and pro-growth policies. Our message was simple and logical: "smaller government...bigger paychecks."

Our platform was solid, but we were still the underdog in the race. If we wanted to generate interest, we had to get creative. So Andy Speth and I went through all of the communities in our district and figured out their total federal tax liability. Then we flipped through the *Congressional Pig Book*, an anthology of pork barrel projects assembled by Citizens Against Government Waste, and matched each town's tax total with projects in the book. For example, one community's tax bill was $11.4 million, roughly the equivalent of what Congress had spent to put an airstrip in a Pennsylvania congressman's backyard. Another owed $10.7 million, around the same amount that the National Park Service had paid to build a few extravagant lodges for its park rangers. Those homes cost $330 per square foot to construct, compared to the national average of $62.75.

We peppered my stump speech with these examples, and to drive the point home, we raided Andy's kids' toy chest for props: a Mattel toy airplane for the airstrip, a Lincoln Logs house representing the park service waste. Pretty soon, we were getting invites to local chambers of commerce, Rotary meetings, and Kiwanis Clubs. The presentation was entertaining, and a lot of voters found the message compelling: *Send me to Washington, D.C., and I'll protect your paycheck. I won't let Congress spend your money on wasteful projects like this.*

Our message was amplified when my opponent, Lydia Spottswood, attacked me for supporting Social Security reform during a late September debate. I wasn't afraid to talk specifics when it came to entitlement programs, and as we each made our key points, Spottswood explained that she would be willing to lift the cap on the Social Security taxes that workers pay. That one admission became a key distinction that defined the rest of the campaign: Lydia Spottswood wanted to raise taxes, and I wanted to lower them.

By October, we were gaining traction in the polls. My opponent outspent me, and she had a lot of help from the unions and the Democratic Congressional Campaign Committee. But our upstart operation was a force to be reckoned with. We worked our tails off. We barely slept. We were scrappy. And we ran a very focused campaign.

Later, my opponent's campaign manager would confess to Andy that they had a hard time keeping pace with our energy and enthusiasm for the race.

"I used to call our candidate at seven in the morning," he said. "I'd tell her, 'The Ryans have been on the road since five a.m. We need to get to work! The day hasn't even started and we're two hours behind!'"

By the time Election Night rolled around, a lot of people were predicting a Ryan victory, but our team took nothing for granted. We worked up until the last hour on the last day. Tobin and Oakleigh held signs in Racine all afternoon on Election Day, something most Republicans wouldn't do because they assumed someone from our party couldn't persuade people there to vote for them. We didn't put much stock in that bit of conventional wisdom. We fought for every vote.

That night, our campaign team and supporters gathered at a family restaurant in Burlington. The space was small, so we brought in an RV, which we parked in the lot outside and used as our war room. Tobin, my mom, Oakleigh, Andy, and my old boss, Bob Kasten, all sat together in that RV waiting for the returns to come in. It was almost as crowded as the restaurant with campaign staff reviewing spreadsheets and field reports—and family members and friends who kept sneaking in and asking for updates.

When we got our first numbers in, Tobin started looking them over. Bob Kasten peered over his shoulder and his eyes got big.

"Those are the early returns?" Bob asked.

"Yeah," Tobin said.

"Wow. You guys are going to win this thing!" said Bob.

"How can you say that?" asked Tobin. "These numbers are so low."

We were so new to canvassing and grassroots politics that we didn't realize how quickly those small figures in early precincts could turn into a landslide district wide.

When all the ballots were counted, I ended up winning by fourteen points—in a year when Republicans actually lost seats in the House. It wasn't a good night for the Republican Party, but it was a great night for the Ryan family.

The news stations declared our victory pretty early in the evening. My mom, Tobin, Oakleigh, Janet, and Stan stood behind me as I gave my victory speech. I said what we all were thinking: I wished my dad could be there. I hoped somewhere he was looking down on us, proud of this moment and the campaign we ran.

In just a few short months, I would take the oath of office and become the second-youngest member in the House. I was entering the battle of ideas. I was swimming.

CHAPTER 3

Lesser of Two Evils

The period between the 1998 election and the swearing-in ceremony in January 1999 was complete and utter chaos. The House of Representatives continued on its march toward the impeachment of President Clinton, which created turmoil among the Democrats. And after the disappointing midterms, things got ugly on our side of the aisle.

In the fall of 1998, House Speaker Newt Gingrich led an effort to nationalize the upcoming election, trying to tie Democratic candidates in key districts throughout the country to President Clinton's problems. It backfired horribly. In my own race, we watched our momentum evaporate as soon as the National Republican Congressional Committee put ads about Monica Lewinsky on the air. Only after it became clear that these ads were harming, not helping, its candidates did the NRCC stop running them.

When the ads came down in our district, our momentum picked up again. Other candidates weren't so lucky; the focus on impeachment wounded them deeply and they never recovered. Gingrich had predicted that his strategy would pick up thirty seats. It ultimately lost us five. That didn't just dampen morale; it made history. Since 1934, no president's party had been able to pick up House seats in a midterm election. And yet, here was Bill Clinton, plagued by scandal, paring our Republican House majority back to just twelve seats. When we were sworn in that January, our party would have the chamber's slimmest majority in thirty-three years. It was a good lesson: You can't simply run against your opponent; you have to stand *for* something.

The election was held on a Tuesday. By Friday morning, Congressman Bob Livingston of Louisiana announced plans to oust Gingrich as Speaker. Hours later, Gingrich chose to relinquish the gavel rather than go down in defeat. The opening sent several members scrambling to test the waters for a run for Speaker and other leadership posts.

That was the scene as our freshman class gathered in mid-November for new-member orientation. Two big questions loomed over the week: Who would lead the majority when we returned in January? And who would cast the ultimate vote on impeachment—members of the lame-duck Congress on their way out or those of us waiting to be sworn in?

For a few days, there was a real possibility that my first vote as a member of Congress would help decide the president's fate. That was when I got my first invitation to the White House.

President Clinton's welcome reception took place on an evening during orientation. There were forty members in our freshman class—seventeen Republicans and twenty-three Democrats. That night, many of us made our way through the tall gate at the edge of the White House grounds and checked in at the guardhouse. From there, we walked up the driveway and past the patch of gravel where reporters deliver breaking news. The lawn was littered with mic stands, cameras, and klieg lights that gave off a blinding glow.

I reached the great white columns of the North Portico and walked into the entrance hall, where the president and First Lady typically greeted heads of state before dinners. I turned left and made my way upstairs to the first family's residence on the second floor. There, I found myself standing in front of the Treaty Room, where President William McKinley ended the Spanish-American War and President John F. Kennedy signed the Partial Nuclear Test Ban Treaty.

I bumped into one of the president's aides.

"Are you having a good night?" he asked.

"Yeah," I said. "This is amazing. Do you guys hold an event up here every time a new Congress comes in?"

"No," he said. Then he leaned in and lowered his voice. "Actually, this is the first time I've ever been up in these rooms before."

It quickly dawned on me that this wouldn't be a regular occurrence, so I decided to wander around with my friend Mark Green, who'd just been elected in Wisconsin's Eighth Congressional District. We stood in front of the famous painting of President Kennedy, deep in thought. We wandered down to the first floor and glanced into the Diplomatic Room, where President Franklin D. Roosevelt had delivered his fireside chats during the Great Depression. We walked through the Cross Hall, where Abraham Lincoln greeted visitors in 1863 right before signing the Emancipation Proclamation. There was a sense of history and duty in every room. I've been fortunate to make several return trips to the White House, and that feeling never quite wears off. It was the perfect way to start our first week in our new jobs.

Back up in the residence, Mark and I visited with Donna Shalala, the secretary of health and human services. Donna once served as the chancellor of the University of Wisconsin–Madison, and the Democrats used that to their advantage in 1998, sending her to campaign against Mark and me. There were no hard feelings, but it was still surreal to be talking Badgers football in the Lincoln Bedroom with someone who, not long ago, had been rooting for our defeat.

Over the course of the evening, I walked through the Yellow

Oval Room, which had been renovated by Jackie Kennedy, and out onto the Truman Balcony. The balcony was the subject of great controversy back when President Harry S. Truman decided to build it in 1947. Critics complained loudly that it would ruin the architectural aesthetics of the White House. Truman pressed on anyway. Then, while it was being built, engineers discovered the whole house was structurally unsound, forcing a costly twenty-seven-month renovation. But looking out across the South Lawn at the Washington Monument on a clear night, I could understand why Truman thought that balcony was worth the trouble.

I was taking in the view, name tag on my lapel and Diet Coke in hand, when I sensed someone walk up alongside me.

"Paul Ryan of Wisconsin." I recognized the raspy Arkansas accent before I even saw his face. "Congratulations on your race."

"Mr. President," I said, shaking his hand. "It's a pleasure to meet you."

"You too," he said, nodding. "You too."

There I was, all alone with the leader of the free world, the opportunity to discuss anything unexpectedly right in front of me. Before I could get a word out, President Clinton turned to me.

"Son, exactly how old *are* you?"

That was a question I'd get a lot over the next couple of years. I was twenty-eight, and my new job offered constant reminders that I probably looked even younger.

Once during my first term I was rushing to a vote and forgot to put my congressional pin on the lapel of my suit jacket. The Capitol Hill police officer stationed outside the House floor stopped me in the hall, blocking me from walking any farther.

"Sorry, no staff allowed," he said, raising an arm to hold me back.

"Actually, I'm going in to vote," I said.

He laughed. "Yeah, right. Nice try."

"No really, it's true," I said, and I pulled out my voting card to show him that I was actually a member of Congress.

The police officer just shook his head. "Man," he said, "you guys are getting younger and younger every year."

Being elected at such an early age, I was careful to be respectful of people who had more wisdom and experience. Growing up, my mom used to say, "You have two ears and one mouth. Use them in that proportion." That pretty much summed up my approach to my first term.

Congressional orientation was useful, but what I really wanted was an education in how to be an effective representative. You can't read that in a book or learn it in a seminar. To get that kind of knowledge, you have to seek it out from the people who have earned it one bill, one vote, and one hearing at a time. So I looked around, picked out legislators who were really effective, and invited them to breakfast or lunch. It didn't matter to me if a member was liberal or conservative, a Republican or a Democrat, a relative newcomer or a seasoned old-timer. If they had been able to accomplish big things in the battle of ideas, I wanted to talk with them.

I ended up with some unlikely dining companions. Among them was Barney Frank, who was about to begin his ninth term as a member of the Massachusetts delegation. If Ted Kennedy was the liberal lion of the Senate, Frank was his counterpart in the House. On every issue, he was about as far away from me ideologically as a person could get. But he was also incredibly effective, and I figured that despite our differences, he could probably teach me a thing or two. *What's the harm in talking to him?* I thought.

So we met for breakfast one morning in the members-only dining room on the House side of the Capitol. I asked him the same question I posed to everyone I met with: What do you know now that you wish you'd known when you started out?

In his trademark thick accent and rapid-fire cadence—relics of a boyhood spent in Bayonne, New Jersey—Frank said, "Look, too many people come here and they try to be a jack-of-all-trades. They end up being about a mile wide and an inch deep. Everybody does that around here. And you know what? They're just passing time. They're bit players."

Then Frank paused and looked me right in the eye. "If you want to be effective," he said, punctuating his words by jabbing his finger into the table, "*do not be a generalist*. Don't spread yourself too thin. Specialize in two or three things, study up, and know those issues better than anybody else. Get yourself on the relevant committees, know everything there is to know about your issues, and then you can start setting policy in those areas." It ended up being the best advice I got.

Wisdom from members like Barney Frank and my work with senators Kasten and Brownback put me just far enough ahead of the curve that I felt comfortable and quickly learned to juggle my new responsibilities. Then, just as I was getting my bearings, the most unexpected thing happened: I had lunch with Janna Little.

After the campaign ended, all the adrenaline left my body. I was worn out, and by the time I returned to D.C. in January, I had come down with the flu. After long days in meetings, I'd drag myself back to the hotel where I was staying and kept a weary schedule of soup and sleep.

One night I was about to turn in when I got a call from my friend Mark Neuman. This was another Mark Neuman, not to be confused with the congressman. I don't know what the odds are, but two men with nearly identical names have had a role in key moments in my life. Mark had just picked up his girlfriend and was headed into the city.

"Get dressed. You're going to a party," Mark said. "We're coming to pick you up."

"Mark, no way. I'm sick. I'm not going anywhere," I protested.

Mark said, "You told me you wanted to get to know Janna Little. Well, this is your best chance. We will be at your hotel in twenty minutes."

Janna Little and I had both been staffers on Capitol Hill. A few years earlier, when I was working for Senator Brownback, I'd seen her across the room at the annual Congressional Sportsmen's Caucus banquet, where she was helping out with the auction.

Over the next few weeks, I asked around about her. Janna was an Oklahoma Democrat. She went to Wellesley College, a prestigious all-women's school in New England. She was well respected around Capitol Hill and was going to law school at night.

I don't know what it was, but she was on my mind. Most important, in a city where relationships don't always run too deep, my sense was Janna was as authentic as you could get. She reminded me of someone I would have met in Janesville.

But much to my disappointment and despite a fair bit of effort, our paths didn't really cross again except for the occasional hello in big groups. I let Mark, a mutual friend, know that I was hoping for a reintroduction so I could make a more lasting impression.

Janna's last name was "Little" and her friend Carolyn's last name was "Small." As luck would have it, they shared the same birthday: January 8. This coincidence inspired the Little-Small birthday party, a celebration to mark the day they both turned thirty.

At the party, Mark made good on his promise and reintroduced me to Janna. She was, as always, warm and kind.

"Congratulations on winning your race," she said, smiling.

"Thanks," I said. Then I nervously mumbled some incoherent small talk before mustering the courage to ask her to lunch sometime.

She agreed, and a couple of weeks later, we found ourselves at Two Quail, a restaurant tucked into the first floor of some row houses a couple of blocks away from the Senate side of the Capitol.

The Senate was voting on the Clinton impeachment that day, and as we walked over to lunch, demonstrators filled the sidewalks with banners and signs.

Two Quail was what passed for ambiance on Capitol Hill. Busy staffers liked its location; just minutes from the office, it allowed everyone to make time to mark special occasions between work meetings and floor votes. But walking into the establishment was a bit like stepping into a bizarre dream. The place was covered in busy floral wallpaper, and an odd arrangement of artwork and knick-knacks covered every possible inch of wall space. Its most famous decorative feature was a mounted deer head draped in pearls.

Not that I was really paying attention to any of that. As Janna and I talked over lunch, I felt like I was at peace and excited at the same time. For starters, we had a lot in common. We both loved the outdoors, and we were both from small towns. Janna and her two younger sisters had grown up in Madill, Oklahoma, which—with fewer than four thousand people—is even smaller than Janesville. But it wasn't just our similarities that drew me in; it was all of the qualities that set Janna apart. The nation's capital is the kind of place that tends to attract big personalities. Janna stood out for her quiet confidence and calm presence. She was down to earth and unassuming and incredibly smart. Halfway through lunch, I knew that this was the woman I wanted to marry.

We started dating soon after. We spent a lot of time outdoors: backpacking, fishing, going to the beach. She even came out hunting with me.

I eventually traveled to Oklahoma to ask Janna's mom and dad, Prudence and Dan Little, for their blessing to propose. Like any man who's ever made that request, I was nervous, but Dan and Pru took it easy on me and gave their support immediately. I didn't know it at the time, but their encouragement was more than just the start of a new chapter in my life; it was the beginning of being part of a new family. Prudence, who lost her long fight with cancer in 2010, was one of the smartest and most insightful women I have ever known. A small-town Iowa girl who studied at Wellesley and finished first in her class at law school, she was an impressive role model for Janna and her two sisters. And over the years, Dan has become, for all intents and purposes, my dad. His presence in my life has given me back the confidant and fatherly influence I lost when I was sixteen years old.

That April, I took Janna up to the Levihns' cottage on Big Saint Germain Lake in Wisconsin, a favorite childhood fishing spot. The Badgers were playing in the semifinals of the Final Four basketball tournament, and at halftime I suggested we take a walk out to the lake and have a beer. The minutes went by, and Janna began to figure out that something was up as my beloved Badgers became an afterthought. Finally, I got down on one knee and asked her to marry me. The Badgers' defeat that night didn't even register as we called our families to tell them the news.

When the engagement announcement ran in the *Milwaukee Journal Sentinel* that spring, the write-up mentioned that I liked to hunt. "Ryan," the *Journal Sentinel* explained, "does his own skinning and butchering." Janna read that line aloud with a fair bit of amusement.

"How funny," she said. "I can just imagine what my friends are thinking now."

* * *

During my first term in office, I took Barney Frank's advice and began to carve out a spot in the battle over economic policy. When I first got to Congress, few members were taking an active interest in the budget. Some people find the minutiae of fiscal matters daunting or boring or both, but somehow I had a knack for the subject. In politics, there are people who like the excitement of making history or the thrill of speaking before a big crowd during a campaign. Those things are great, but what I like is wading through the data and policy. For me, those numbers aren't just dollars or trends. They represent ways we could move the country in a better direction and make a positive difference in people's lives.

I got a spot on two committees involved in economic policy— Budget and Banking—and I kept my head down and hit the books. When I first ran for Congress, I'd told voters that I wanted to reform Social Security and put it on a path toward solvency. What I learned as part of the Budget Committee's Task Force on Social Security only reinforced my resolve.

At the task force, when they start talking about entitlement programs, everyone pulls out the heavy books, the wall charts, and the spreadsheets. It's easy to let your eyes glaze over and tune out. But my mind kept going back to our house in Janesville and the fall of 1986. When my dad died, I saw government make a difference for the better in our lives. Social Security was there for my grandmother, and the program's survivor benefits helped us. Before I could even vote, I saw the difference programs like Medicare and Social Security could make for people in old age and during tough times. But the more I studied up, the more worried I got—and I shared my concerns with my constituents.

During my first two years in Congress, I held dozens of town hall meetings in my district. I'd take questions on any topic, but I'd always start each event the same way: by talking about Social Security.

Together, Andy Speth and I tried to figure out how to explain the incredibly complex program—and its money troubles—in simple, personal terms. Since our idea to use his kids' toys as props in my campaign speeches worked so well, we printed up a bunch of Monopoly-style money and big stacks of index cards labeled "IOU."

At each event, we'd ask for volunteers and assign them roles: Sally the Taxpayer, Joe the Retiree, the Social Security Administration, Congress, the administration, and the U.S. Treasury. Then, we'd start moving the paper around.

"Sally the Taxpayer, give $500 to the Social Security Administration," I'd direct. "Okay, good. Now, Social Security, you give $200 to Joe the Retiree."

Everyone would look confused. "Wait a minute," the person playing Joe would inevitably say. "Why am I getting Sally's money? Where's the money I paid in when I was working? What happened to my Social Security account?"

With that, we'd be off to the races, explaining that Social Security, created in 1935 and designed to provide economic security to the disabled, the retired, and families coping with the death of a parent or a spouse, doesn't have a pile of money waiting for you when you turn sixty-five. It is a pay-as-you-go system, meaning that taxes paid by current workers cover the benefits of current retirees.

"That's part of the problem," I'd tell the man cast as Joe. "Every person who pays into the system relies on the next generation of workers to make good on the program's promises to them. Now, so far, that's been working pretty well. Social Security has been able to meet its obligations to citizens. In fact, for all but eleven years of its existence, the money it's taken in through taxes has either met or exceeded the amount of money it needed to pay out. But, starting with President Johnson, here's what the government did with those surplus funds."

I'd ask the person playing the role of the Social Security Administration to give the leftover money to the guy who was standing in for Congress. In turn, he'd give the money to the person playing the administration, and "Congress" would give "Social Security" a big stack of IOUs.

"Basically," I'd explain, "the government invests any surplus funds in special government-backed bonds, leaving a stack of IOUs for future beneficiaries. The government then uses that money to pay for other programs. Social Security has really become a slush fund for members of Congress, allowing them to fund pet projects and avoid making hard decisions about how to keep costs in other areas of the government under control."

At this point, without fail, people would start to get really upset. That's unreal, they'd say. Washington shouldn't be allowed to do things this way.

Then I'd explain that things were about to get a lot worse because of demographic trends. First, the Baby Boomer generation was getting ready to retire, and the coming flood of new retirees threatened to overload the system. In 1950, there were sixteen workers for every retiree. By the time the Baby Boomer wave hit, there would be just over three workers per beneficiary. That shrinking ratio meant there wouldn't be enough tax income to keep the system flush with cash.

Furthermore, people were simply living longer, meaning the total amount of benefits each American would draw over the course of his or her lifetime continued to grow. Together, these two factors—an influx of retirees and longer life spans—meant Social Security was headed for catastrophe.

I'd talk with my constituents about the charts I had seen where the line that represented what we were spending on Social Security stretched far above the line representing the tax revenue we'd take in. I knew the white space between those two lines represented people—just like my grandmother and my mom—who were counting on their Social Security benefits and would find the government unable to keep the promises it had made. When we reached that point, we'd have nothing left but painful choices. We could either slash benefits or raise taxes in real time. Whichever path we chose, the impact would be devastating.

I felt passionately that we had to head off the coming catastrophe, and I'll admit that early in my career, I had a tendency to focus on trying to persuade people and making my point. Janna helped me slow down and really listen to what people were saying to me. Early in our marriage, she started coming to some of my events. One day, she gently said to me, "Are you up for a little constructive criticism?"

"Sure," I replied. "What's up?"

"Look," she said, "sometimes you have to take a minute. People aren't necessarily coming to these events because they want to hear what you think; they want *you* to hear what *they* think. Listen to them. Really consider what they are saying to you, especially if they disagree with you."

Janna was right. The more I listened, the more I learned from and about the people I represent. It's been said that in any good marriage each partner makes the other person better. That's certainly been true for me. One of the ways Janna has helped me is that she's made me a better listener. She helps ensure that what constituents share with us really sinks in.

At the end of every town hall, people would come up and talk to me, and I found out that a lot of them shared my concerns about Social Security. I've planned out my retirement, they would say, and I'm counting on it. An entitlement crisis was coming, and the people I served understood that the sooner we dealt with it, the better off we would be.

My solution was twofold. First, we would put Social Security funds in the proverbial "lockbox," which would prevent the program from being raided to pay for other things. Second, we would allow every citizen to share in our country's economic prosperity by reforming Social Security to look more like the Thrift Savings Plan, a benefit available to every member of Congress and federal employee.

The Thrift Savings Plan allows federal workers to set aside pretax income and invest it in the market. I wanted to reform Social Security in ways that would give young people the same opportunity. Instead of inheriting a stack of IOUs, Americans would be able to place a generous portion of their Social Security taxes into a personal retirement account that Social Security would invest in the market. The accounts would be subject to proper safeguards and age indexing, meaning the investment strategy for their money would become more conservative as individuals got closer to retirement age.

Everyone would own their account; it would be their property. It would give them their own piece of the American economy and a better rate of return. And Social Security would be put on the path toward solvency instead of bankruptcy.

In 2001, a budget surplus of over $230 billion meant that Social Security reform was finally a real possibility, and it seemed to have a determined advocate in President George W. Bush. In his first inaugural address, the president promised to take on entitlement reform. In February, he appeared before a joint session of Congress and pledged to provide younger workers with personal retirement accounts. That spring, he formed a commission headed by Senator Daniel Patrick Moynihan and Richard Parsons of AOL-Time Warner. Their task was to come up with recommendations that reflected the president's key priorities for reform, including the creation of personal accounts.

These were promising signs, but it was tough to gauge the administration's commitment, especially because I knew there were real skeptics in their ranks. Early in the president's first term, my friend Rob Portman arranged for a few of us to meet with Dick Cheney, the new vice president. At the time, Rob had served almost eight years in the House, representing the Second Congressional District of Ohio. Having been a key advisor in the 1990s to the first President Bush, he was the natural choice in 2001 to serve as the liaison between Republicans in the House and the administration of George W. Bush.

Our meeting took place in a small conference room on the third floor of the Capitol Building. Vice President Cheney sat at one end of the table. Rob was seated next to him and the rest of us took up the other spots. Rob moderated, giving each member of Congress a few minutes to pitch the vice president on our top priority for the administration's first term. When it got to me, I used my two minutes to discuss Social Security.

"The surplus has given us a huge opportunity," I explained. "If we dedicate the Social Security surplus to reform, we can shore up the program and end the raid on the trust fund." I talked about the opportunity to create a real ownership society, how workers could actually own a piece of the free enterprise system through these reforms.

As soon as I finished my pitch, Vice President Cheney said, "Yeah, we're not going to do that." Then he looked at the person sitting next to me, signaling that he was ready to hear the next idea. His terse reply was the verbal equivalent of someone swatting an annoying mosquito from his face.

I wanted a strong commitment from the new administration, but I knew even that wouldn't ensure the reform effort would sail smoothly through Congress. Some members felt the budget surplus should be used solely for a large tax cut instead. Tax cuts alone, they argued, were the priority; reforming Social Security could be put off for another day. Others, like me, wanted a more modest tax cut so that the rest of the surplus money could fully fund reform and the transition to personal accounts, which I argued was also good pro-growth policy. Yet, even among my fellow reformers, there was a debate about how big these new accounts should be, how the transition should work, and what kinds of safeguards we ought to put in place.

On the morning of September 11, 2001, I joined a handful of members of Congress at the White House to continue the budget surplus debate. Over breakfast with Ken Mehlman, the president's political director, we discussed the proposals. I repeated my case for using part of the surplus to fund Social Security reform and the rest to reduce the tax burden. It was, I argued, a win-win.

We kept on talking, unaware that life was already changing in a city 230 miles away. As we left the White House that morning, we learned that two planes had flown into the Twin Towers in New York City. Minutes after we drove away from the White House grounds, American Airlines Flight 77 crashed into the Pentagon.

*   *   *

At the end of that terrifying and devastating week, Andy and I got in a car and made the long trip home to Janesville. All I can remember about that drive are the American flags. They were everywhere—in car windows, on truck antennas, hanging from overpasses and bridges. The entire journey through Maryland, Pennsylvania, Ohio, Indiana, and Illinois was bathed in red, white, and blue.

All along, I held out hope that when we reached Janesville, things might start to feel a little bit normal again. But as I walked in the front door of our house, I couldn't shake the disquiet and unease that had been with me all week. It felt like nothing would ever be the same. And, in a lot of ways, it wouldn't.

*   *   *

After 9/11, our focus in Congress rightly shifted to terrorism and national security. My colleagues with military or intelligence experience had a natural contribution to make. I decided to figure out how I could use my economics background to help.

It was clear to me that one of the best tools in our foreign policy arsenal was trade. So, from my spot on the Ways and Means

Committee, I helped move trade agreements forward. I also cofounded the Middle East Economic Partnership Caucus, which aimed to strengthen relations between our country and Middle Eastern nations through economic engagement.

But I was still hopeful that we could make progress on reforming Social Security, even though national security was now our top priority. Then came the economic downturn, the effort to rebuild and recover after 9/11, and the war in Afghanistan—all of which strained the Treasury.

External events—the weak economy and threats from our enemies—impacted the government's budget priorities. While that was understandable, it was also true that the Republican Party strayed from its core principle of spending discipline.

For much of my early years in Congress, big-spending Republicans dominated our caucus. They held several of the congressional chairmanships and some of our leadership posts. If the growth of government, constant overspending, and a weakness for earmarks are the measure, these Republicans were indistinguishable from Democrats. They earmarked like crazy and grew the size of government instead of reining it in.

Those of us who argued for fiscal restraint often found ourselves in the minority of the majority. We didn't have the numbers we needed to right the ship. Our only leverage was our vote—and often that wasn't much leverage at all, since we were increasingly given bad choices and forced to vote for the lesser of two evils.

Take, for example, the Medicare Prescription Drug, Improvement, and Modernization Act. Since its creation in 1965, Medicare has provided health-care coverage for Americans who are over the age of sixty-five or have a permanent disability. Preventive care, hospital stays, and visits with physicians had long been part of the program. By 2000, many were calling for an overhaul that would add a prescription drug benefit as well.

President George W. Bush had campaigned on a promise to add prescription coverage to traditional Medicare. During his first term, between 2000 and 2003, the White House, House, and Senate offered competing proposals that tried to make good on the pledge.

The administration's initial plan was bold, conservative policy, but unfortunately, it was quickly derailed by Republican leaders on Capitol Hill. After that, for conservatives, each round was more depressing than the last. The low point came when Senate Democrats pitched a plan that would have cost $600 billion over ten years.

When the dust settled in June 2003, two Medicare modernization proposals were left standing—one in the Senate and one in the House. The House bill was worrisome in a lot of ways. It created a new federal entitlement that wasn't paid for, which offended my conservative core. That said, my colleagues and I were able to amend the bill so that it included some good reforms.

For example, one of our greatest challenges was—and is—the continued explosion of health-care costs. The best way to combat that problem is by promoting greater competition in the private marketplace, requiring providers to better serve the patient. And the best way to encourage that kind of competition is to put patients in charge of their health-care spending.

So I participated in an effort to add a provision to the House version of the Medicare bill that allowed Americans enrolled in high-deductible insurance plans to put pretax income into a Health Savings Account, or HSA. People could then use the money in their HSAs to pay for prescription drug copays, health services, and medical devices.

The HSA provision was a good first step toward bending the cost curve in health care. Because patients were spending their own money, they would have an incentive to ask questions, shop around, and get the best deal. The competition for their health-care dollars would, in turn, help keep costs down. Together, some colleagues and

I got several Republicans to sign a letter stating they wouldn't vote for the bill unless it included full-fledged HSAs, and I successfully managed it as an amendment on the floor.

Together, conservatives in the House also added Medicare Advantage to the legislation. Under this new health-care program, seniors would be able to use their Medicare dollars to purchase a private insurance plan that best met their needs. In wonk-speak, that kind of program is similar to what is called "premium support." Medicare provides the resources, the individual makes the choice, and the government offers financial support to help the individual pay their premiums. It's similar to how members of Congress get their health coverage—and it's a concept that we should replicate for all of Medicare, because it offers more affordable options, higher-quality care, and real security for seniors.

So, when the final House proposal came up for a vote, I was torn. It had the HSAs I fought for. It included Medicare Advantage, which I liked. And although it introduced a new entitlement, the drug benefit was delivered through the private insurance system. On the whole, it wasn't ideal, but it moved the ball forward toward broader, conservative goals.

The House proposal was certainly much better than the alternative, a version of the bill produced by the Senate Finance Committee. The Senate proposal didn't contain offsets, either, but it also didn't include HSAs or the Medicare Advantage plans. It was just another big, government-run entitlement with no connection to the private market.

As the vote on the House bill approached, I was still trying to decide which way I would go. It was going to be close, and President Bush was calling members to shore up support. When we spoke, I explained my overriding concern: both bills added too much to the debt.

The president waited until I was done and said, "Listen, I am going to sign into law a prescription drug benefit. You guys in the House are going to decide which one I sign. Am I going to sign the one with HSAs and private plans, or am I going to sign the Senate bill? That's your choice."

That was frustrating. But it was also the truth. I knew I had two options. I could walk away, throw up my hands, and vote no. That would allow me to disown the outcome. But if I helped defeat the House bill, I would also be knowingly helping the Senate's big-government bill become law. It was a tough moment in my career. I could have kept my hands clean and remained ideologically pure, but my conscience told me that it would have been wrong to let the worse option win just because the better option wasn't 100 percent perfect. I knew I'd get bloodied up, but I felt an obligation to influence the outcome for the better—and I trusted that in the end the people would recognize the good sense of my vote.

The Medicare modernization bill was one of many pieces of legislation during those years that put me in the position of having to practice defensive voting. The bill I wanted wasn't offered, so I had to choose between two that were both flawed. The only comfort was that my vote helped prevent a far worse piece of legislation from becoming law.

As a member of a legislative body, you don't always get the choices you want to vote on. Sometimes you are forced to choose between the lesser of two evils. This is an unhappy reality in the lawmaking process, but the answer can't be simply to oppose every proposal that doesn't have your complete approval. I've seen firsthand the damage that approach can do.

After the 2008 presidential election, the economy was in a tailspin and we got word that the major auto companies were going down. The administration came to Congress with a plan. Earlier in the session, unrelated to the economic distress, we had passed an energy bill that authorized $25 billion in loans for the auto industry so they could retrofit their factories to make more green cars. I had opposed the money and voted against the bill. I felt it was corporate welfare and just more green pork we couldn't afford and they didn't need. But by then, Republicans didn't control the House. Nancy Pelosi brought it to the floor, the House and Senate passed it, and President Bush signed it.

Now, with the economic crisis in full swing, the Bush administration wanted to take that previously approved money and use it to help save the car companies. Not long after they pitched their proposal, I ran into Josh Bolten, the president's chief of staff, at a going-away dinner for a mutual friend. He asked me which way I was leaning on their proposal. I explained that my instinct was to vote no. I'd been against the fund they were tapping from the beginning, and I didn't think we had the resources to bail the car companies out.

"Look," he said, "I understand your position. But if we don't get the $25 billion from the Department of Energy, then we're going to use TARP to shore up the auto companies."

The prospect of using TARP, the Troubled Asset Relief Program, horrified me. That money was supposed to be used for buying toxic assets to stop the credit markets from crashing, not for bailing out these companies. It would set a troubling precedent for all-new government intervention into the economy.

Josh explained that the administration would not let the car companies go down on its watch. They were not going to leave office like Herbert Hoover.

The choice was clear: I could either vote to reallocate the green-car fund, or I could vote no and help ensure that they used TARP. If I did the latter, I'd be contributing to an open-ended bailout, because TARP had virtually no limits on it.

I went back to my office after that dinner and gave the vote a lot of thought. I decided that if the support was there to shore up the auto companies, I would rather they got the money that had been assigned to a program I opposed. That would put the funds to a better use and prevent the administration from tapping TARP.

When the time came, the House passed the bill and I voted yes. When it got to the Senate, Jim DeMint, a conservative from South Carolina, led an effort that killed it. Sure enough, the administration then used TARP funds instead. It set a dangerous precedent, allowing the federal government to expand the program into other areas. And the money originally allocated for the task grew from $25 billion to $65 billion, much of which the American taxpayers will never get back.

In the end, an effort meant to stop the auto bailout actually caused an even worse outcome. The bailout still happened, but it cost more money and set a dangerous precedent. The whole affair was a good reminder that votes that look "pure" can really pave the way for a more harmful policy. That outcome is anything but a victory for our party, our country, or our people.

Congressman Jim Sensenbrenner, my close friend and colleague from Wisconsin, used to tease me about my anguish over such votes. "It's your Catholic guilt," he would say.

I just know that in Congress, you have to do the best thing under the circumstances you're in and then be willing to take the heat. If you can make things better and move the outcome toward conservative principles, then you must have the courage and the wisdom to say yes. You've got to be willing to take criticism—even from your friends—and trust that the people will understand that governing requires trade-offs. That was how it was with my votes on the Medicare overhaul and funding for the auto companies.

On those votes and others during that time, a lot of conservatives felt discouraged. We often commiserated at meetings of the House Republican Study Committee, or the RSC.

The committee was formed in 1973 as a conservative check on the power of Republican House leadership. While its focus has shifted over the years, its core mission has always been the protection and promotion of key conservative causes like a strong national defense, a balanced budget, and the Second Amendment. I'd joined the committee during my first term.

During the Bush years, members of the RSC were united by a shared frustration over federal spending. To his credit, early in his first term, President Bush had vowed to put an end to wasteful boondoggles pursued at taxpayer expense. To drive the point home, he released a budget proposal in 2002 that included several passages chastising Congress for its earmarks.

The RSC backed the president's words up with actions. Together in the House we fought against an appropriations process that was increasingly out of control. We tried backbencher, guerilla tactics on the floor, proposing amendments and voting against bills and rules. We went to Speaker Dennis Hastert and others in the leadership and asked them to change course. But we barely made a dent in the process, and federal spending continued to grow at an unsustainable rate.

In the House, we had exhausted all of our options. So, at our next meeting with the president, the RSC decided to speak with him directly about our concerns.

Together, we sat on couches in the Yellow Oval Room, a few steps from the balcony where I first met Bill Clinton. One by one, we each discussed an issue we felt was in need of presidential support.

When it was my turn, I said, "Mr. President, we need you to get involved and help us rein in spending. The earmark culture is wrong. It's corrupt, and it's not who we are. You've got to weigh in. It's the only way we can turn this around."

The president thanked us for coming down to the White House.

Regarding spending, he noted that he shared our concerns. But he felt that as part of the Republican majority, we should be able to fix those bills before they reached his desk.

I explained that we had done what we could, but we were in the minority of the majority. Our options were limited.

"We've lost the fight," I said. "We need you to rein in the caucus. We need you to send a message."

The president nodded sympathetically. He understood and sympathized with our position, but he explained that his focus had to be on keeping the country safe from another attack. He was counting on House Speaker Dennis Hastert and Senate Majority Leader Bill Frist to pay the bills and keep the trains running on time, and he felt that a veto would undercut them. If we wanted to change the bills, we'd have to do it in the House.

That was when I knew the cavalry wasn't coming. There was no higher authority that could weigh in, get everyone in line, and make sure that we governed according to our principles. While the president was understandably preoccupied with national security, it was clear that when it came to fiscal policy our party was adrift. My colleagues and I would continue to be confronted by inferior bills and lousy choices.

Taken together, these experiences taught me valuable lessons about how the House and Senate operate, and I came away with an even deeper appreciation for the role of congressional leadership. Who holds the top posts really matters because the decisions they make at the outset determine the votes that every member has to take and how much good we can achieve for our country and our fellow citizens.

My disappointment over the lack of fiscal restraint was compounded by our failure to make any progress on shoring up our entitlement programs, the true drivers of our debt. After the administration abandoned Social Security reform in 2001 in favor of a tax cut, people cautioned me against moving forward on my own. Entitlement programs were like the third rail on a subway track: electrified. Touching them was political suicide. I decided the problem was too important to go unresolved. I wrote a big Social Security reform bill with Senator John Sununu of New Hampshire. When people tried to discourage me, I told them, "It's too late. I'm hugging the third rail like a koala bear."

The Ryan-Sununu bill didn't get much traction until after the 2004 campaign, when President Bush announced he would pursue Social Security reform in his second term. Ultimately, the Bush administration sought much smaller personal retirement accounts than the ones John Sununu and I had proposed. But, like the House version of the Medicare Part D bill, it was better than the alternative. Unfortunately, the effort to persuade Americans and their elected representatives to support the reform was flawed from the start. The Bush administration had the engineering guys running the marketing department, and even when the president told Americans that in a newly reformed Social Security system, "this money is in your name, in your account—it's not just a program, it's your property," somehow the argument just didn't get through.

Despite problems with the outreach, we managed to get a major concession from the House leadership before the August recess in 2005. Majority Leader Tom DeLay and Bill Thomas, the chairman of the Ways and Means Committee, agreed that after the summer break they would bring our reform bill, which included personal retirement accounts, to the House floor for a vote.

Then Hurricane Katrina hit. The devastation was incredible and the response was woefully inadequate. By the time we returned from recess, the administration was struggling. House leadership didn't want to risk the politics of bringing Social Security to the floor, and the administration wasn't in a strong enough position to pursue it. The whole effort completely fizzled away.

At the beginning of the Bush years, I had been excited about what we could accomplish in the majority. By 2006, I was deeply disappointed. On matters of domestic policy, we weren't rising to big challenges like entitlement reform. Instead, we were growing the size of government and incurring deeper and deeper debt. We were failing to live up to our conservative principles of limited government and spending restraint.

We lost our way. And, in the 2006 elections, we lost control of the Senate and the House.

*   *   *

Under the new schedule imposed by Speaker Nancy Pelosi, the House was in session five days a week. That left me with just over forty-eight hours every weekend to get back home and see Janna and our three kids. Meanwhile, divided government made it nearly impossible to advance any proposals or ideas.

I'd been discouraged when I was in the minority of the majority, and I was disappointed in my party. We had strayed from our principles and failed to lead on the big issues. But the thought of the Left calling all the shots was downright depressing. For the first time, I started thinking about leaving Congress and doing something else with my life. I missed Janesville. I missed my family. And I didn't see much opportunity to get things done.

One morning after a particularly frustrating week, I got up at five a.m. and hiked out into the woods to go bowhunting. I was in a treestand watching the sun come up when I remembered something my dad used to say to me as a kid: "Son, you're either part of the problem, or you're part of the solution." He usually said that when I was being part of the problem.

I hadn't come to Congress to just go along with the crowd. I wanted to do big and serious things. I realized it wasn't enough to keep choosing between two bad options and voting for the lesser of two evils. And I certainly didn't want to be just one more voice in the chorus of "no." I thought, to hell with the consequences, I was going to push the kind of conservatism I believed in.

By the time I got back to my truck that morning, I had decided that I was going to put out a very specific proposal detailing how we could head off the impending budgetary crisis we faced. I knew it was a political risk. In fact, I thought there was a very real possibility that it would end my political career. But I knew that I would rather be who I was, say what I believed, and lose than continue getting reelected by playing it safe.

The way I thought about it was "do or die." Janna and I later joked that it was my "Jerry Maguire Moment."

I started by seeking the top spot at the House Budget Committee. It required leapfrogging several more senior members of the committee. But I was able to persuade my colleagues, and in January 2007, I became the ranking member of the committee, which is the top position for the minority party.

With additional staff and new resources at my disposal, I began writing a document that would eventually become known as the "Roadmap for America's Future." It took the best ideas we could develop for getting our fiscal house in order and put them in one comprehensive plan. The Roadmap reformed Medicare, Medicaid, and Social Security. It outlined policy proposals to make health insurance affordable and accessible to all. It simplified our tax code and did away with barriers to economic growth.

In all, the proposals in the Roadmap would have added up to a solution to our entitlement crisis. They would have restored fiscal order and held federal taxes to the post–World War II average as a percentage of the economy. And they represented the best budgetary policy for growing our economy, which would in turn provide Americans with greater opportunities and good-paying jobs.

I worked on the plan for well over a year. I consulted with

actuaries at Medicare and Social Security. And I got feedback from the Congressional Budget Office. I solicited input from economists, and continually refined the proposals with my staff in the dingy basement rooms of the Cannon House Office Building. After putting all the pieces together, I introduced my plan as H.R. 6110, The Roadmap for America's Future Act of 2008.

At first, we heard nothing but crickets. A presidential contest was heating up, and campaign platitudes trumped policy details. But soon enough, the critics took a look and started to pile on. Some on the Left sensed a political opportunity; others on the Right worried about the political risks.

A lot of people said I was crazy—and compared to many others, they were being nice. The political pundits couldn't believe I'd put all of my proposals in one document. The GOP's professional consultants and pollsters worried aloud that the Democrats would beat us over the head with the Roadmap in the upcoming November elections and prevent us from taking back the House and Senate.

The National Republican Congressional Committee, the entity in charge of electing Republicans to the House, told every candidate running that year to stay away from my plan—and from me. Don't cosponsor it, don't support it, and don't talk about it.

In May, shortly after introducing the proposal, I sat down for what I'd hoped would be a productive conversation with the political staff at the NRCC. I offered to help them think through how to message the policy ideas in the plan. But the more I volunteered to assist them, the more irritated they seemed.

They made it clear that they believed the Roadmap would probably cost our party a congressional majority—and they strategized accordingly. Later, in August, when their press shop learned that MSNBC was trying to get an NRCC-endorsed candidate to talk about the Roadmap on TV, an alert went out far and wide:

"MSNBC is trying to convince a Republican candidate to go on the Dylan Ratigan Show tonight and support the Paul Ryan Roadmap, therefore supporting Social Security privatization. Please do NOT accept this invitation; it will not end well. In addition, if you receive any questions about the Roadmap, please contact me immediately before answering any questions."

In criticizing the Roadmap, the NRCC had a lot of company. I was ostracized for putting the plan out there, and I didn't have much support. The original roadmap attracted only eight cosponsors—and almost all of them were my colleagues from the Republican Study Committee.

On the day he decided to join the effort, Jeb Hensarling of Texas came to see me.

"If you're willing to stick your neck out like this, I have an obligation to stand with you," he said.

Tim Walberg of Michigan felt the same way. He came to me one day and said, "Paul, I want to sign on to the bill. When can I cosponsor it?"

"Tim, I can't let you do that," I said. Tim was at the top of the Democrats' target list for 2008. He was courageous, but signing on would have meant certain defeat.

"Sign on next January, after you've been reelected," I said.

Tim lost that fall, but he'd make his way back to Congress by 2011—in time to vote for the second iteration of our budget plan.

* * *

When I first started working on the Roadmap in 2007, I based my projections on consultations I'd had with several economists and the Congressional Budget Office. They all agreed a fiscal crisis was coming, but their calculations indicated we had time to prevent it from happening. On all the charts they showed me, the really worrisome lines—the ones that dipped deep into the red—were at least a decade out.

Then, in 2008, the dominoes started to fall. First, the Federal Reserve engineered the buyout of Bear Stearns. Then, the government placed Fannie Mae and Freddie Mac into conservatorship, and next, Lehman Brothers filed for bankruptcy, sending a shock wave through the economy. By the end of September, Washington Mutual had collapsed, while Goldman Sachs and Morgan Stanley had morphed into bank holding companies.

Every night the news broadcasts led with footage of people walking out onto a New York City street, the contents of their desks in boxes. Soon, that turmoil on Wall Street rippled across Main Street, including in Janesville, where the GM plant was closing its doors.

As ranking member of the Budget Committee, I felt I had a duty to make sense of the events as they unfolded and try to figure out if there was anything we could do to stop the bleeding. I was on the phone with Ben Bernanke, the chair of the Federal Reserve, and Treasury secretary Hank Paulson constantly—sometimes multiple times a day.

One night, the House was in the midst of a late-night session when I got word that Ben was trying to reach me. I made my way to a phone in the cloakroom that's next to the House floor and dialed the number my staff had given to me.

"I'm glad they found you," Ben said, dour but calm. "I didn't want to wait."

Ben and I had known each other for some time. Very little seemed to rattle him, but on this night, he sounded deeply worried.

"Listen, the guys just sent over the latest runs of the economic scenarios that are about to hit."

"How bad are they?" I asked.

"Pretty bad." Ben's voice was crackling with uncertainty and fear. "If our models are right, then we're looking at a great recession. I think unemployment could go as high as 10 percent. If prices drop in a deflationary spiral, we could be looking at a whole string of bankruptcies, and a real crash."

I was also talking almost hourly with members of my staff on the Budget Committee. I'll never forget the night we sat down with their new calculations. It was late in the evening and I was exhausted. We'd been on high alert for weeks, and no one was getting much sleep. I walked down to a windowless office in the bowels of the Cannon Office Building, where my staff laid dozens of new charts and graphs out in front of me.

All of the problems had moved up. The doomsday scenario we'd thought was looming out on the horizon was happening here and now.

As I flipped through the charts and scanned the new numbers, I realized that the crisis was much worse than we'd even imagined. Not only were millions of people going to lose their jobs, but we could be facing a depression, and surely a severe recession. On top of that, all of the problems we thought were a decade away were upon us now. We were looking at running trillion-dollar deficits. It would be years before we'd see an economic recovery.

We couldn't afford to choose between the lesser of two evils anymore. It was time to lead.

CHAPTER 4

The Battle of Ideas

Just before eleven p.m., Fox News called Virginia for Barack Obama. It was Election Night 2008, and anchors Megyn Kelly and Brit Hume were discussing his strong support among newly registered voters and independents. Things were looking good in the First District of Wisconsin, but I was thinking about my friend, Tim Walberg, the congressman from Michigan who had wanted to cosponsor the Roadmap.

Tim had the same kind of district as mine—blue-collar, a tight margin between Republicans and Democrats. He had the same voting record and the same principles. But he was probably going to lose, and he wasn't alone.

Election Night 2008 felt like the moment of reckoning, and I was frustrated. Our party had grown timid. It was contradicting its own principles. It wasn't backing up conservatives like Tim who needed support in their reelection bids.

When Fox News called and asked if I would be willing to do a live interview that night, I decided to drop any pretense of being polite or deferential. Brit Hume gave me an opening to say what I thought out loud, and I took it.

"Where does the Republican Party go from here?" asked Brit.

"We need a house cleaning in our party," I said. "Let's make this the election that's a turnaround for the Republican Party. That's what we have to get out of this evening."

A few minutes after I wrapped up with Brit, Fox News called California for Senator Barack Obama, a milestone that gave him 275 electoral votes and the presidency.

The election also gave House Democrats an even greater majority; the gap between the two parties now stood at twenty-one seats. The general sense among the remaining Republicans was that we had to push out the deadwood and usher in bold leaders and proposals. And the collapse of the financial system gave our mission a deeper urgency. We had to get serious about our nation's economy and the size of our government.

What worried me most was that the Republican Party wasn't up to the task. We'd become lazy and tired. We were complicit in creating many of the problems we now faced. We'd become just another party of big spending and big government.

I knew if we were going to save the country, first we would have to change the Republican Party from within.

For starters, we needed to step up and really engage in the battle of ideas. We had to be bold, get specific, and accept the risks that entailed. We had to put our ideas in writing and make the case for them in each campaign. We had to engage with Americans from every walk of life and deliver solutions that expanded opportunities for all. And we had to have the courage to defend our proposals when they came under attack.

Real change was necessary, and if the Republican Party was going to make that change, then we had to lead. We had to win elections not by merely attacking our opponents or offering vague generalities, but by running on our ideas so that we could win a mandate. Going forward, we would have to be all in.

To our surprise, many of us who had been backbenchers during the Bush years finally started gaining traction. More and more people came out of the woodwork to support our efforts. We had lost everything, and nothing the old guard tried was working.

But now we were in the minority, and to get things done, our party needed an army. We needed to build a conservative governing majority again—this time with men and women who wouldn't go wobbly when they came to Washington. In 2009, my colleagues and I set out to find them.

Along those lines, I'd been strategizing with two close friends. I'd met Eric Cantor about eight years earlier when he was elected to represent Virginia's Seventh Congressional District. We served on the Ways and Means Committee together, and he rose through the House leadership quickly, becoming chief deputy whip by 2003. Very conservative and smart, he could always be counted on for shrewd analysis and tactical advice, delivered in his subtle Southern drawl.

Kevin McCarthy arrived a little later, in 2007. He was a native Californian, gregarious and laid-back. At six thirty every morning, Kevin would wake up and join a bipartisan group of us in the House gym. Over tough P90X sessions, we all got to know each other. Kevin is a guy who knows how to build a team and get it to work toward a common goal, a skill that I would come to appreciate.

Eric, Kevin, and I had each been discouraged and frustrated by recent events. For years, we had watched our party recruit people who simply saw Congress as their next promotion. That strategy filled our ranks with local career politicians whose greatest goal was to become federal career politicians. Once elected, they were beholden to the earmark culture because they needed to deliver for their districts.

During the 2008 cycle, Eric, Kevin, and I sought to fix that problem by creating a recruitment program called Young Guns, a name adapted from a magazine article about our work. Candidly, I still hate that name, but I'm proud of the effort.

The idea was to go out and find bright, talented, principled leaders who would support a conservative agenda—and wouldn't bolt when the going got tough. Once we identified good prospects, we offered them advice and fund-raising help in exchange for meeting key benchmarks in their candidacy.

Our effort was about more than just recruitment, though; it was ultimately about creating and implementing good policy. In that regard, our first task after the election was to answer President-Elect Obama's call for proposals that could get the American economy out of crisis.

In January 2009, millions were out of work and foreclosures kept racking up while economic growth stalled. Eric and House Minority Leader John Boehner convened the House Republican Economic Working Group, which produced a plan to jump-start the economy by providing tax relief, responsible housing and health-care reforms, and immediate help for those looking for a job.

The Democrats had a plan, too—a grab bag of congressional appropriators' pet projects, all of which, we were assured, were "shovel ready." In reality, with a price tag of $787 billion, it was just a spectacular waste of money. It took me all of a minute to figure out it wouldn't get the economy growing again and decide to vote against it.

In late January, John and Eric met with the president to discuss the competing proposals. They detailed the Republican alternative and were encouraged by the president's feedback. Yet at the same time he promised to work with us, he gave Nancy Pelosi and Harry Reid the green light to jam their stimulus bill through Congress. The American Recovery and Reinvestment Act passed the House without any Republican input—or any of our votes. Our alternative was attacked and then ignored. It was a sign of things to come.

* * *

In the president's first address to Congress, he made it clear that health-care reform would be a key priority. Left unsaid was that his administration's approach in pursuit of that goal would marry deeply entrenched ideology with the brutal efficiency of machine politics.

Between February and late September 2009, every House and Senate proposal that moved forward included the "public option," a provision championed by the liberal wing of the Democratic Party that would create a government-run insurance agency. Republicans were extremely worried about the impact that the public option would have on the cost and quality of health care. However, even putting that provision aside, the House version of the legislation was a monstrosity. It contained more than two thousand pages of rules, mandates, taxes, fees, and fines. It forced Americans to purchase insurance or pay a penalty, a provision that would be enforced by the IRS. Even with all the revenue it raised through taxes on medical device companies and others, the plan still needed to raid $716 billion from Medicare to make the numbers work. It would spend trillions over ten years, and it grew the size of the federal bureaucracy.

A particularly pernicious expansion of government was the creation of the Independent Payment Advisory Board, a board of fifteen so-called experts empowered to put price controls on Medicare that would lead to inferior care and restricted access for seniors. The board was designed to work around Congress and disregard the interests of Medicare recipients. Instead of empowering 50 million seniors with more control over their care, the administration put fifteen unelected bureaucrats in charge. I just found that setup outrageous—both in terms of my adherence to constitutional self-government and my commitment to preserving Medicare.

Of course, my biggest objection to the bill was that it gave the government tasks that it's simply not equipped to carry out. Adapting to consumers' needs, offering better choices in price and quality, keeping costs down—those are all things that market-based solutions can better deliver. I raised these concerns in meetings I had with the health-care community as part of my work on the Ways and Means Committee. The responses I got were unsettling.

As group after group came in to see me, I asked, *Why are you cooperating with this bill? I can count dozens of provisions in here that are going to make it harder for doctors and nurses to care for their patients. This is going to make it more difficult for people to get quality care.*

Everyone gave me the same response: We're either at the table or on the menu. If we don't participate, the bill could end up a lot worse for us than it is now.

Finally, I stopped someone midsentence. "I keep hearing that phrase. Where is this coming from?"

Apparently that was the key talking point being used by both the president's staff and the bill drafters in Congress. The message had clearly gotten through. To a person, everyone I met with was convinced that they had to shape up and cooperate if they wanted to be cut in on the deal. Otherwise, Democratic leaders and staff heavily implied, we will eviscerate you.

I'd heard about stuff like this, but I'd never actually seen it in action before. This was smashmouth, raw-power politics. The Left was using intimidation and legislative extortion to get its way. Obamacare was the application of a big-government philosophy by any means necessary.

The House debated the bill late into the evening on Saturday, November 7. As speaker after speaker compared it to Medicare and Social Security, I sat there wondering, *Do they know that those programs are headed for bankruptcy?* Putting aside my philosophy about the proper role of government, I wondered how they could support the creation of a new entitlement that people would come to rely on but we could not afford. When it came to Obamacare, the political reality was that we could not stop it, but due to the fiscal pressure it would put on the Treasury, someday soon we'd be talking about how to cut the program. To knowingly put Americans in such an untenable position just struck me as the height of irresponsibility.

*   *   *

When Barack Obama took the oath of office, I adopted a wait-and-see approach to our forty-fourth president. I knew that ideologically he was a liberal progressive, but he talked like a centrist. I was hoping that he might keep his campaign promises to change the tone in Washington by being inclusive and open to everyone's ideas. I thought that when it came to governing, he might prove to be pragmatic and willing to work across the aisle.

The stimulus and the debate over Obamacare had been discouraging, but then in late January 2010 something interesting happened: President Obama decided to meet with House Republicans.

The GOP House Retreat is a policy event, an opportunity for our chamber's Republican members to get together and discuss ideas and strategy. That year, our meeting came at an important moment: The House and Senate were trying to reconcile their different versions of the health-care bill, and I had just released the newest iteration of my budget plan, an updated Roadmap with some further policy improvements.

As we met to discuss these developments, President Obama not only agreed to talk with us, he was willing to take questions. As we took our seats at lunch, the back of the room was busy with reporters, cameras, and lights.

The president's speech was substantive and its central theme was bipartisanship. "I've said this before," he said, "but I'm a big believer not just in the value of a loyal opposition, but in its necessity.... Having differences of opinion, having a real debate about matters of domestic policy...it's absolutely essential."

It was a different tone from the one that had marked the first year of his presidency. Of course, one could chalk all that up to scripted remarks. For me, the most promising parts of the event were the unscripted moments, when he responded to our questions extemporaneously.

I was sitting at a table in the front of the room, located by the right-hand corner of the stage, with my family. When I got up to ask my question, the president stopped me.

"Is this your crew right here, by the way?" he said.

Yes, I said, introducing him to Liza, Charlie, Sam, and Janna. "Say hi to everybody," I told the kids. They waved, which got a few laughs, including one from the president.

Then we got down to business. I used my time to ask about the increases in spending during his term. I also pitched my bipartisan proposal with Democratic senator Russ Feingold to create a constitutional version of the line-item veto so Congress could cut extraneous spending and waste. I didn't get very far with my spending question, but on the line-item veto, the president agreed. "This is an area where we can have a serious conversation," he said.

My question time over, I sat down and listened to the rest of the exchange. To my surprise, President Obama later referenced my budget proposal, which had been out for only two days.

"I think Paul, for example, head of the Budget Committee, has looked at the budget and has made a serious proposal," President Obama said. "I've read it. I can tell you what's in it. And there are some ideas in there that I would agree with, but there are some ideas that we should have a healthy debate about because I don't agree with them."

The president's comments struck me as an olive branch.

Unfortunately, within seventy-two hours, his budget director took that branch and hit me in the face with it. In a news conference, Peter Orszag went after the Roadmap. Then congressional Democrats followed his lead in a conference call with reporters. Soon after, Nancy Pelosi criticized it in a speech before the Democratic National Committee. They apparently saw my budget plan as a critical weapon in their 2010 midterm campaign strategy.

It became clear that the president wasn't laying the groundwork for a bipartisan compromise; he was gearing up for a fight. He had praised the Roadmap to elevate it, so that when his allies trashed it, all eyes would be watching. It was classic good cop/bad cop. He was just setting us up for the hit.

The debate over the budget meant that this was becoming a struggle over the first principles of government. I didn't think much of the Democrats' style, but I did welcome the debate. The Roadmap is a philosophical document. It lays out a vision for the country— one that offers economic prosperity and fiscal responsibility. I took their bit of political theater as an invitation to debate our different approaches forthrightly, but I would do so respectfully. Soon, I got my chance.

* * *

In early January, Democratic leaders in the Senate and the House had announced that they were close to reconciling the differences between each chamber's health-care bills. Then Republican Scott Brown won a special election in Massachusetts to fill what had been Ted Kennedy's Senate seat, costing the Democrats their supermajority in that chamber and stalling all health-reform-related activity.

In an attempt to revive his key legislative priority, President Obama released a proposal that looked a lot like the Senate bill and invited a bipartisan group down to the Blair House to discuss health care. The summit also allowed him to fulfill his campaign promise to put the health-care negotiations on C-SPAN, something he was getting a lot of public pressure to do.

Together, nearly forty of us trekked over to Blair House and crammed into chairs set up at long conference tables arranged in a square. To my left was John Kline of Minnesota, the ranking member on the Education and Labor Committee. To my right, Marsha Blackburn of Tennessee.

Instead of a true negotiation, the whole meeting quickly turned into a charade. It felt as if we were each debating the president; he responded to most comments directly, and frankly, he was just running out the clock. It was clear that the administration had no intention of seriously considering any of our ideas. Meanwhile, in an attempt to keep things cordial, everyone on our side of the aisle was holding back from really tearing into the problems with the president's proposal.

I was getting frustrated. I was ticked off that the summit had turned out to be nothing more than a publicity stunt, and yet I knew we probably weren't going to have another opportunity to make our case like this again. So when my turn came, I went straight after the basic flaws in his proposal. I focused in on the budgetary problems, the empty promises, and didn't hold back.

"This bill does not control costs," I said. "This bill does not reduce deficits. Instead, this bill adds a new entitlement at a time when we have no idea how to pay for the entitlements we already have."

But, for me, the most important point was one I had made months earlier on the House floor. "When you take a look at this," I told the president at Blair House, "it's really deeper than the deficits or the budget gimmicks or the actuarial analysis. There really is a difference between us...and it's basically this: We don't think the government should be in control of all of this. We want people to be in control."

When the day wrapped up, President Obama walked over to me. "We should sit down and talk about this stuff," the president said.

"Sounds good. You know how to reach me," I replied.

He chuckled. "I do."

Given the new reality in the Senate, I thought the president might reach out to those of us in the House. We never heard from him. Instead, a month after the Blair House Summit, Nancy Pelosi declared, "We have to pass the bill so that you can find out what's in it."

To overcome the problem of Scott Brown's election, they decided to ram the Senate bill through the House. Instead of scaling back their ambitions and looking for a bipartisan win, they chose to muscle through their deeply flawed bill. They abused the legislative process, deceived pro-life Democrats, and bought off senators with special carve-outs. For them, the effectiveness of the policy was less important than the ideology.

Yet, when it came time for the House to vote on the Senate's bill, the fate of Obamacare was still uncertain. Passing the legislation would require a handful of Democratic holdouts to vote yes. One of those uncertain votes was my good friend Bart Stupak, a Democrat from Michigan.

Bart was what's known as a bell cow in the House. Get him to come into the barn and a lot of other members would follow him. In this case, he could influence a handful of critical votes. With such a thin vote margin, Bart and his allies would prove essential for the bill to become law. But Bart had serious reservations about Obamacare.

Bart and I worked out every morning in the House gym together. We may not have always seen eye to eye politically, but we actually have a fair bit in common. We're both die-hard Packer fans. We come from the same part of the country. And we're also both Catholics, so Obamacare raised serious concerns for us in terms of federal funding for abortion and the protection of religious liberty. It's always been a principle of our nation that the government shouldn't force people to violate their religious beliefs, and yet Obamacare included mandates that would have compelled many Catholics to defy either federal law or the teachings of their faith. That didn't sit well with several members on both sides of the aisle, including Bart and me.

Usually we don't talk politics during our workouts, but this issue weighed heavily on Bart. He was a committed pro-life legislator, and he prided himself on advocating for the conscience rights of his constituents. Obamacare, as drafted, would make it easier to fund the ending of innocent life, and it lacked sufficient protections for religious liberty. Bart asked his Democratic colleagues a lot of tough questions in an attempt to square his vote with his beliefs, and the answers he was getting weren't very comforting.

So we suspended our unwritten rule and spent a few mornings talking about Obamacare. Bart would occasionally replay the talking points he'd been given and gauge my response. Then he'd push back some more on his party's leadership. Over time, it became clear that the back-and-forth was taking its toll on Bart. The Obama machine couldn't put him on the menu, but it wore him down in other ways.

On the day of the vote, Bart and the administration were at an impasse. He wanted assurances that the bill complied with what's known as the Hyde Amendment, a long-standing policy that prevents federal money from being used to fund abortions. In an effort to appease Bart, President Obama said he would issue an executive order later that clarified that the Hyde Amendment applied to Obamacare.

We all knew that executive order wouldn't be worth the paper it was printed on. Those orders are simply a promise to interpret the law a certain way, but they can be undone just as quickly as they are issued. In order for the promise to be meaningful, it needed to be in the law that Congress passed and the president signed. So it was a fig leaf, but Bart wanted to believe. They just wore him down.

On the day of the vote, Bart announced his support at a press conference in the Capitol, and by the time I saw him on the floor that night, he looked exhausted. He cast his vote in favor of the bill, and with that, the bell cow brought six votes into the barn, and Obamacare passed.

That vote ultimately cost Bart his seat; in 2010, facing certain defeat, he decided not to run for reelection. I watched a good friend give up his career in public service for a law that has undercut an issue he cares about and now put the Catholic Church and millions of religious Americans in a deep struggle against the U.S. government. It was one of my sadder days in Congress.

*   *   *

The controversy over Obamacare—both in substance and process—did not go unnoticed. It added fuel to the growing Tea Party movement, one of the most important developments in politics in recent memory. Countless Americans, fed up with the excesses of the federal government, got involved and began to move the debate.

I first sensed that the movement was gaining ground in August 2009, when Tea Partiers started flocking to my events back home. Over the years, I have done more than 550 listening sessions in my district. Usually, we gather in the city council's chambers, a public library, or a classroom. A good showing in a big city is ninety to a hundred people. In a small town, we're lucky if fifteen people attend. But when Andy and I drove up for our first meeting during recess that summer, there were lines around the block. Hundreds of people were waiting. We couldn't fit everyone in and had to turn folks away.

We decided to switch the locations for our events, upgrading from libraries to high school gymnasiums and auditoriums. Even those weren't big enough; the fire marshals were still turning people away.

Wow, I thought, *this thing is real.*

Compared to my colleagues on the other side of the aisle, I had an easy go of it that summer. I shared my constituents' concerns and authored reforms they supported. They were angry about government overreach and especially Obamacare, and they wanted to register their displeasure and tell me to keep on fighting. I thanked them and assured them I would.

Every once in a while, the Democrats would send hecklers in with a few talking points. *How can you be against Obamacare?* they'd ask. *Isn't health care a right?*

I'd reply that it wasn't a right, and framing it that way was dangerous to our liberty. To say it's a government-granted right means that government is in charge of your health care. I think *you* should be in charge of your health care.

The Tea Party was not a passing fad; it was a growing, enduring movement. It was boosting citizen participation, always a good thing. And it was inspiring a lot of citizens to run for Congress as well. The Young Guns program that Eric, Kevin, and I started in 2007 proved to be a good complement to the Tea Party's energy. Heading into the 2010 election, we supported ninety-two candidates. One of them was a fellow Wisconsinite, Sean Duffy.

A lot of people remembered Sean as the lumberjack from MTV's *The Real World*. But by 2009, he was an accomplished lawyer, serving as the district attorney for Ashland County up in the northern part of our state. He was a bright, energetic guy and the father of five; I'd seen him at various events over the years and gotten to know him well.

Wisconsin's Seventh Congressional District is a beautiful place. Starting just north of Highway 29, it's sparsely populated woodlands all the way up to Lake Superior. In 2009, the district was represented by Democrat David Obey, who was thought to be unbeatable. Obey was the longest-serving member of Congress in our state's history, with a tenure that spanned forty years. As chairman of the House Appropriations Committee, he was also responsible for a lot of the waste and mismanagement that the Tea Party was railing against.

When I saw the long lines at town halls in August, I thought of Sean. I knew he was interested in running for Congress. So I called and told him, "This is it. Do it now."

The next few months were a perfect illustration of how Kevin, Eric, and I had hoped the Young Guns program would work. I hit the road, campaigning for Sean. There are more people and businesses down in our part of the state, so I helped him out with fundraising, as well. Sean was an effective, tireless candidate, and Obey saw the writing on the wall. He dropped out of the race, preparing the way for Sean's victory that fall.

That year, my office heard from challengers in dozens of states. I didn't know them and had never spoken with them, but they were endorsing and running on the Roadmap.

"I just endorsed your budget," they'd say. "Now, how do I respond to this attack I'm getting? How do we defend this thing?"

The campaign committees weren't helping these candidates because they still weren't sold on my plan. So, in our personal time, a few members of my staff and I tried to help their campaigns weather the storm, make a persuasive case for our solutions, and stay on offense.

Election Day 2010 brought huge victories for Republican candidates. The party dramatically increased its share of state House and Senate seats, resulting in a takeover of both chambers in twenty-five states. It was the biggest victory since 1928, and the largest swing in the U.S. House of Representatives in sixty-two years. We elected 87 new Republicans, 62 of them candidates we had recruited for the Young Guns program.

In 2010, we went out and recruited a conservative army for the battle of ideas. And in 2011, that army became the House majority. We had been given a mandate, and we were ready to get things done.

* * *

In February 2011, President Obama released his budget proposal for the next fiscal year. Calling his $3.73 trillion budget one of "tough choices and sacrifices," the president failed to address the toughest choice of all: how to reform our entitlement programs.

Now chairman of the House Budget Committee, I again offered an alternative. I revised my Roadmap, working to build consensus with my colleagues while maintaining the boldness of the vision. In April, with my Budget Committee colleagues, I released the new plan, now titled "The Path to Prosperity." This iteration reduced federal spending by $6.2 trillion over ten years. It lowered taxes, balanced the budget, and repealed Obamacare. It also saved our entitlement programs through a series of reforms, including a premium support model for Medicare.

While earlier Roadmap introductions were met with little immediate fanfare, this budget shook up the debate. And not long after I released it, I got an invitation to attend a speech that President Obama was going to deliver at George Washington University.

In the weeks following the midterm election, it seemed like the president was preparing to take a page out of Bill Clinton's playbook: When the Republicans take over Congress, move to the middle. By adopting this approach, Clinton had been able to work with Republicans and pass welfare reform, a legislative victory that helped assure his reelection in 1996.

My colleagues and I were led to believe that Obama would do the same thing with the budget. Within days of the election, the administration began reaching out. I started hearing regularly from Tim Geithner, the secretary of the treasury, and Gene Sperling, the director of the National Economic Council. Our conversations went beyond the basic niceties. They asked for my ideas and ran theirs by me. It seemed like the administration was feeling things out and getting ready to triangulate.

If they wanted to do that, they had the perfect vehicle for it. In December, the National Commission on Fiscal Responsibility and Reform had wrapped up its work. The commission was commonly referred to as Bowles-Simpson after its cochairmen, Democrat Erskine Bowles and Republican Alan Simpson. President Obama had created it through an executive order and tasked it with improving the country's fiscal situation. In total, there were eighteen members of the commission. Six were from the House of Representatives, including Jeb Hensarling of Texas, Dave Camp of Michigan, and me.

Yet, after a little more than five months of deliberations, the commission couldn't agree on a plan, and Bowles and Simpson released their recommendations without the support of the entire group. Jeb, Dave, and I had all voted against it. We had three reasons for withholding our backing: It didn't get a handle on health-care costs, which is a primary driver of our debt; it made deep cuts to defense; and it called for a huge tax increase.

But it was a starting point and it had some Republican support. The easiest way for the president to moderate would be to embrace the Bowles-Simpson report, and it certainly seemed as if he was leaning that way. Erskine Bowles and I had become good friends, and he was reporting back to me, "I think we're making progress. I think the president is coming around."

The day of the speech, Jeb, Dave, and I piled into Jeb's Jeep Cherokee and drove to the university. We spent the car ride over trying to guess what the president would say. Every option we considered assumed the president would triangulate, endorsing Bowles-Simpson and portraying us as radicals for opposing it and himself as the reasonable moderate for embracing it.

When we got to the university auditorium where the speech was going to be delivered, we were surprised to find that seats were reserved for us in the front row.

"Definitely a full embrace of Bowles-Simpson," I said to Dave and Jeb, pointing to the index cards with our names, which were taped to three chairs.

We took our seats, and I started chatting with some GW students sitting behind us. Erskine came over to say hello. That was when I noticed a photographer with a huge telephoto lens aimed at us instead of the stage. *That's kind of weird*, I thought.

President Obama walked out to the podium, which was no more than twenty feet from us, and began his speech. About a third of the way through, he got to the heart of our fiscal problems.

"Around two-thirds of our budget is spent on Medicare, Medicaid, Social Security, and national security," he said. "Programs like unemployment insurance, student loans, veterans' benefits, and tax credits for working families take up another 20 percent. What's left, after interest on the debt, is just 12 percent for everything else. That's 12 percent for all of our other national priorities like education and clean energy; medical research and transportation; food safety and keeping our air and water clean. Up until now, the cuts proposed by a lot of folks in Washington have focused almost exclusively on that 12 percent. But cuts to that 12 percent alone won't solve the problem."

All right, I thought. *We're getting somewhere.*

"A serious plan," he said, would require "tough decisions and support from leaders in both parties. And above all, it will require us to choose a vision of the America we want to see five and ten and twenty years down the road."

I nodded along in agreement. And then things changed.

The president proceeded to list every step in the Path to Prosperity, grossly mischaracterizing them in the most partisan way possible. He described our budget as "changing the basic social compact in America." He called it neither "serious" nor "courageous." Then he accused our plan of taking away health insurance from 50 million Americans.

"Who are these 50 million Americans?" he asked. "Many are somebody's grandparents...Many are poor children. Some are middle-class families who have children with autism or Down's syndrome....These are the Americans we'd be telling to fend for themselves."

His false attacks were offensive, even by the low standards for discourse and civility in Washington, D.C.

At that moment, a friend and budget ally, Tom Price, was watching the speech from his House office. He fired off an e-mail to Jeb, Dave, and me: "You guys should consider leaving right now."

The three of us looked at each other. I knew the guy with the telephoto lens was waiting for a visible reaction. I didn't want to give the White House the satisfaction. Instead, we whispered out of the sides of our mouths.

"Do you think we should leave?" asked Dave.

"We probably should stay," I said.

"Yeah," said Jeb. "That might make things worse."

"Let's leave right after, then," said Dave.

"Okay," I said.

So out of respect for the office of the presidency—not for the man haranguing me twenty feet away—we agreed to wait until he finished.

The president continued talking, explaining that he had gathered us to offer his own "more balanced approach," so I started taking notes. *No point in wasting the time I spent coming over here*, I thought.

I rested a legal pad on one knee and my phone on the other, and I started tallying up and scribbling down the planks of the president's plan.

He promised cuts in spending, but then laid out six general areas that he would not touch. He promised to reduce the cost of health care by implementing Obamacare and making vague changes to reduce waste and inefficiency.

He's almost made his way through the domestic discretionary spending in the budget, I thought. *Total savings: $0.*

Then he got to the defense budget. "Over the last two years, Secretary Bob Gates has courageously taken on wasteful spending, saving $400 billion in current and future spending. I believe we can do that again."

Bob Gates was an honest broker, and I'd seen his recommendations. He'd outlined a budget for the department that was doable, and he'd offered up cuts that could be achieved without risking the readiness of our armed forces. I knew where he had drawn the line between reducing waste and redundancy and jeopardizing our military by denying our troops the equipment they needed in the field. The cuts the president was proposing crossed that line.

But more important, his proposal revealed a misunderstanding of how defense budgets are produced. Providing for the national defense is the first mission of the federal government. Of all of the budgets within the government, it's the one that most needs to be strategy-driven, not numbers-driven, because the safety of our troops and the security of our nation are involved. The president was choosing a number and saying the Department of Defense had to meet it. When it comes to national defense, things are done the other way around. First we define the mission. Then we write the budget that can achieve it.

I kept writing down the president's numbers on my legal pad and comparing it to Bowles-Simpson in my head. In the end, his plan offered all of two concrete fiscal proposals: cutting the Department of Defense and raising taxes in a bad economy. Suddenly it was clear.

This is who he is, I thought. *Savage defense. Demagogue Republicans. Don't triangulate. Don't moderate. Go all in.*

The president closed his speech with some fluff about bipartisanship—hailing the great achievements of leaders like Ronald Reagan and Tip O'Neill. But we'd heard enough empty talk, and as soon as he was done and left the room, Dave, Jeb, and I headed out to our car.

As we got to the exit, I felt someone tapping my shoulder. Gene Sperling, the president's top economic advisor, had rushed over to follow me out. He insisted no one knew I was coming to the speech.

"Gene," I said, "he just poisoned the well."

We were silent until we got back into Jeb's Jeep. Once the doors were closed, we unloaded.

"What the hell was that?" I asked.

"That was an ambush!" Jeb said.

"This guy is off the rails. That stuff about children with Down's syndrome? That was just absolutely outrageous," said Dave.

"He's not going to work with us," I said. "He basically just told us he is going to fight us every step of the way. Even on the budget."

We were just floored. We couldn't believe it.

I hopped on my BlackBerry and started trading e-mails furiously with Conor Sweeney, my communications director on the Budget Committee.

I typed "DO A PRESS CONFERENCE" in the Subject line and hit Send.

Two seconds later, my BlackBerry rang. It was Cantor.

"What the hell just happened? Let's set up a press conference."

"Absolutely," I said. "Conor is already on it."

I hung up. My phone rang again. It was Erskine.

"Paul, I'm so sorry," he said, "I'm ashamed of what just happened.

I cannot believe the president just did that. I apologize. That was reprehensible behavior and I'm ashamed of it as a Democrat."

"Erskine," I said, "I appreciate the call, but you don't have to apologize. You didn't say it; he did."

"I know but I just...I just can't...I've never seen anything like that before. I'm going to have harsh words with the president about this. I'm going to talk with him about this."

Soon after we pulled up to the Capitol Building, Dave, Jeb, and I joined Eric at the press conference.

"I am sincerely disappointed that the president, at a moment when we are putting ideas on the table to try and engage in a thoughtful dialogue to fix this country's economic and fiscal problems, decides to pour on the campaign rhetoric, launch his reelection...and make it that much harder for the two parties to come together with mutual respect of one another to get things done." I delivered my statement, and I meant every word. I'd been hoping to see leadership, and instead we got empty partisanship. It was a complete letdown.

Later in the day, Alan Simpson called me.

"Paul, I just couldn't believe it. That was awful. Afterward, I went out and almost threw up in the tulips." Alan Simpson has always had a special way with words.

For the first two years, it had been hard to read our president. Deep down, was he an ideologue or a pragmatist? Was raw power politics his style, or just the actions of his senior staff, who had been given too much latitude? Did the stimulus bill and the health-care bill reflect his own hard-Left commitments, or was he trying to appease his base? Would he ever reach across the aisle, respond to our efforts to reach out and work with us?

That speech answered all of those questions for me. At the Wisconsin Dairy Breakfast, we serve bacon, eggs, and milk, and we have a saying about the meal: The chicken and the cow are involved, but the pig is committed. That day, I realized this president was committed. If we were going to head off a fiscal crisis and fix our economy, we were going to need a different president.

* * *

The president was right about one thing: We did have two different visions for the future of America. He was just deeply dishonest about the one we had proposed and where his would lead.

By late 2011, the center of political attention was the next presidential race, and I was concerned, because it seemed like none of the candidates was really drawing a clear distinction between a conservative vision and the president's. In fact, someone from Mitt Romney's team gave an interview and explained that they saw the election as being overwhelmingly about Obama's economic record. That prompted me to call over to Mitt's campaign.

"Look," I said, "I have to tell you that when you say things like that it's like fingernails on a chalkboard to conservatives. This guy is good. He's gifted. We're not going to beat him like that."

It was fairly silent on the other end.

"I'm just calling because I want to help," I explained. "I think Mitt's the best in the field. But it has to be more than just a referendum on Obama. Americans have to feel like there's a viable alternative being offered in this race."

The voice on the other end spoke up. "This is really good. Let's keep this line of communication open. This is really helpful."

So I wrote Mitt a few memos. In December 2011, as the Republican primary was about to get under way, I sent one titled, "A Choice of Two Futures." In it, I argued that issuing a referendum on the Obama presidency and offering voters a choice were not mutually exclusive strategies.

I encouraged Mitt to think about the referendum as being not just about the unemployment number or our debt, but as being about the American Idea and what it means in the lives of those he hoped to serve. Our country was founded on the principles of free enterprise, limited government, individual freedom, and a strong national defense. Those founding principles made real opportunity and unprecedented prosperity possible. The president's true failure was that he was pulling us away from all of that.

However, our party also had to offer voters a real alternative. In my view, the election needed to be framed as a choice between our vision of principled reform and expanded opportunity, and the president's vision, which would lead to a government-centered society, less freedom, more debt, and economic decline.

I wrote to Mitt that the "moral, fiscal, and economic case" for such a campaign strategy "is simply this: We cannot afford to win by default." Having lived through the failed Social Security push in 2005, I knew that the next president would need a mandate, not just a victory. That meant Mitt needed to run on specific policies so he would be able to implement them when he won.

I sent the memo off, and I forwarded additional thoughts as they came to me. Then, on January 10, I turned on the television to watch Mitt declare victory in the New Hampshire GOP primary. The first half of his speech hit the referendum theme hard, offering a stark assessment of how President Obama's first three years had failed to restore the American Idea. Mitt then offered a full-throated defense of economic freedom and free enterprise.

Inside a room full of excited supporters at Southern New Hampshire University, Mitt declared, "We must offer an alternative vision." The last third of the speech was a full articulation of the choice in the election.

"President Obama wants to 'fundamentally transform' America," said Mitt. "We want to restore America to the founding principles that made this country great.

"He wants to turn America into a European-style entitlement society. We want to ensure that we remain a free and prosperous land of opportunity....

"This president puts his faith in government. We put our faith in the American people."

On he went, point by point and policy by policy, laying out the difference between the conservative vision and the Obama agenda. As soon as the speech wrapped up, I hopped on my iPad and sent off a quick e-mail to one of the campaign's advisors: "Mitt nailed it tonight; speech was great."

*   *   *

By the time I joined the ticket in early August, Mitt had endured a long primary and fought his way through twenty-three debates. Bloodied up, he limped into the spring as the presumptive GOP nominee, but he was unable to spend any of his general election money until September. The Obama machine took the opportunity to carpet-bomb key states with millions of dollars in negative ads that portrayed Mitt as rich, heartless, and out of touch. It was clear that the final three months would require not only that we campaign tirelessly, but also that we outsmart our opponents tactically and strategically.

Every week, Mitt would meet with the senior staff to go over the most recent polling data, finance numbers, and get-out-the-vote reports. With all the information laid out in front of them, the inner circle would calibrate the message, move around resources, and plan events. After I officially joined the ticket, I began participating in the campaign's strategy sessions via Skype.

Mitt was challenging an incumbent saddled with a bad economy and weak popularity. Historically, the preferred strategy in those circumstances is to make the election a referendum on your opponent's record. But that approach just ran against my instincts. In all of my races—not just as an incumbent, but also as a challenger—I'd been successful precisely because I had offered voters a choice. I'd always felt like the specificity of my proposals and my willingness to be candid about my ideas had been my greatest strengths. Early on, I shared those insights with the team.

I was a late addition to the campaign, and it's a real testament to Mitt and his staff that they took the time to hear me out. I was asking them to consider a different approach, and they gave the idea a full hearing. Together, we debated the pros and cons of expanding our message beyond a referendum on Obama's first term and framing the election as a choice between two visions. But ultimately, the team decided to use August, September, and early October to continue to give voters a reason to fire the president instead.

The strategy set, I focused on the job I had to do as a running mate. I needed a good rollout, a good convention speech, and a good debate. Those were my duties.

In executing them, I was prepared to experience a whole new level of press scrutiny. I knew I would have to defend my record, past statements, and the Roadmap. But I hadn't realized the attention that the press would pay to little things.

For example, I'd been climbing in Colorado since I was a kid, including several of the state's "Fourteeners," mountains with altitudes of over fourteen thousand feet. A few years earlier a local reporter asked me how many Fourteeners I had climbed. I had never really counted them up before. I told him I'd done a whole bunch of repeats, but I thought I'd probably done about thirty to forty climbs. The reporter's write-up paraphrased our conversation and left the impression that I'd claimed to climb forty of the famous peaks.

In September, seemingly out of nowhere, the campaign started getting questions from reporters who wanted an inventory of all of the Fourteeners I'd ascended. A liberal political organization had sent out a press release titled, "Did 'Lyin' Ryan' Really Climb Forty Colorado Fourteeners?"

Conor Sweeney found me and asked if I had any proof documenting all of the mountains I had scaled over the course of my lifetime. Tobin and I spent an entire flight flipping through a guidebook and scanning a map, trying to figure out which mountains I had climbed since I was twelve years old. The final tally was a couple of dozen peaks, totaling thirty or forty climbs. Eventually the local reporter posted a blog item with his original interview notes, which made clear I had not claimed to climb forty separate Fourteeners. But we lost precious hours trying to clear up the controversy.

When people started coming at me and questioning my integrity, it was stomach churning. The hardest were the self-inflicted wounds, like when I recalled the wrong marathon time from a race I ran during college. We lost another couple of days cleaning up that mess in the press.

I could see the narrative that was developing out of these tiny bits of information. I had too much record and policy experience to be portrayed as stupid. I suppose being married to someone as open-minded and big-hearted as Janna made it hard to cast me as an evil guy. But a sloppy paraphrase here, a poor recollection there, and pretty soon I was being labeled a liar.

It made for a tough transition. I quickly realized that there was no margin for error. For the first month, my mantra was "survive." Get the convention speech right. Do the debate prep. Live up to my end of the bargain.

I was also focused on being there for my family. It's true what they say about the scrutiny and lack of privacy being harder on spouses, and Janna is probably more private than most. So I worried about my family's loss of anonymity and how the campaign was affecting them.

To my surprise, Janna and our kids actually handled the transition even better than I did. Liza, Charlie, and Sam joined us out on the road most weekends, and let me tell you: There is nothing like seeing this country through your kids' eyes.

I still remember Charlie, shy and serious, looking out the window of a bus as all the scenes of America—big cities, cornfields, mountains, and crowds of people—passed by. It reminded me of those car trips with my dad, when he was so eager for us to see the different corners of our country. But no one needed to tell Charlie to absorb; he was quick to take it all in.

Then there was Sam, our youngest, as happy as could be, like when he ran back onto the plane in Alabama to tell me all about the Huntsville Space and Rocket Center. When we arrived in the convention hall in Tampa, he quickly figured out that it had something to do with balloons, elephants, and Dad, and that was all it took to get him fired up. Soon enough, he became a favorite of the traveling press corps, giving impromptu press conferences on hard-hitting topics like his Halloween costume.

I think Liza may have had more fun than any of us, though. She loved the rallies. The energy of the campaign was a perfect match for her personality. One day as we were standing backstage, a photographer came by and snapped a candid shot. In it, Janna and I are smiling, and Liza is photobombing us with a wassup pose. On days when the campaign trail was tiring and the press scrutiny was grueling, Liza reminded us that it really was a great experience and we needed to enjoy it and have a good time.

Together, our whole family got to see parts of the country we'd never visited before. And we formed relationships we'll never forget. We became very close with the staff that traveled with us. Between Janna, the kids, and me, we had dozens of Secret Service agents on our detail, and all of them were caring men and women who made great sacrifices on our behalf. Then there were another twelve staff members from the campaign team—and our pilot, our copilot, and the people who manned the airplane cabin. As we flew around the country, everyone became a big family. Surprisingly, we even developed a respectful relationship with our press corps. Sometimes we'd meet them down in a banquet room at the hotel and have a few beers—off the record (to their chagrin).

By far, it was the Americans who showed up to our rallies who were the best part of the campaign. After every event, I'd walk along the rope line, talking with people and signing hats or posters. The most touching thing was when they would lean in and say, "I'm praying for you and your family." Often they'd hand me a strand of rosary beads. By November, we had a whole box full of them. I'd look at it and think about all of those people and their prayers. It was deeply moving and very humbling.

I was particularly grateful for those prayers as I prepared for my debate with Joe Biden. Nationally televised debates are a challenging forum, and my opponent was not only a skilled debater, but he also had a lot of experience with the format. He'd run for president twice, and had debated Sarah Palin in 2008 as his party's VP nominee.

To help me prepare, we hauled around a brown leather briefcase that contained about forty pounds of talking points, news reports, and briefing documents. In between campaign stops and interviews, I would study up for our mock debate sessions, where attorney Ted Olson played the role of Joe Biden.

Of all the strategies that Biden could employ, our team thought two were most likely: He could play it straight, as he had in 2008, and make his points by being disciplined and direct. Or he could try to throw me off my game by acting unpredictably. We referred to these possibilities as "Normal Joe" and "Uncle Joe," respectively.

The "Uncle Joe" strategy would be risky for Biden; voters could find it off-putting and it could lead to gaffes. But it was also risky for me.

Given our age gap, I thought a lot about the VP debate in 2004, when John Edwards had appeared out of his depth next to a composed, confident Dick Cheney. No one wants to be the young, eager guy getting schooled by the elder statesman.

But the possibility that "Uncle Joe" might show up on debate night wouldn't neutralize the age issue; in fact, it could heighten it. Early on, someone warned me that if I let Biden get under my skin, the scene unfolding on the television screen would be an agitated forty-two-year-old debating an erratic sixty-nine-year-old. In those encounters, no one comes off looking particularly well, but the older and more experienced debater usually prevails.

To prepare me for this possibility, Ted Olson adopted the "unpredictable" strategy in our mock debates. In his seventies, Ted's most notable features are his wire-rim glasses, reddish-blond hair, and calm demeanor. He was once the solicitor general of the United States, and he's argued dozens of cases before the Supreme Court, including those arising out of the 2000 Bush v. Gore election.

An excellent litigator, Ted was the ideal mock debate partner. His arguments were forceful and persuasive, but his behavior was distracting. He would sigh loudly or interrupt me or roll his eyes. A couple of times, he would gesture wildly while I was mid-answer, motioning in a way that seemed to say, *Can you believe this guy?!?*

At the time, I remember thinking that Ted might be overplaying the part. Surely Joe Biden wasn't going to act that way in a vice presidential debate. But when the night finally arrived, I was grateful for Ted and his antics, as it didn't take long to figure out which Joe showed up. It was clear that Biden was trying to get me to lose my cool by acting so strangely. I didn't take the bait and delivered most of the points I was hoping to make.

When the debate was over, I felt very good. I'd fulfilled my official VP duties and was really enjoying the campaign.

Mitt had tapped Mike Leavitt, an old friend and the former governor of Utah, to head up the transition team in the event we won.

Mike and I started holding conference calls frequently. We worked on the first budget Mitt would introduce and a two-hundred-day plan for his administration. I began to see, more clearly than I had before, that we were going to come out swinging and tackle all of the big problems. Our mission was to pull $2 trillion of capital in from the sidelines and jump-start the economy with certainty and free-market, pro-growth policies. Then we were going to get our fiscal affairs in order by putting in place a plan to balance the budget and pay down the debt.

In the closing month of the campaign, I was getting really excited about the prospect of actually winning and governing. I also refocused on strategy. Things seemed to be moving in the right direction, and our internal numbers were looking good. On the road, it was hard to make a dispassionate assessment of the race as the crowds swelled and enthusiasm soared. The consensus among our team was that a new, forward-looking message could give us the boost we needed to finish strong. So, for the last three weeks of the campaign, we made what we called our "closing arguments."

Our message: This election is a choice. A vote for us is a vote to save the American Idea.

*   *   *

On Election Day, I woke up and went to the Hedberg Public Library in Janesville with Janna, Liza, Charlie, and Sam. It was where I cast my first vote for president and most of my ballots since.

Together, my family and I walked through the lobby and said hello to some friends and neighbors along the way. When I got to the voting booths, I saw Marjorie Reed. Marjorie is a family friend, and our kids love her. She always sends them little Irish keepsakes on Saint Patrick's Day. That morning, she gave me my paper ballot and a hug for good luck. Charlie went with Janna, while Liza and Sam followed me.

Liza dragged her finger across the paper and found my name in two spots—one in the list of candidates for the First District's congressional race, and the other under MITT ROMNEY, CANDIDATE FOR PRESIDENT.

When Janna and Charlie were done, they joined us. We stood together as Liza proofed my work, making sure I didn't miss any boxes that I needed to check. Then our family walked over to the voting machine and fed my ballot in.

I thought that morning about my first campaign in 1998. I thought about my dad and the lesson I learned from his death: Life is really short, so you'd better get serious and make it count. I thought about the path that stretched from a sad August morning in 1986 to this emotional November homecoming—and all the people and places along the way. *That* was how I got *here*.

I also thought about Jack Kemp—his example and his message that ideas matter and actions count. That morning, it felt like the tide was turning in the battle of ideas. It had been a long fight. In the House, we finally had a conservative majority that had been specific and put out a plan. Our presidential candidate had embraced big parts of it, and now we were asking the American people for their support. If Mitt and I could pull out a victory, we would have a mandate—and all the disappointment and despair so many Americans had been feeling would soon be behind us. We were on our way.

Our challenge had been formidable, but not insurmountable—and we had given it our all. I had high hopes that Mitt and I would be able to deliver an electoral victory, and then, a real recovery.

After I cast my ballot, I hopped on a flight. First we stopped in Cleveland, Ohio, for a quick campaign event with Mitt. As I got on his campaign plane, I saw him sitting down, surrounded by friends, and working on his iPad.

I sat down next to him, excited to be in the final hours of our campaign. Both of our voices were hoarse from too many stump speeches, but Mitt and I felt confident. It was looking good. We were doing well with turnout.

Together, we visited with volunteers at a local campaign office and grabbed lunch at Wendy's. Then I took off for Richmond, Virginia. At our final events there was a sense of intensity and enthusiasm that seemed like a good omen.

After Richmond, it was on to Boston. When we landed, I called Matt Rhoades, our campaign manager, and Rich Beeson, our political director. I was surprised by what I heard. There were long lines at the polls in the Democratic bastions. Early reports from supporters in key states contradicted our projections going into Election Day. And Project ORCA, our voter intelligence and turnout infrastructure, had gone down. For the rest of the day we were reduced to getting our news about the election from CNN's Wolf Blitzer and Fox's Megyn Kelly.

Nothing was really breaking our way, and that seemed to confirm a sense of apprehension that Janna couldn't shake right before the election. On our last night home in Janesville before we returned for Election Day, we finally had a quiet moment together to sit and reflect on everything.

"I'm worried," Janna said. "None of the public polls look like the internal numbers you're getting from the campaign. If it doesn't work out, I just want you to be prepared."

"I have to believe we can win," I told her. "I don't know if I can do what Mitt needs me to if I look at it any other way."

"I know," Janna said. "I just feel like you need to get your mind right on this. I think that on some level you need to brace yourself for the possibility we might lose—and that will be hard, but we'll be okay."

I'd had that same lingering doubt in my mind, but I also knew I had a job to do and so I pushed it away. But when everything started going wrong on Election Day, the doubt started to bubble up.

This is happening. We may actually lose this thing.

By early evening, our VP group merged again with the Romney family and senior campaign staff. Sam had gone to bed, but Liza and Charlie wanted to stay up, so Janna and I brought them in the motorcade. Things were looking uncertain, and it was a very somber ride.

We met up with Mitt and Ann at the Westin Hotel on Boston's waterfront. As we waited, we talked about how stunned we were by the news that was coming in. The networks were starting to call Ohio for Obama, which would put victory out of reach. Matt Rhoades spoke with Ohio senator Rob Portman. When he got off the phone, he turned to Mitt and said, "It doesn't look good."

We went back into a suite with our families. Soon, Matt came in and said, "It's not going to happen. It's over."

"Then it's time to do the honorable thing," Mitt said. "I'll call the president."

Mitt's son, Tagg, and I joined him in the other room while he made the call. There wasn't much to be said, and the exchange with the president was brief and polite. After Mitt put down the phone, there was silence in the room. A few moments passed, and then he said, "I just feel so bad for the country."

No one who knows the man would take such a comment the wrong way. Mitt is a humble guy, and there wasn't a bit of ego in his reaction to defeat. Sure, on a personal level, he must have felt the way anyone would when they've given their all and come up short. There's no reward for coming in second in presidential politics. Losing an election is tough, it is personal, and it is final.

At the same time, Mitt's concerns about the future of our country weren't just lines he was reading from a teleprompter. From my first conversations with him before I was even selected, I knew this was a serious man truly alarmed at the drift of events under President Obama. America got a glimpse of that fellow in the first presidential debate, when Mitt set the standard for all such debates to come.

Now, with the contest over, it would be four more years of "fundamental transformation," four more years of putting off the coming fiscal crisis instead of trying to avert it. All of that, too, was the price of defeat. Our chance to set a new direction had slipped away—and not by cruel misfortune, but by vote of the majority.

I'm not one to dwell too much on might-have-beens, although now and then my mind does go back to the great partnership I might have had with a President Mitt Romney. He didn't just look the part in 2012—he had what it took to fill the role, and I believe he would have been one of our finest presidents. He is honorable, principled, and fiercely intelligent. He was ready and worthy, and at his best, candidate Romney was a very impressive sight.

That night, as the Romneys and the Ryans all took the long elevator ride down to a ballroom full of staffers and supporters, the loss was starting to set in—as was my own realization that a great partnership with someone I now considered a dear friend had come to an abrupt end.

Janna and I stood offstage with Ann and her sons as Mitt conceded and wished President Obama the best. I looked around and saw some tears, but many in the room were simply too stunned to cry.

Afterward, Janna and I stayed behind for a while to talk with the Romneys. We didn't have much to say; we just weren't ready to say good-bye.

Finally, Mitt looked at me and asked, "You were reelected to Congress, right?"

"Yes," I replied.

A moment of silence passed between us.

"What are you guys in the House going to do now?"

I stood there, staring at the wall for what seemed like an eternity. "I don't know."

PART TWO

Where We Go from Here

CHAPTER 5

Beyond Makers and Takers

In July 2012, our local fairground was full of families, farmers, and visitors who had traveled to Janesville for the Rock County 4-H Fair. One of the oldest 4-H fairs in the United States, it might be the only place where you can get cheese curds, a funnel cake, a gyro, and a baked potato all in one stop.

I've been going since I was a boy. The fairgrounds were close to our house, and my friends and I would ride our bikes there every day with our pockets loaded up with money we'd made mowing lawns. We'd spend our limited funds on the midway, with its games, rides, and junk food.

My most vivid memory of the fair occurred during what I'll call the Year of the Zipper. That ride was a gigantic contraption of spinning steel. The attendant would strap you in a cage and then the thing would spin around like a hamster wheel, all the while rotating along a big axis. Every year, I went to the fair intending to give it a try, and every year, I went home disappointed that I hadn't forced myself to get in line. When I was around twelve years old, I finally worked up the courage. Enough to say it didn't end well, and I haven't been on it since. Even now, when I see my kids eyeing the Zipper, I am more than happy to sit it out.

I also remember fondly the year that my sister, Janet, was the 4-H Fair Queen, which bestowed upon her the privilege of walking through the animal barns with a sash and tiara. My dad joked that we had come a long way from shanty Irish to having royalty in the family.

These days, Janna and I enjoy taking Liza, Charlie, and Sam. When they were younger, they loved seeing the farm animals and climbing around in the corn crib (think of it as a sandbox filled with dried kernels). Janna loves taking the kids to see the kinds of sheep she used to show at the county fair in Oklahoma. As they've gotten older, it's all about the rides—especially on wristband day, when a plastic bracelet buys unlimited turns on the various attractions.

Every year, we head out to the fair as a family, and I spend an afternoon standing at the local Republican Party tent, meeting anyone who wanders up. A few elected officials are always there, chatting and watching the fair go by. Often people will take a minute away from the action to seek advice about a problem or share an idea.

That July, I'd been shaking hands and talking with people for a while when I saw a man making his way over to me. He was wearing a shirt that pledged allegiance to a local Democratic candidate.

"Hey, Paul," he said as he got closer, "I just need a minute. I'm from the Democrats' tent, and I just wanted to come over here and give you a piece of my mind."

He got up close and asked, "Who, exactly, are the takers?"

"Excuse me?" I replied.

"The makers and the takers," he said. "I know who the makers are, but who are the takers? Is it the person who lost their job and is on unemployment benefits? Is it the veteran who served in Iraq and gets their medical care through the VA? When you talk about the takers, who exactly do you mean?"

He turned out to be a very forceful and eloquent guy. So I stood there, listening without interrupting.

I'd started using the phrase "makers and takers" nearly three years earlier, after the Tax Foundation issued a study comparing how much families receive in government spending with how much they pay in taxes. If a family's share of government spending exceeded the amount it paid in taxes, the study's authors deemed them "receivers." If a family's share of government spending was less than the amount they paid in taxes, the authors described them as "givers." The analysis revealed that 60 percent of American families were already net "receivers," and under President Obama's policies for things like cap-and-trade and health care, that number would grow to 70 percent.

The phrase "givers and receivers" was similar to another term that had been making the rounds among thinkers and legislators in Washington: "makers and takers." A couple of books had used some variation of the phrase in their titles, and it snuck into the vocabulary that many, including me, regularly used.

At the time, it seemed convenient shorthand for a serious issue. Over the years, in ways large and small, we've slowly been adding to the number of benefits that government provides an increasing number of our citizens. Some of those benefits are worthy, laudable commitments. For example, we should ensure that there's a safety net that can catch people when they fall on hard times, and that the elderly have some guaranteed level of income and health security.

Other benefits aren't really the responsibility of government or the kind of thing we can afford—like unemployment benefits for millionaires, which costs taxpayers in the neighborhood of $30 million each year. Yet, in recent years, we've seen a push toward—and a reluctance to address—these kinds of programs from both sides of the aisle.

If we keep going on this way, soon we'll reach a tipping point where there are too many people receiving government benefits and not enough people to pay for those benefits. That's an untenable problem. The receivers cannot receive more than the givers can give.

Even so, while the problem it depicts is real and worrisome, the phrase "makers and takers" communicated a lot more than just the dilemma I was trying to describe. That day at the fair was the first time I really heard the way it sounded. As I stood there, listening to the guy from the Democrats' tent lay into me, I thought, *Holy cow. He's right.*

At the end of the day, I met back up with Janna and the kids. Together, we walked back to my truck and drove home, but I couldn't stop thinking about what that guy had said. Who was a taker? My mom, who is on Medicare? Me at eighteen years old, using the Social Security survivor's benefits we got after my father's death to go to college? My buddy John Ramsdell, who had been unemployed and used job-training benefits to get back on his feet?

We're just lumping people in this category without any regard for their personal stories, I thought. *It sounds like we're saying that people who are struggling are deadbeats, as if they haven't made it already or aren't trying hard enough.*

That was not what I meant. The idea of people struggling and striving to get ahead—that's what our country is all about. On that journey, they're not "takers"; they're trying to make something of themselves. We shouldn't disparage that.

Although he doesn't know it, that guy taught me a valuable lesson that day. It took me a while to completely come around, but I soon realized that the phrase I'd been using implied a certain judgment about the group that receives government benefits—one that is in deep conflict with the American Idea.

*   *   *

The American Idea is our nation's most unique and powerful contribution to the world. It describes a way of life made possible by our commitment to the principles of freedom and equality—and rooted in our respect for every person's natural rights.

We can understand the American Idea in philosophical terms—as the expression of those principles in ideas like the opportunity to rise, the rule of law, and the American Dream.

We can understand it in political terms—as a system of government that is at once both energetic enough to meet our needs and limited enough to preserve our freedoms.

We can understand it in human terms—as the vital space between the individual and the state, the space where family, community, and civil society thrive. As the conviction that we're all in this together and have a duty to protect the vulnerable.

We can understand it in cultural terms—as the notion that a free society requires a virtuous citizenry.

And we can understand it in economic terms—as the belief that broadly shared prosperity is best achieved by allowing individual creativity and ingenuity to emerge and evolve. This understanding, of course, assumes that productive enterprise and free choices in the market—not the edicts of centralized command—should shape our economy.

The American Idea is a way of life—one that enables each person to chart their own course, pursue their own happiness, and govern their own lives.

Why is this so special?

For most of human history, a very different idea reigned supreme: the idea that a few were born to rule, and everyone else was destined to obey. The common man lived to serve the king, the despot, or the state. They were subjects, serfs, or slaves.

Our forefathers rebelled against this long-held belief. To this day, America is exceptional in part because it was the first country explicitly founded on the ideas of natural rights, human equality, and self-governance. It was the first to take these articles of faith and write them into law. It was the first to tell the world—and to prove by its example—that the best government rests on the consent of the governed. It was the first to proclaim that our rights come not from rulers, but from God.

The American Idea is a vision of human equality in a just and free society, and the Founders created the best political system for advancing that idea. First came the Declaration of Independence, which can be thought of as the birth certificate for the American Idea. The Declaration established that the power of government was legitimate only to the extent that it secured the rights and expressed the consent of the people—a truly radical claim.

The challenge was to make a government strong and energetic enough to do its job, but not so much so that it would overwhelm the people and destroy liberty. "If men were angels, no government would be necessary," James Madison wrote in *The Federalist Papers*. "In framing a government which is to be administered by men over men, the great difficulty lies in this: you must first enable the government to control the governed; and in the next place oblige it to control itself."

The Founders did this by writing a Constitution that divided and limited government, leaving the powers not explicitly granted to the federal government with the states and the people. The federal government was limited so that freedom, opportunity, and civil society could flourish. Its core duties were protecting the nation and maintaining its independence, upholding the rule of law and securing our rights, and doing the things necessary and proper to fulfill its basic tasks. The very structure of government would limit it and focus it on forming a more perfect union and securing the blessings of liberty.

In other words, the Founders believed that the primary purpose of government was to do a few things very well but otherwise respect the space between the individual citizen and government—the space where family, community, the marketplace, and civil society thrive.

So in addition to our birth certificate, the Founders gave us the blueprint for a free and just society. Limiting government and freeing up the formative institutions of civil society makes safety and security, self-government and liberty, opportunity and social mobility available to everyone. It has led to unprecedented prosperity and unrivaled opportunity. It's done more to help the poor than any other economic system designed by man, and it remains a beacon of hope for the rest of the world.

But the American Idea is not self-sustaining. That part, too, is up to us.

In using the phrase "makers and takers," I was trying to describe one of the practical challenges that could eventually undermine the American Idea. But at the fair that day, I realized I'd been careless with my language. The phrase gave insult where none was intended. Ultimately it was also ineffective, because the problem I was trying to describe was not about our people. Rather, it is rooted in a very different philosophy of government that I believe threatens to destroy the American Idea.

* * *

The Progressive Party was founded in Madison, Wisconsin, about forty minutes from my home as a vehicle for native son Robert "Fighting Bob" La Follette's 1924 presidential campaign. A Republican politician known for his fiery oratory, La Follette was the leading advocate for the Wisconsin Idea, the Badger State's contribution to progressive reforms.

When I was growing up, our family was fairly apolitical, but as Wisconsinites, we were well aware of La Follette's past crusades in government. The influence of the progressive movement was always in the air, and La Follette, a former governor, congressman, and senator, was given the hero's treatment in our history lessons at school. One of our greatest high school rivals is Madison's La Follette High.

To get a sense of La Follette's importance to Wisconsin, one need only walk through Statuary Hall in the U.S. Capitol. The hall sits between the ornate Rotunda and the chamber where members of the House of Representatives deliberate. Starting in 1864, each state was invited to select two influential citizens, carve their likeness into stone, and place their statues in the hall. For one of Wisconsin's two slots, our state chose La Follette.

These days, I pass his white marble figure every time I walk through the hall. If you look at him from just the right angle, Fighting Bob bears a slight resemblance to Martin Sheen, the actor who played the president on *The West Wing*. La Follette is seated in a chair, leaning to one side, and kind of lurching forward—which is to say that he looks like a man who could stand up at any moment and still hold his own.

Of course, during his lifetime, La Follette fought for and against lots of things, animated by the ideas of the progressive movement. The movement's rise coincided perfectly with his own, having hit its peak between 1890 and 1920, a period known as the Progressive Era.

At the time, the country was grappling with changes brought on by industrialization and urbanization. Key thinkers and political leaders sought to reform our economy, government, and society in ways that would allow the nation to adapt to new conditions.

And to be fair, the movement gained support for good reason. Hardworking families faced real hardships. There was rampant corruption in government at all levels. Big business formed common cause with big government—at the little guy's expense. Monopolies cornered markets. Families lived and worked in filth and danger. Progressives won at the ballot box because they spoke to these concerns.

Much like today, government had lost its way. But instead of renewing the American Idea, progressives went in a very different direction. In their search for ideas and inspiration, some came to believe that there are no foundational truths, just different but equally valid points of view. Moreover, they decided that there were no permanent principles or natural rights, only historical claims that changed with the times. So much for self-evident truths.

Instead, these progressives looked to the methods of science to guide government and society. Consider the work of Charles Darwin, who documented the evolutionary capacity of animals, including human beings. Progressives took Darwin's ideas and misapplied them to every aspect of society, arguing that even government—and the country as a whole—was like a living organism and must be made to adapt, progress, and advance. Instead of fixed and enduring principles by which to govern, progressives prefer "living documents" more easily tailored to their ever-expanding agenda.

Such thinking led progressives to view the work of the Founders—their arguments, their assumptions, the system of government they set up—as outmoded and insufficient for the challenges of more modern times. The aim of progressivism, as Ronald J. Pestritto and William Atto have observed, was to get past, "or move beyond, the political principles of the American founding."

My friend Matthew Spalding calls this a "refounding"—a moment that, for progressives at least, signaled "the end of the old order and the birth of a new republic—based on a new theory of the state, a new understanding of rights, a new concept of national community, and a new doctrine of the 'living' Constitution."

The government envisioned by the progressives would be unlimited so that it could more easily adapt to changing conditions and times—and easily be deployed to alleviate all manner of ills and achieve a whole host of goals. It was a vision in which Congress didn't so much legislate as oversee the activities of unelected bureaucrats directed by the president. Governing, progressives argued, was better conducted by experts, who they felt could be trusted to remain objective and above the fray. They would toil away in executive and independent agencies where they could apply scientific knowledge to every aspect of the human condition, improving society through the rules and regulations they devised.

Our forefathers believed in the ability of men and women to govern themselves, and they distrusted unchecked power, which was why they limited government and encouraged a robust civil society. Progressives, on the other hand, thought it better to govern men, and therefore, they sought a much larger and more active central government with the ability to reach further into our lives. This distinction forms the core of the debate we find ourselves in today.

*   *   *

The progressive impulse was what animated Wisconsin's La Follette to form the National Progressive Republican League. But much to his disappointment, the progressives backed Theodore Roosevelt (instead of him) in 1912 as their candidate for president. That election was a three-way race between Roosevelt, Democrat Woodrow Wilson, and GOP nominee William Howard Taft. Wilson prevailed and brought the new progressive paradigm into the political mainstream.

Wilson was the quintessential progressive. He understood that the American Idea stood in the way of progressive reforms, so he took aim at the founding documents. He argued that the Declaration of Independence was not a document for every season, but relevant only in its moment. He went so far as to claim that the Declaration was merely "a long enumerated [list] of the issues of the year 1776," and that we shouldn't "repeat the preface"—that is, the part that talks about self-evident truths and certain inalienable rights. When it came to the Constitution, he was just as dismissive, arguing in his 1912 stump speech that:

> Living political constitutions must be Darwinian in structure and in practice. Society is a living organism and must obey the laws of life, not of mechanics; it must develop.

All that progressives ask or desire is permission—in an era when "development," "evolution," is the scientific word—to interpret the Constitution according to the Darwinian principle; all they ask is recognition of the fact that a nation is a living thing and not a machine.

This approach treated the Constitution as an evolving, living document and prepared the way for the development of a different approach to governing, which the progressives called "administration." By this they meant the centralization and consolidation of administrative government and bureaucratic experts, relatively untethered to the popular branches of government and unencumbered by the Constitution, which would govern and guide us toward a more progressive future and a better society—all with scientific efficiency.

This vision of administration—of central planning, bureaucratic rule, and comprehensive government solutions to every problem—pulls us away from the American Idea. Unfortunately, through fits and starts over the course of the twentieth century, this approach has become central to liberal progressive philosophy in the modern Democratic Party. Franklin Delano Roosevelt's New Deal and Lyndon Johnson's Great Society grew out of this mindset. That does not mean that every idea or particular program associated with those periods is incompatible or cannot be reconciled with our principles, but they must be reformed and restructured so they are compatible with limited government.

Our current president is a throwback to the old progressive philosophy. Of the role of the president, Barack Obama has said, "At the end of the day we're part of a long-running story. We just try to get our paragraph right." It seems like a humble sentiment until one considers the radical direction of Obama's part of the narrative.

So far, his paragraph includes the $787 billion stimulus bill, a takeover of one-sixth of our economy through Obamacare, a legion of new federal regulations affecting just about every facet of the American economy, and the practice of revising laws—even laws of his own devising—without the consent of Congress.

All of this did not help an economy that was underperforming or reduce unemployment, which was still rising. But when it came time to defend his first-term record, Obama laid our problems, particularly those of the middle class, at the feet of the wealthy. Columnist Charles Krauthammer summed up Obama's explanation best:

> The "breathtaking greed of a few" is crushing the middle class. If only the rich paid their "fair share," the middle class would have a chance. Otherwise, government won't have enough funds to "invest" in education and innovation, the golden path to the sunny uplands of economic growth and opportunity.

As Krauthammer observed, the problems currently plaguing the middle class stem from a range of causes, including the explosion of health-care costs, our national debt, and the pressures of a global economy. Yet none of those culprits offered a strong enough rationale for the solution Obama sought to implement: higher taxes, greater regulation, and more federal "investments," like the one we made in the now-bankrupt green energy company Solyndra, which cost taxpayers $528 million.

And while it follows from the progressive disregard for constitutional government, I'm deeply troubled by the extent to which the Obama administration has become lawless, ignoring laws passed by Congress and making up others as they go along. Not only does this make government arbitrary and subject to the whims of the current executive, but important decisions about national questions are made without debate and legislative consent. This shows great contempt for the rule of law, and in this regard, President Obama goes well beyond any of his predecessors. He's made it very difficult—in some cases, perhaps, impossible—to come to any consensus on the serious reforms our country so desperately needs.

Obama's greatest ambition, in word and deed, seems to be the continued imposition of the liberal progressive experiment. His policies represent an ideological mission to reorder the human condition through state action, empowering bureaucrats to decide what's best for everyone rather than allowing citizens to govern themselves.

In the liberal progressive world, that setup supposedly insulates us from risk and hardship, helping navigate the individual away from the shoals of life and toward safer, calmer waters regulated by government. That argument has a certain appeal, especially in times of great turmoil and economic insecurity like what we've been experiencing lately. In fact, the way liberal progressives argue their case can often make things feel less risky—as if it's offering us a lot of gains at minimal expense. Indeed, it is the progressive impulse that drives liberalism to respond to every social problem by advocating more government, more bureaucracy, and spending of more taxpayer's money.

Over the years, I've noticed that liberal progressives don't seem to talk much about the price we pay to pursue their vision—not just in terms of money, but also in restrictions to our freedom and liberty. Of course, it's hard to sell people on the idea of surrendering control of their lives to the state. To really do that, you have to find ways of making the case that sound friendlier and happier, which is why liberal progressivism tends to obscure what you're losing by emphasizing all the great things you're supposedly getting instead.

For a view of what this looks like in action, consider a bit of progressive promotion that was assembled and distributed by the Obama reelection team. In 2012, to help us all picture the bright future that has yet to unfold, their campaign created a fictional character, Julia, and a cartoon titled, "The Life of Julia," that followed our virtual friend from age three to sixty-seven. It's worth revisiting her journey because Julia is the essence of liberal progressivism.

Julia lives an imaginary life filled with moments made possible by the state. She glides from one government program to the next: Head Start, Pell Grants, $10,000 in American Opportunity Tax Credits, federal student loan payments programs, Obamacare, Social Security, and Medicare.

Through it all, nothing comes between Julia and her government. When she needs a job, it magically appears and never goes away. At forty-two years old, she starts her own business with a government loan. No middle-class striving for her: It's all taken care of by the state.

A high point of the story is when Julia experiences the endless benefits of Obamacare, miraculously free of any costs to her or to the economy that supports it. When she needs medical care, Julia enters a wonderland of friendly, efficient government bureaucrats who rush to meet her every need.

By the time Julia reaches sixty-seven years old, Social Security has apparently dodged bankruptcy and provides her with enough in monthly benefits for a comfortable retirement. Medicare is also there and able to deliver the care and medicine she needs.

I can understand the attraction of using a cartoon character to make one's case. After all, it was a lot easier in 2012 to talk about the imaginary "Life of Julia" than the real record of Barack Obama—or of any particular liberal progressive endeavor, for that matter. In a fictional account, all the practical problems that this approach to government creates can be easily explained away, or simply removed from the story entirely.

For example, when it comes to Julia's life, it's always assumed that the private economy is performing well. The money's always there in this vision of lifelong dependency on the state, and workers and taxpayers are somewhere off in the distant background. Problems like the national debt and entitlement programs nearing insolvency have somehow gone away.

Also missing from all of these milestones is any sign of Julia's friends, family, or community. Her son, Zachary, miraculously appears with no discernible contribution from his dad. Watch "The Life of Julia" long enough, and pretty soon it feels like even the woman herself is secondary, a supporting character in her own story. Government now carries the leading role.

"The Life of Julia" also assumes that the government's answer to all of a citizen's wants and needs is an unconditional, immediate yes. But, of course, it never really turns out that way when bureaucrats are in charge.

On this point, the casework that comes through my office every day is instructive. Take, for example, my constituent Chrissy Fields. When I first met Chrissy, she was seventeen years old and very sick. She had a life-threatening heart condition and needed an adjustable pacemaker. The device was available in Europe but hadn't been approved for use in the United States yet. Chrissy's mom had tried everything she could think of to get a compassionate-use waiver from the FDA, but she'd had no success and Chrissy's life was slipping away.

Left without anywhere else to turn, her mom walked into my district office, crying. She told my district director, Danyell Tremmel, she was at the end of her rope. The medical device company was willing to send the pacemaker over from France, but without the compassionate-use waiver, the customs officers here would turn it away. Chrissy didn't have much longer to live, and her only hope was trapped in the bureaucracy of a federal agency.

Danyell called me, and then I called the head of the FDA. I refused to get off of the phone until I talked with him, and when I finally reached him, I said I wasn't willing to take no for an answer.

He promised to look into it, and fifteen minutes later he called back to let me know that the waiver would be approved.

Today, Chrissy is a nurse and living a full life, but what about all of the other people trapped in—or turned away by—our growing federal bureaucracy? If you think Chrissy's battle against the FDA sounds bad, just wait until Obamacare's Independent Payment Advisory Board gets going. Its rulings are all but final, and its domain includes decisions about payments for life-saving treatments and critical care. Under Obamacare, decisions made by the fifteen members of that board could make it impossible for Medicare patients to get treatments that could save or dramatically improve their lives—supposedly in the name of controlling costs.

That's the face of modern liberalism, and from the progressive view of government, it's nothing new. It's a state-centered approach that, at every turn, reverts back to expert rule and political coercion, yet sells itself as the opposite. In the abstract it often sounds like freedom, but in action it undermines liberty, self-government, and the dignity of the individual—and tramples the rule of law.

When it comes to liberal progressive government, the life of Chrissy is a lot closer to the truth than "The Life of Julia." Whatever its friendly airs and philosophical pretentions, liberalism on the business end is blunt, arbitrary, and always sure of itself—no matter how clear its mounting failures are to everyone else. Liberal progressives mean well. The problem is not in their motives; it's in their methods and ideas. When any ideology deals in coercion instead of choice, in decrees to the collective instead of faith in a free people, the results are never good.

*   *   *

In our public discourse, it's become increasingly common to vilify those with whom you disagree. But I don't ascribe evil motives to liberal progressives or Democrats. I'm sure that they sincerely believe that their political philosophy and the policies that flow from it are best for our country and our people.

I just have a very different point of view. Unlike liberal progressives, I don't think the Founders' vision was relevant only in Franklin's time or Jefferson's time or Lincoln's time or our time. Their vision is relevant to all people and all times, as Lincoln put it. I want to apply those timeless principles to the challenges of our moment. I also believe that the Republican Party is the best vehicle for confronting the coercive liberal progressive vision—and reinvigorating the American Idea.

Of course, that only invites the question: If the Republican Party is so well positioned to advance a vision that offers freedom, opportunity, and prosperity, then why does it keep losing presidential elections?

As you might suppose, I've spent a lot of time thinking about that. The GOP ticket has been defeated in four of the last six presidential elections. That's a pretty stunning showing, but even more so considering that between 1968 and 1988, in five out of six presidential elections it was the Republicans who prevailed over the Democrats.

Going into 2012, the stage seemed to be set for a reversal of the Republican Party's fortunes. The fundamentals favored us. The economy during President Obama's first term was bad from beginning to end. An overwhelming number of Americans believed the nation was still in a recession more than three years after it had officially concluded. The president's major domestic achievements—the stimulus package and Obamacare—were highly unpopular. The world was increasingly restive, with events, particularly in the Middle East, going from bad to worse. And President Obama's approval ratings were in a territory generally considered near fatal for an incumbent.

And yet we lost.

Why did we lose? How did it happen? Why does the Republican Party seem to keep losing ground?

I don't have all the answers, but I do know at least part of the GOP's problem—and, therefore, part of the solution—lies in our party's failure to grapple with today's changing world. Our principles are timeless, but we must effectively apply those principles to today's challenges. Our policy solutions must address what families face in their daily lives. And this needs to translate into not just what we champion, but also where and how we make our case.

The liberal progressive strategy is to carve up the electorate and target citizens on the basis of their group identity. The Obama campaign combined this strategy with twenty-first-century technology to devastating effect in 2012. Using sophisticated analysis and voter mobilization techniques, they were able to reach the voting public in ways that defied the conventional wisdom. This is one reason why an unpopular president with the economic and political fundamentals stacked against him was able to prevail.

After our loss, some Republicans focused their frustration not on the tactics, but on the voters—criticizing them for being drawn in by the promise of government benefits tailored to their demographic position. But as Jack Kemp used to say, "Bad-mouthing democracy is the occupational disease of political losers." Blaming voters for listening to—and voting for—a party that speaks directly to their immediate concerns is not a winning strategy. We'd be better served by considering what Republicans are doing wrong—and what we must do to engage with and compete for those voters.

For too long, our party has failed to show how our principles and ideas are relevant to people's everyday lives. The core of our problem is that people don't think we are offering them a better future. The rich, comfortable, cold-hearted Republican who cares about protecting his own wealth from taxes and about little else, indifferent to the hardships of poor people who live in the same country but a different world, is mostly a figure of caricature, and never more so than in the case of our 2012 standard-bearer, Mitt Romney, who remains one of the most earnest, big-hearted people I've ever met in politics. But Democrats are most successful when they run against that caricature; sometimes, it's all they've got. They sure know how to work that image of our party—and, I'll admit, some Republicans sure know how to play into it.

We can go on and on, in policy debates, talking about how government needs to be run more like a business. We can take out the charts and actuarial tables to show all the problems of debt and unfunded liabilities. We can go on forever talking about the enduring principles of conservatism, the high ideals that we Republicans believe in. We might be right on every count, but it's just not the same as showing people that you believe in them, understand their lives, are pulling for them in their struggles, and care whether they make it or not. If we have to go the extra mile to make all of that clear, as Jack Kemp showed us, then let's start doing it. And we won't just be better politicians for the effort, we'll also be better leaders.

Recently, we've missed the opportunity to make our elections a choice between the vision we are offering and the reality that liberal progressive ideology has been delivering. Instead of talking about what we're for, we've only railed against what we oppose. Rather than offering an alternative, we've primarily framed elections merely as referendums on our opponent's performance and ideas. That may be necessary, but it's not sufficient.

As a result, too few people understand what the Republican Party stands for and how our principles will improve our economy, revive our culture, restore upward mobility, and strengthen our international standing. Frankly, we've become lazy and complacent. Instead of doing the hard work of persuading people, we've opted for the easy route, focusing our attention on communities where people already agree with us and trying to turn out the base.

In national elections we make our pitch to areas that are already deep red—communities in the suburbs, exurbs, and rural areas of the South, Midwest, and Mountain West. These places tend to be whiter, older, and better off economically. Going forward, we have to do even more. We have to go to every corner of our country and communicate who we are as a party, what we believe, and how our ideas will actually build a better future for every voter. And we have to do it every year, not just during an election year.

This work is becoming more and more important with each passing election, because the Republican Party is running into the headwinds of shifting demographics. As 2012 illustrated, focusing heavily on simply turning out our traditional coalition is a losing strategy—and it's only going to deliver even more lopsided losses.

In 2012, our campaign carried only 17 percent of the nonwhite vote. Among all African American voters, we captured six percent, and among Hispanics and Asian Americans, we received 27 percent and 26 percent, respectively. It was an admittedly poor showing, and projected growth among these voters will create more problems for the GOP unless we can more effectively communicate how our approach would be as good for them as it would be for all Americans. Hispanics, African Americans, and other minority groups aren't just becoming an increasingly larger percentage of the overall population; they are also starting to vote in greater numbers. The 2012 election marked the first time in history that a higher percentage of African Americans than whites voted in a presidential election.

Surveying this changing political environment, some argue that we need to build a more advanced electoral infrastructure with better technology and turnout capability. And, of course, our party will greatly benefit from an ability to get out the vote on Election Day. No more Project ORCAs, please—let's never let ourselves be outsmarted or outmaneuvered again.

Others argue that we need to transform the Republican Party so that in its principles and policies it is offering something closer to what the Democrats stand for and offer. Why can't we just be "economic conservatives" and forget all the rest?

That would be an enormous mistake. A winning party knows how to play to its strengths, and our greatest strengths are the conviction, intellectual force, and moral idealism of the conservative cause. Take those away, and what's really left? In his own day, Lincoln cautioned Republicans about sacrificing their defining principles for the almighty dollar, a warning we'd do well to remember, too. And talk about playing into a caricature: Democrats portray us as caring only about taxes and economics—and, in response, we're supposed to clear the party platform of everything but taxes and economics?

The way I look at our situation, maybe it's not the core convictions that need broadening—maybe it's the core audience. Conservatism is our party's fighting faith; we just need to fight for the interests and the hopes of more people. And, here again, we could do a lot worse than to follow the example of Jack Kemp.

* * *

In late April and early May 1992, Los Angeles had been rocked by six days of riots in the wake of a trial that acquitted four police officers, most of them white, in the beating of a black man, Rodney King, that had been caught on videotape. When the verdict came down, the city exploded in fire and looting. I was twenty-two years old, and the images on the nightly news were like nothing I'd ever seen.

Of course, the trial, the riots, and their aftermath were about a lot more than a verdict. They were an outlet for years of pent-up frustration about race, poverty, and the lack of economic opportunity in south central Los Angeles. At the time of the riots, unemployment among black men in some Los Angeles neighborhoods was 50 percent.

In the spring of 1992, Jack Kemp was serving in President George Bush's Cabinet as the secretary of housing and urban development. While other people stayed away from LA and waited for the chaos to die down, Jack flew in. He'd grown up in Los Angeles, so for him the riots were personal.

I can vividly remember watching TV and seeing Jack walk through the city's streets with his suit jacket off, tie loosened, and sleeves rolled up. He surveyed the damage and met with community leaders.

I remember watching him and thinking, *That's something else.* It was inspiring.

Jack thought that the answer for what was ailing places like Los Angeles was to give people a stake in their communities "with education, jobs, and ownership." Jack wanted every American to own a piece of where they worked and lived.

One reporter asked him, "Mr. Secretary, you keep saying people should have a stake and home ownership and so on. How are they going to have a stake when they don't have any money?"

"Well," Jack replied, "the way to get money and capital and credit into the inner cities of America and the barrios and ghettos of America is to do something radically different than just transferring wealth through government bureaucracies. It is to empower people directly."

In one short answer, Jack conveyed the power of the American Idea—and the hard limits of liberal progressivism.

Jack had been bringing the message of conservatism to the inner city long before the LA riots, and he continued that work long after that story left the front page. When I arrived at Empower America, his calendar was full of events in places where Democrats had a political monopoly. He would visit housing projects, community meetings, and halfway houses. His message was always the same: The American Idea is not just for the suburbs or white communities or people who want to work on Wall Street. It is universal, and if we pursue the right policies, then you can share in the prosperity, too.

When I worked for Jack at Empower America, he was always my boss more than a buddy, but he invested time in young staff and tried to help them learn. His investment transformed me in a lot of ways. I remember watching him speak and thinking, *Now this is my brand of conservatism.* And today, even more than back then, the Republican Party could use a big dose of Jack's idealism and energy.

We could start by being a lot more inclusive in how we talk about our country's challenges and opportunities. Jack used to say, "People don't care how much you know until they know how much you care." The simple fact is there are whole communities of Americans who don't think the Republican Party and its leaders care about them. How do you care? Same as in the rest of life—by *being there*, showing up, and listening instead of just talking. It's easy for people in struggling communities to think of Republican leaders in caricature when, basically, they never see us in person. They hear *about* us, instead of *from* us, and that's got to change.

In my district, there are a lot of African American and Hispanic citizens who live in the cities of Beloit, Racine, and Kenosha. When I was first elected in 1998, I knew that since those towns were Democratic strongholds, most of these citizens had probably not voted for me. But I was their congressman and it was my responsibility to represent them, too. I couldn't do that if I didn't know them, so I decided to go into the community and get a conversation going.

I started by visiting our local black churches. I wanted to do it in a way that was low-key and wasn't about trying to pose for cameras or get publicity. So the only thing I did to prepare for each visit was call the pastor and ask him if I could come by.

Walking into those churches on Sundays was a revelation. As a Catholic, I'm used to an hour-long service that's fairly predictable and sedate. We engage in "Catholic Calisthenics"—we sit, we stand, we kneel, and we make the sign of the cross repeatedly. If, during the homily, any Catholic ever called out "Amen!" "That's right!" or "Halleluiah!" the ushers would start to get nervous.

It's a different deal at a black church, of course. And if anyone's faith ever needs some perking up, that's the place to go. I always tried to get into the spirit of things with dancing, clapping, and singing out in the pews. It was a small mercy in 2012 that no videotapes of my dancing ever surfaced.

After one service, a few people came up to give me some friendly grief about my moves. That got us all talking, and in time we got to know each other—well enough that they didn't hesitate to say when they disagreed with me or thought I'd gotten a vote wrong. That happened a lot, in fact. But at least they were telling *me*, personally, instead of just some pollster canvassing the neighborhood. And I was hearing it directly, instead of just listening to some consultant who's been studying the latest numbers from a pollster. There's nothing like firsthand knowledge in politics. Sometimes the most effective move is simply to walk up and introduce yourself.

I went to these churches off and on until my kids got a bit older and it became more of a priority to attend Mass on Sunday as a family. But I really miss my visits to those services in Beloit, Racine, and Kenosha. I loved the music, the spirit, the deep faith, and the sense of community. And I enjoyed getting to know the people I work for there.

Around the same time, I started reaching out in other ways. I don't speak fluent Spanish, and I knew that could be a barrier in communicating with some of our Hispanic citizens. I had heard great things about Teresa Mora, a woman who had been working as the outreach coordinator for the Spanish Center of Southeastern

Wisconsin. Teresa was born in Mexico and immigrated to America at an early age. From what we knew, she was fairly apolitical, and we weren't sure if she would want to work for a Republican. We approached her and she agreed to come on board. She's made a tremendous difference in our community, ensuring Hispanic citizens of the First District are heard. Ever since my first term, Teresa has helped me organize our Hispanic listening sessions, which have been invaluable to me. What I learned from Teresa is that knowing the policy doesn't mean much if you don't know the community. I don't know much Spanish, but I do know that if you show people respect and take their concerns seriously, then—on a vital level—you are speaking the same language.

I was reminded of that truth at a recent town hall in Janesville, when a young Hispanic woman got up and shared her story with me. When she was younger, her parents brought her to the United States, and Janesville is the only home she has ever known. She's a good student; she went to Parker High School and is now finishing her bachelor's degree at the University of Wisconsin in Milwaukee. When she graduates, she wants to go to medical school so she can become a doctor and come back and serve our community. The problem is that because of how she came to our country she is ineligible for in-state tuition and unable to receive federal student aid. She wanted to know what we could do to help students like her—and why I voted to defund an executive order that President Obama had signed making students in her position eligible for state and federal aid.

I explained the reasons for my vote, which went straight to the Constitution and the rule of law. I support immigration reform, and that includes a way for her to pursue her dreams here in Wisconsin. But good reforms in law usually come about by lawful means, and that hadn't happened this time. It was not for the president to rewrite our laws unilaterally. He has no such constitutional authority. And when a president shows so little respect for the law, how are we in Congress supposed to respect his decisions? And since he lacks the authority to take such actions, how does this approach really help the students such as the young woman at that town hall, who will only be put in greater limbo by the legal and legislative wrangling that will inevitably ensue?

A better way—and one which I support—would be for Congress to pass, and the president to sign, legislation that would offer a legal pathway for unauthorized immigrants whose parents brought them here as children. And, of course, we must also secure the border, enforce the interior, and address other pressing immigration issues this way.

I'm sure it wasn't exactly an answer she could agree with. I don't know if I convinced her that my position was the right one. But going forward, the person with that position is someone she has met, someone who cared enough to show up in her neighborhood and give a straight answer to her question. At my listening sessions in some areas, I'm still a Republican in a Democratic stronghold, but at least I'm not a stranger. In politics, that's how things can start to change.

It's a step we've been able to take in the African American neighborhoods of the First District as well. After I was first elected, I reached out to an African American county board member in Racine for advice about how to make my town halls more inviting for everyone, and African American voters especially. He suggested we go into their communities and hold listening sessions there. So that's what we did.

My first outings, I have to admit, weren't always smooth going. Often someone would get up and explain a problem they were having in their neighborhood. Sometimes that was followed by the question, *How much federal money can you secure to help us address that?*

Every time I got a question like that, I replied that I wanted to solve their problems not by delivering more money, because that wasn't the real solution. Instead, I wanted to empower the members of our community to address our challenges. It was the Jack Kemp message, but probably could have used more of the Jack Kemp style. I got denounced here and there by prominent local Democrats, but that didn't really bother me. I kept coming back and kept listening. It sharpened my focus for those town halls, and if nothing else I proved that I cared about everyone in the district—not just enough people to make it a "safe" district for Republicans.

I had heard the usual advice, in so many words—*don't go there, you'll never get their vote.* And there were people in the audience at those events who had been told, "The Republican Party hates you. It has nothing to offer you." Experience taught me that—on both sides of that equation—the conventional wisdom is wrong. We all have a lot to gain by talking to each other, even if at the end of all of our talking we still disagree.

I've been at this for over fifteen years now, and I certainly haven't earned the support of all of the African American and Hispanic constituents I serve yet. For a long time, the Republican Party just didn't engage these communities. Earning support is going to require a long-term commitment to a conversation about principles and policies. We can't just parachute in for a photo op before an election. The only way to generate respect and a better understanding of our motives and ideas is to keep visiting and talking and opening the lines of communication. There are a lot of preconceptions I have to overcome, and that's true of most Republicans. It's really challenging, but it's something our party needs to do. Otherwise, we won't be able to convince our fellow Americans that we care about them— and that our ideas can help create a better life for them and their children.

We need to get back to our message of opportunity, upward mobility, and economic growth, the American Idea, and its promise for everyone. We need to make the case for greater freedom instead of ceding personal choices or responsibilities to the state. We need to emphasize the dignity of work and the primacy of civic institutions. And we need to explain how that vision is relevant and meaningful for every person—no matter their color, creed, occupation, or station in life.

For the Republican Party, this is a matter of practical necessity. Preaching to the choir isn't working, and by the way, the choir is shrinking. But, for me, it's about a lot more than that. It's about our common humanity, and the duties we owe to one another. I am inspired by Jack Kemp's example that we shouldn't isolate people; we Republicans should include them. That's the only way those same people, when they vote, will start to include us.

* * *

Last Christmas, my son Charlie and I volunteered at our parish's homeless shelter. We helped set up the beds and serve the meals. As my son and I were putting the salad out, a guy approached me. His clothes and his hair were disheveled, and his eyes were bloodshot. It took me a minute to place him, but I knew I recognized him. Then it clicked—we were about the same age and he'd gone to Parker, the other high school in town.

"Hey, Paul," he said.

"Hey," I said, "Merry Christmas. You doing okay? Let's catch up."

We went over to one of the empty tables off along the side of the room. He told me that he'd been homeless for about a year. As is so often the case, his hard times started with addiction and then snowballed from there. Now he didn't have a job and he was out on the street.

We talked about his struggles, about how the people at places like our parish center were helping him find his way. He told me that he was working hard to get his life back on track. And then, in a moment that was both surprising and moving, he asked how I was doing. With everything going on in his life, he was concerned about me.

As we talked a bit about my job, our conversation turned to events in Washington, D.C. He became animated as he shared with me his feelings about our country—how he hoped we could remain a place where there was opportunity enough for everybody, where there were second chances for people who'd hit a hard stretch of road, like him.

It's a common Democratic talking point that the Republican vision is relevant or appealing only to wealthy white guys. Our conversation was one more reminder that nothing could be further from the truth. The American Idea has resonance and relevance for all of us because it speaks to everyone, regardless of our moment in history or station in life.

The Republican Party must be the keeper of the American Idea, which is why it's critical that we get our act together. As Jack Kemp once said, "It is not enough that the Republican Party somehow survives. It is not enough that it enjoy mild success, that it only wins enough elections to hang on as a minority political party. What is really necessary to the system is that the GOP become the *dominant* party in America. . . . I don't mean this as a partisan, but as an American."

The Republican Party has to speak to every American. We need to address practical problems and offer a meaningful choice. That means we can't just talk about what we're against. We need to start talking more about the policies we're offering and how they can make a difference. And to do that, we need a plan.

CHAPTER 6

Simpler, Smaller, Smarter

On a warm evening in mid-October 2013, I met up with my cousin on the street behind the Capitol building. We were hoping to grab dinner and catch up, but my iPhone kept vibrating. Finally I looked at the screen.

URGENT: MEETING IN THE SPEAKER'S OFFICE NOW.

I said a quick good-bye, walked back to the Capitol, and made my way over to Speaker John Boehner's office. When I got there, a handful of colleagues were already seated at the long table that ran the length of the room. I took a spot at one end with a couple of other committee chairmen. Boehner sat at the other end, slouched in his chair. He looked haggard.

For weeks, John had been working around the clock, trying to head off a government shutdown. We were quickly coming to the point where there would be no turning back. As a last-ditch effort, he'd worked with House conservatives on a proposal that would have kept the government open while expressing opposition to Obamacare. Word of the idea had leaked and outside conservative groups had rebelled, creating consternation that rippled through the caucus.

John has the hardest job in the House, and life prepared him for it well. He grew up in a big Irish Catholic family in southern Ohio. One of twelve kids, John worked in his dad's bar, Andy's, which is named after his grandfather. He waited tables, made drinks, mopped floors, and kept things from getting too rowdy. In short, he's used to mediating disagreements over a smoke and a drink—and achieving a good outcome before a brawl can break out.

One thing I like about John is that he always speaks his mind. You know where he stands and what he thinks. That may be standard practice in most places, but it's a refreshing approach for Washington, D.C.

Of course, there are times when even John needs to keep his cards close to the vest. But you can generally tell how things are going by how long it takes him to light up a cigarette. If it's a good meeting, he might go without one. If things are tense or frustrating, he'll start about halfway through. On this night, he was already smoking when we got there.

"We tried to get the votes, but we're not even close. There's no way this is going to pass."

Then Speaker Boehner leaned his head back into the chair and took a drag from his cigarette, pausing to ponder the moment.

"It looks like we're going into a shutdown," he said. "And I don't know how long it's going to last."

Exhale.

"Anybody have any ideas?"

*   *   *

As we got closer to the point of no return, I had a meeting with a close colleague. He's a true conservative from a deep-red district and a bell cow who can bring a lot of votes with him. Persuading him to vote for the stopgap spending bill was our best hope of avoiding what I believed would be a calamity for our party and our country.

For weeks, a few conservatives in the Senate and some outside groups had been claiming that the House could unilaterally defund Obamacare by refusing to fund the government. That's not how the law works. Obamacare is an entitlement; its spending levels are not set by the annual appropriations process. The House can't unilaterally defund it or eliminate it. And even if we managed to shut the government down, entitlements like Social Security, Medicare, *and now Obamacare* continue operating. To actually stop it, the House and Senate would have to pass a new bill. And even if we could get a Democrat-led Senate to do that, President Obama would never sign it into law.

In short, the strategy our colleagues had been promoting was flawed from beginning to end. It was a suicide mission. But a lot of members were more afraid of what would happen if they didn't jump off the cliff.

"The problem is that I can't be seen as complicit in any effort that advances Obamacare," my colleague said, "and no matter what the facts are, that's how it's going to look with prominent Republicans out there saying the opposite."

I kept explaining the facts and voicing my concern that a needless shutdown would harm our credibility as a governing party. I was around when Newt Gingrich led the shutdown in 1995, I explained. I saw the damage it did. We couldn't afford to take a hit like that again—not for a strategy that had no hope of advancing our core principles.

"Paul," he said, "I'm happy to vote to fund the government, but we have to shut it down first. That way, we can prove what you're saying—that it doesn't stop Obamacare. But if I vote to stop the shutdown beforehand, then I could be cast as being in favor of Obamacare. I just can't do that."

"So let me get this straight," I said. "As long as we shut the government down, therefore proving that Obamacare still lives, then you're okay with taking the same vote you won't take now. You'll vote to fund the government."

"Yes," he replied, "that's right."

Wow, I thought. *This can't be the full measure of our party and our movement. If it is, we're dead, and the country is lost.*

* * *

The shutdown wasn't a disagreement over principles, or even policies. Rather, it is proof of what happens to a party when it's defined primarily by what it opposes, instead of by its ideas.

To be fair, in most cases, Republican opposition over the last six years has been a position of principle. Conservatives in the House and Senate have tried to stop policies that grow the government at the expense of freedom. Many also see themselves as watchmen sent to Washington, D.C., to ensure that as a party, we don't lose our way again.

Those are positive developments. But governing is about much more than just opposing bad ideas, and criticism isn't all there is to campaigning. Making the Republican Party a majority party again will require both sides of the equation—opposing lousy policies and advancing better ideas. We must continue to point out how the liberal progressive vision takes us further away from the American Idea, but we must also offer an alternative vision that can restore it. Then we have to run on it and win on it so we can put that vision into action.

Furthermore, it is only when we have a sense of what we're aiming for that we can tell the difference between a worthwhile compromise and a worthless one. We must show where our principles would take us so we can figure out how to get there in practice.

That was the philosophy behind the first Roadmap, back in 2008. At the time, I knew I was taking a political risk—and I probably wouldn't get everything I wanted—but I hoped to get things moving in the right direction again. I remember thinking that the subsequent debate might last four or five years. I'm an optimist at heart, and I figured somewhere around 2012 or 2013 we'd be able to reach a bipartisan agreement to avert an entitlement crisis and jump-start our economy.

Of course, it didn't quite work out that way. Today, we're still dealing with many of the same problems that the original Road-map addressed—and they've only grown more pressing with time. We're also facing new challenges—including a terribly designed health-care entitlement and other results of six years of liberal pro-gressive policies.

Unfortunately, our government isn't well positioned to overcome these challenges. Today, our bureaucracy is basically the junk closet at the end of the hallway. Over the years, we've thrown stuff in there, piling it high and deep. If you open the doors, everything comes crashing down. You're left to wonder, *How did we end up with such a mess?*

That's the government we've got, but clearly it's not the one we want or need. The task now is not to put the mess to some better use but rather to reform it, so that we have a government that can address our country's twenty-first-century challenges in ways that are consistent with our constitutional principles and our priorities. And that starts with the question: What do we think the govern-ment ought to do?

Today, there is widespread agreement that the government should provide some measure of health and retirement security. It should maintain a robust safety net, particularly for those who are unable to help themselves, and help able-bodied Americans who have fallen on tough times—like my old acquaintance who showed up last year in a Janesville homeless shelter—get back on the lad-der of life and reach their potential. It must encourage economic growth by supporting free enterprise and the talents and ingenuity of our citizenry. It must protect the space where civil society thrives.

And it must fulfill its primary responsibility, which is to provide for the national defense and implement a foreign policy that defends America's interests and values internationally.

What holds these aims together? A vision of a government that can sustain the preconditions and space for people to thrive, while protecting them from the greatest risks of modern life.

That's a very different vision, by the way, than the assertive, hyperactive role for government that today's liberal progressive Left is pursuing. In their vision, government defines success, strictly prescribes roles and outcomes, tries to replace our civic institutions, and manages much of our economy and national life. And because the liberal progressive vision imagines a far more intrusive and ambitious role for government, it ultimately ends up failing to meet the government's most basic obligations.

Under liberal progressive policies, the federal government has grown too unwieldy and unresponsive. It is increasingly denying people the liberty to shape important aspects of their lives, like how they get their health care or what sort of education their children should receive. In short, liberal progressivism's method for fulfilling the government's missions isn't working—and, what's more, it's ill-suited to the times we're living in. The ironic thing about "progressivism" is that it's terribly old-fashioned and hasn't kept up with American life.

A generation used to the quick access of an iTunes playlist, an Amazon wish list, and an instant search on Google isn't looking for one-size-fits-all, centralized bureaucratic planning or control. Nor do they necessarily think in terms of "big" or "small" when it comes to their government. They think in terms of efficiency and innovation. They want to be able to customize government services to fit the priorities in their lives. They're looking for a government that is geared toward meeting their needs and limited enough to let individual creativity and economic opportunity thrive. A philosophy of government that limits the state and makes room for society to find creative ways to solve problems and produce opportunities is much better suited to these twenty-first-century needs and expectations.

That's why conservatives are offering reforms that can streamline government, making it nimbler and more responsive. Only then can it fulfill its duties efficiently and effectively. Conservatives don't want to eliminate the government; we want to limit and reorient the government so that it can focus on what it is supposed to do.

For conservatives, the central question is: How can we make government simpler, smaller, and smarter? In 2012, that was our test for every policy we proposed. But our plans were built for a party that held the presidency, and when we lost, the way forward wasn't immediately clear.

* * *

I'll admit that in the wake of the 2012 election, I found myself in a bit of a funk. I'm not easily discouraged, but that election was the first I'd lost—and it was a tough one to lose. Plus, I didn't really have a lot of time to process the defeat. I had to get back to work, passing a budget, helping constituents, and taking new votes.

For those first six months back, I was doing my job, but it felt like I was going through the motions. I'd always had a plan for what I wanted to tackle next. And now, for the first time ever, I didn't have a next move. People seemed to sense that, and they were generous with their advice. More than a few tried to convince me that I should throw myself into laying the groundwork for a presidential campaign in 2016. Get out on the road, they said. Head to some primary states. Staff up and lock down donors and supporters.

I appreciated their interest and advice, but that course of action wasn't really appealing. I felt like it was too soon to think about 2016. Not to mention that if I went that route, I would be making the next few years all about me and my own ambitions. I would have to constantly think about how every little move I made positioned me vis-a-vis any possible primary competitor. *That is no way to go through life*, I thought. *That's just not who I am.*

But if the answer wasn't getting ready to run for the presidency immediately, what would the next couple of years be about? How would I pick myself up? What was I going to do to get excited about my work again?

I knew I had to reset, and so, like so many challenging moments in my life, I would go out hunting early in the morning before the sun was up. And this time, I had a new companion with me.

My daughter, Liza, had taken her hunter safety course and gotten her certificate in 2012. For Christmas, Janna and I gave her a deer rifle. On our next trip to Oklahoma to visit Janna's dad, Liza came out with me. As I watched her, I couldn't stop thinking about how quickly she and her brothers were getting older as well as the kind of country we're leaving them. Out with my daughter that day, I think I understood my own parents—all of their hopes and anxieties, all of their dreams for my siblings and me—better than I ever had before. That morning, Liza bagged a really nice ten-point buck; an accomplishment I had not achieved until well into my twenties. Moments like that really help clear the mind.

Soon, the way forward was clear. The things I really care about—advancing good policy and helping our country—hadn't changed. And it was time to open up a conversation about where we go from here.

In my treestands and on flights back and forth between Janesville and Washington, D.C., I started thinking about what it would take to get our country back on track, whether we had enough time to get things right, and frankly, if we could win the elections necessary to get the job done. I decided we needed to offer a vision of what full-spectrum conservatism looks like. I wanted to help provide an agenda that gets the basics right, so the country can thrive.

I started developing a slate of policies that would reorganize the junk closet, making government simpler, smaller, and smarter so that it can effectively fulfill its proper role again and help Americans recover the promise of our country. It is not a solution for every problem we face, but it reflects our commitment to ensure that America has the most dynamic society, most prosperous economy, most capable military, and most able citizenry in the world. It is, in other words, an application of the conservative idea of government's role made real through concrete public policy.

Entitlement and Health-Care Reform

Social Security is the third rail of American politics. Touch it, you're dead.

—KIRK O'DONNELL, CHIEF AIDE TO THEN
HOUSE SPEAKER TIP O'NEILL

Before Barack Obama took office, there were two high-water marks for liberal progressivism in the United States. The first occurred between 1933 and 1938, when President Franklin D. Roosevelt shepherded through a series of policies known as the New Deal. The second was in the 1960s, when President Lyndon Johnson unveiled and implemented a sweeping agenda of domestic programs known as the Great Society.

Both sets of policy initiatives aimed to address problems that were dire and real. For FDR, it was the Great Depression. For Johnson, it was deep and persistent poverty and the injustice of racism. Each responded by creating federal programs to overcome these problems, and their legacies include entitlements that Americans have come to rely upon and appreciate—Medicare, Medicaid, and Social Security.

After Barack Obama was elected, he enacted another new entitlement: Obamacare. Much like Johnson and Roosevelt, the president was trying to solve a real problem when he passed and signed the Affordable Care Act. In 2010, the health-care sector was broken, 50 million Americans were uninsured, health care cost too much, and there was widespread agreement in both political parties that the status quo was unacceptable. To address these problems, President Obama and his allies chose a distinctly liberal-progressive solution that heavily regulated the insurance and health-care industries, and imposed mandates on citizens and businesses that did not behave as required while providing taxpayer-funded subsidies for those that did.

Our major entitlement programs—Social Security, Medicare, Medicaid, and now Obamacare—were created and implemented using the liberal-progressive model of bureaucratic control and open-ended design. As a result, they're delivering benefits ineffectively, approaching bankruptcy, and threatening our country's fiscal health. They are also on the verge of creating real hardship for our citizens.

Collectively, Social Security, Medicare, and Medicaid are the key drivers of our national debt. In 1970, they consumed about 20 percent of the federal budget. Today they account for over 47 percent. By 2066, these three programs—and the new spending for Obamacare—will swallow up nearly 100 percent of all federal revenues; meaning everything else the federal government does will have to be paid for with borrowed money. Add in the growing cost of the national debt, and these programs will consume all federal revenues by 2030.

To get a sense of the scope of our entitlement crisis, it helps to look at each program individually. First, consider Social Security, which—as I explained in chapter 3—uses a pay-as-you-go system to collect revenues and distribute benefits. That model has more or less worked for decades, but it's headed for catastrophe. More and more Baby Boomers are becoming eligible—at a rate of about ten thousand a day—putting enormous strain on the system. Furthermore, the ratio of workers to retirees has been declining at an alarming rate, meaning it will eventually be impossible to raise enough money from today's workers to keep the program's promises to retirees. To make matters worse, Social Security has been dipping into its trust fund, the pool of IOUs from the Treasury for all the payroll taxes paid in by workers over the years, and that fund will be exhausted in 2033.

Then there's Medicare, which mostly provides health insurance for Americans over the age of sixty-five. Medicare is also grappling with the Baby Boomer wave, but by far its biggest challenge is the overall explosion of health-care costs. At its inception in 1966, Medicare cost roughly $900 million. In 2013, the program's price tag had grown to $492 billion. By 2024, the Congressional Budget Office expects costs to reach $858 billion. The Medicare Trustees Report indicates that the long-term financial sustainability of the program will be in jeopardy in the near future. And, as with Social Security, Medicare's hospital insurance fund is also set to dry up, but sooner—in 2026.

The third major entitlement is Medicaid, which provides health care to low-income Americans. Medicaid is a joint federal-state program; it is administered by states, and financed by both the states and the federal government.

More than 72 million Americans received health care through Medicaid at some point in 2013. That year, the federal government's share of the program's total cost was $265 billion, and the states contributed another $181 billion. Sums that high inevitably raise the question: What kind of results does that much money buy? The answer, unfortunately, is wholly unsatisfactory. A recent study found Medicaid "had no significant effect" on a series of key health outcomes, meaning that—when it came to one's health—there was little difference between being on Medicaid and being uninsured.

So here we have a program that is straining state and federal budgets, and providing low-quality care to patients. It's the kind of situation that begs for new thinking and better ideas. But rather than reform the program, Obamacare expanded it by changing the eligibility requirements so that millions more could qualify.

Thanks to a Supreme Court decision in June 2012, states can opt out of this expansion. But if the Obama administration has its way, nearly 16 million more people would enroll in Medicaid. As it stands today, the Congressional Budget Office expects the program's rolls to grow to 93 million Americans by 2024. To pay for all of these new enrollees, the federal share of Medicaid spending will double—to $576 billion—in the next decade.

Of course, Obamacare did more than expand Medicaid; it created a whole new entitlement and began a government takeover of one-sixth of our economy. It was the wrong solution for a broken system—the federal role was already far too great and harmful, and Obamacare simply gave Washington an even more central and ill-conceived part to play.

To understand what is wrong with Obamacare, it helps to understand what was wrong with our health-care system as it existed before the law's enactment in 2010. That system was woefully inadequate, particularly because it created powerful incentives for higher spending and higher costs—which, in turn, made health insurance unaffordable for millions of Americans while driving our government toward bankruptcy.

As I just noted, Medicare and Medicaid were a big part of that problem. To compensate for the below-market payments they receive, Medicare providers simply perform more procedures, leading to vast waste and overuse of resources. Medicaid, meanwhile, encourages state legislators and officials to push for greater spending and discourages fiscal discipline—since state officials can claim credit for more generous benefits while the federal taxpayer foots at least half the cost.

Moreover, there is a powerful, open-ended tax incentive for employer-provided insurance coverage. The money that employers spend on workers' coverage isn't considered part of a workers' taxable income, which encourages higher spending on premiums.

That incentive came to be almost by accident. During World War II, the federal government imposed wage and price controls, and employers needed a new way to convince potential employees from the smaller pool of available workers to come and work for them. So they started offering health insurance coverage, and eventually the IRS ruled that those benefits would not be counted as taxable income and Congress encouraged the practice by writing it into law.

Over the years, what started as a way to attract workers has become the defining feature of our health-care sector. One of the greatest problems with this third-party payment system is the way it contributes to rising health-care costs. As it should be, companies can deduct their cost of providing health insurance for their employees, just like they deduct the wages they pay. But unlike wages, employees do not pay taxes on the income they receive in the form of health-care benefits. Naturally, this encourages employers to offer more expensive plans, and it shields the employees from understanding the true cost of their health insurance. In turn, they use more benefits and drive up the price of those services for everyone else. What's worse is the fact that this tax benefit is tied to a person's job, not the worker. So if a person loses their job, changes their job, or becomes self-employed, the tax benefit does not stay with them. In essence, the tax code discriminates against people who do not get health insurance from their jobs.

All of these badly misaligned incentives are really versions of the same problem: The American market in health insurance has not been much of a market at all. In a true market, people know how much they are paying and can measure the quality of what they are getting. Third parties don't subsidize the costs, so they aren't inflated artificially. And the scale isn't unfairly tipped in favor of one kind of consumer over another. In the health-care sector as it developed in America in the postwar era, none of those market forces was at play, and we've paid the price in cost and access to care.

Supporters of Obamacare claimed their new entitlement would solve these problems, but in many ways it's only made things worse. The law didn't fix Medicare—it simply took more than $700 billion out of the program to pay for a new entitlement without changing its basic design or shoring up its finances. It didn't fix Medicaid—it just vastly increased the size of that broken program. It didn't correct the enormous distortion created by the tax exclusion for employer-provided coverage. It just doubled down on all the worst parts of the system.

Obamacare itself is built upon a flawed foundation. It uses price controls and attempts to drive costs down by paying providers less, which will force them to drop patients or deliver lower-quality care. It puts bureaucrats in charge of major decisions about life-saving treatments and drugs. It tries to nationalize the regulation of a health-care sector that works on a state-by-state basis. It dumps large numbers of the uninsured onto Medicaid, which already struggles to provide access to doctors and other providers for its current benefi-ciaries. And it raids more than $700 billion from Medicare to fuel a new $1.9 trillion open-ended entitlement.

In all of these ways Obamacare embodies the Left's government-centered understanding of American life. The law was based on the premise that the problem with American health care was that it wasn't subject to enough government control. The reality is roughly the opposite.

* * *

Our entitlement programs just aren't well designed to achieve their key goals in a sustainable way. The drafters of the New Deal, the Great Society, and Obamacare favored the administrative state and an expansive government over the private economy and the market's approach to continuous innovation and bottom-up problem solving. I believe that we need to reform them by introducing more competition, greater consumer choice, and market pressures for more cost effectiveness. By doing so, we can better protect those with the greatest needs. Policies that reflect those principles can save and improve Medicare, Medicaid, and the private insurance system for generations to come—and help right our fiscal ship.

Solving our entitlement crisis starts with finally making health care a true market, empowering patients instead of bureaucrats and making our programs more efficient and easier to use.

For starters, I would repeal Obamacare and replace it with market-based, patient-centered reforms. For able-bodied Americans under the age of sixty-five, we would replace the inefficient tax treatment of employer-provided health care with a portable, refundable tax credit that Americans could use to purchase coverage and get care. At the same time, it is vital we continue the current tax incentive for employers to offer insurance to their workers.

But rather than attaching a person's health-care tax benefit to their job, each person should have a tax credit that is theirs to take with them regardless of their employment status. You can then take your plan with you from job to job—and hang on to your insurance even when a job might be hard to find.

The tax credit wouldn't just make insurance portable. It would also help solve the problem of cost inflation by transforming our health-care sector into a functioning market. For workers who get coverage through their employers, their tax credit would go to their Health Savings Account to help pay for any out-of-pocket costs, like premiums and deductibles—or they could buy separate insurance, if they wish. And everyone else would now have a tax credit they could use to purchase insurance in the private market, where insurers would compete for their business.

Soon, health care would start to look like a real market with transparent prices, easy access to information about quality, and more choices. Americans will be empowered to choose the insurance plan that offers them the best quality for the lowest cost. When millions of Americans are making their own health decisions, it's going to drive the cost of health care down. Instead of top-down price controls imposed by bureaucrats, we're offering bottom-up competition driven by millions of customers.

For a sense of the kind of difference that would make, consider what has happened to Lasik eye surgery over the years. Lasik is an elective procedure that came of age outside of our existing health-care sector. People pay for it out of pocket, meaning it's a true market. And over time the surgery has gotten better and cheaper. I got Lasik in 2000, and the procedure has been revolutionized two or three times since then. The laser your doctor uses today is much more sophisticated, and the procedure is less expensive. So it's not that health care is immune from market forces; it's that they haven't been applied yet.

That's why the current system is such a mess, as my family's experiences with tonsillectomies have made clear. Over the last few years, we have had three tonsillectomies in our family. Every procedure was done with the same doctor and at the same hospital, but each of them cost a very different price.

When we got our bill for my son Charlie's surgery it included $1,400 for "recovery." It turns out we paid over a thousand dollars for Charlie to sit in a La-Z-Boy, eat Jell-O, watch *SpongeBob SquarePants*, and wait for the anesthesia to wear off.

And all of that is downright reasonable compared to how we picked our doctor. The only reason we knew who to go see is because I have a buddy who's a doctor in Janesville, and I asked him who he'd pick if he had to schedule a tonsillectomy for his own kids.

Why couldn't I find out what the "recovery" service would cost beforehand so I could call around and compare? Why can't I find out about the quality of care that's available at a certain hospital? Or whether a doctor is a quality practitioner?

I should be able to go online and find out who has the best track record, where I can get the best outcome, and what a routine procedure is going to cost. By transforming our health sector into a market, these reforms will enable patients to answer all those questions, save money, and get better care.

What's more, the alternative I'm proposing doesn't come with any of the unpleasant features of Obamacare. There are no mandates, fees, or penalties. And you can use your tax credit to choose the plan that works best for you rather than one that satisfies a government bureaucrat in Washington.

Instead of creating a budget-busting new entitlement involving over one-sixth of our economy, this policy uses market incentives to drive insurers and providers to offer consumers more appealing products and services at a lower cost. This fundamental shift in approach— from government-centered to patient-centered health care—will yield big dividends. It will mean more choices, patient freedom, and better care. It will dramatically expand access to quality, affordable coverage, especially for society's most vulnerable. And it will do it without raising taxes or adding one dime to the national debt.

For those who will turn sixty-five in 2024, my plan reforms Medicare using an approach known as premium support. Future retirees would receive financial support for the plan of their choice, with more support available for the poor and the sick. This is similar to how federal employees now get their health-care coverage. Under my reforms, seniors could choose to stay with a traditional fee-for-service plan, similar to Medicare today, or they could select from a list of comprehensive private policies that deliver all of their traditional Medicare benefits in one plan.

My approach doesn't raid $700 billion from Medicare to get up and going. In fact, it keeps those savings for Medicare. And with additional support for those with preexisting conditions, people can get affordable coverage regardless of their health status.

These reforms aren't just hopeful theories; we have real proof that they work. Back in 2003, I was torn about my vote on the Medicare Modernization Act (MMA). Ultimately, a factor that weighed heavily in favor of voting yes was the bill's inclusion of what are called Medicare Advantage plans. These plans operate in a very similar way to the reforms I'm currently proposing for Medicare.

Since we passed the MMA, it's become clear that people really like Medicare Advantage. Enrollment has risen rapidly—from 5.3 million people in 2004 to 14.4 million in 2013. The program's popularity has a lot to do with how effectively it delivers benefits and the innovative features it offers, which may not be available through traditional fee-for-service Medicare. In one study, 94 percent of seniors enrolled in Medicare Advantage said they were satisfied with the care they received and 81 percent were happy with the costs they paid out of pocket.

Just as we need to turn the power to make choices back to workers and seniors in health care and Medicare, we also need to give states more freedom and flexibility to decide how to best deliver benefits through Medicaid. Today, the program is governed by a misguided, one-size-fits-all approach that imposes mandates and requirements on state governments. But we all know that what works in Wisconsin won't necessarily work well in California or New York. These states are different and so are their citizens' needs.

We should send federal Medicaid dollars back to the states through per capita grants. This approach gives each state the flexibility to tailor its Medicaid program and implement it in ways that better address its citizens' unique needs. Today, the care that Medicaid patients receive is often substandard, in part because it's subject to the demands of federal bureaucrats. Under these reforms, states will be able to give their citizens better options, improved outcomes, and greater access to quality care.

Finally, we must protect Social Security. Drawing upon the ideas presented in the original Roadmap, a sensible reform would slightly pare back the growth in future benefits for higher-income people and slowly increase the retirement age to reflect longevity over time. This should be done without affecting the benefits of anyone in or near retirement. Then, building on the legislation that former senator John Sununu and I offered in 2004, I would propose the creation of optional personal retirement accounts. That way, younger workers can invest in their own account, which will be managed by Social Security for their retirement and can deliver a much better rate of return.

By introducing personal accounts into the current system, we can ensure your money is working for you. While there are many ways of allowing such accounts to be created (either using your existing payroll taxes or with additional voluntary contributions, for instance), any of the major approaches to such reforms allow you to build a nest egg and accumulate assets as you contribute to the program. Your account would have safeguards so that the level of risk you can assume is dialed back as you get closer to retirement age. That not only ensures that your money will be there for you in retirement; it also means you actually own your retirement fund and can pass it on to your family. The federal employee Thrift Savings Plan, which is a benefit offered to Members of Congress and federal workers, shows that such a plan can help people prepare for retirement.

Economic Growth

When you tax something more you get less of it, and when you tax something less, you get more of it.

—ARTHUR LAFFER, STEPHEN MOORE,
AND JONATHAN WILLIAMS

Any fair accounting of history has to acknowledge that when Barack Obama first took office, our nation was in the throes of a serious economic crisis. Major financial institutions were folding, the economy was shedding jobs, and the national debt was $10.6 trillion.

The two major political parties have two very different philosophies when it comes to economic policy, especially during the kind of recession we were experiencing in 2009. And again, the difference comes down to whether, when we think of America, we think first of society or government.

Many Democrats believe government spending creates demand and, in turn, jobs and economic growth. They propose we pay for that spending by borrowing money and raising taxes on the "rich."

The first problem with this approach is that we can't afford it. As I write, the debt is over $17 trillion and climbing. That's $55,000 for every man, woman, and child. A recent report by the Congressional Budget Office predicts the debt will grow nearly $10 trillion by 2024, for a total of $27 trillion. The deficit is projected to again top $1 trillion per year by 2022, and the interest we pay on the national debt will nearly quadruple over the next decade.

Even if we raised taxes on the wealthy, it wouldn't be enough to make a meaningful dent in our debt. Let's say we define the "rich" as people who make $1 million or more a year. In 2012, several Democrats introduced the Paying A Fair Share Act, which would have raised taxes and required anyone making that much money to pay 30 percent or more of their income in taxes. It would have generated $4.7 billion a year, which in 2012 was the equivalent of one week's interest on the national debt.

The second problem with the Democrats' approach is that, even if we could afford it, more government spending won't generate the kind of economic growth we need. We know because the

Obama administration tried it. Consider the $787 billion stimulus bill that was passed in the president's first term. It didn't create 2.5 million "shovel-ready" jobs or keep unemployment below 8 percent. Proponents of the stimulus bill hoped that a dollar of government spending—financed in this case from higher government borrowing—would generate more than a dollar of economic activity. This so-called multiplier implies there's a free lunch to be had from more government spending, despite the fact that every dollar that the government spends is a dollar that has come from the private sector either through higher borrowing or higher taxes. Unfortunately, a growing body of research supports the common-sense idea that the government is no better at spending the public's money than the public itself.

And while the unemployment rate today is considerably lower than the recession high of 10 percent, the employment picture isn't really improving. Rather, the labor force is shrinking. In April 2014, labor force participation was only 63 percent—a thirty-five-year low. In other words, if the labor force participation rate had remained steady and many able-bodied adults had not given up looking for work, then the unemployment rate would be 9.1 percent today. And in early 2014, the CBO determined that Obamacare—even with all of its spending—will reduce work in the economy by the equivalent of another two million workers by 2017.

The bottom line is that when you tax something, you get less of it. So when we tax prosperity and success, we get less of each—and we need more of both so we can get the economy working for everyone again.

Conservatives believe the answer is to grow our economy. Rather than divvying up a pie that is shrinking, we want to pursue policies that will make it bigger—and give everyone a greater slice in the form of more opportunities and true prosperity. If that's our goal, then reforming the tax code, ending corporate cronyism and welfare, reducing our regulatory burden, reforming our broken immigration system, and fixing the Federal Reserve are good places to start.

Tax Reform

It's a good thing we don't get all the government we pay for.
—WILL ROGERS

Our tax code is in need of a major overhaul. The last time we reformed it in a significant way was in 1986, when Ronald Reagan worked with congressional Democrats to simplify the code and lower rates. Since then, we've added loopholes, exclusions, and deductions back in—many of which benefit specific industries or try to encourage, or discourage, certain behaviors. In total, Congress has made almost five thousand changes to the tax code since 2001. To put that in perspective, that's an average of more than one change every single day.

Today, our tax code contains almost four million words. It's seven times as long as *War and Peace* and more than 880 times longer than our Constitution. It's a complex web of deductions, exemptions, and exclusions that's incredibly difficult to figure out.

It takes Americans more than six billion hours each year to prepare and file their tax returns at a cost of $168 billion. That's a tremendous waste of time and money, all to meet what should be a pretty straightforward obligation.

A simplified tax code would narrow the number of rates for individuals and families from seven brackets down to two. Low- and middle-income families would pay a marginal rate of 10 percent, with a tax rate of 25 percent for anyone earning more.

These lower tax rates are made possible by broadening the tax base. Rather than fully eliminating all tax preferences, we can circumscribe some in a way that allows low- and middle-income families to benefit the same as the wealthy. Today, the disproportionate share of tax expenditures favor the wealthy. It'd be more sensible and more productive if the wealthiest Americans and corporations devoted fewer resources to accountants that help them find the right tax shelters and to lobbyists that help preserve them. Tax rates would be lower for all Americans. Any existing preferences should prioritize working families struggling to make ends meet.

I would also get rid of the alternative minimum tax, a parallel, decades-old income tax that requires millions of Americans to do their taxes twice and needlessly complicates the code. And by increasing the standard deductions, millions more families could fill out their taxes on the simple two-page IRS 1040EZ form. These reforms would ease the burden on families and businesses that are currently forced to navigate a broken code.

We must also reduce our corporate tax rate, which is currently the highest in the industrialized world. Today, businesses are subject to a 35 percent rate at the federal level, and then an average of over 4 percent at other levels of government. That puts our country at a serious disadvantage in a global economy, where businesses can pick up stakes and move their operations elsewhere.

Let me give you an example of how damaging this situation is to economic growth—and job creation. For years, I've been trying to convince a Fortune 100 company to build an operation in Kenosha County, which could eventually create as many as twelve thousand jobs in Wisconsin. It should be an easy decision; the company already owns over five hundred acres there, its leadership is unhappy with its current location, and the enterprise needs to expand. But, so far, I've had little success in making the case.

I asked the company's CEO why he wouldn't build in Wisconsin. He replied, "It's not about Wisconsin. I'm not building anywhere in the U.S. My board won't let me do it."

Instead, they're expanding in Ireland because the corporate tax rate there is 12.5 percent. That's the choice: 12.5 percent in Ireland or over 35 percent here. It's no wonder that the *Wall Street Journal* found that between 2009 and 2012, at least ten major companies have either moved or announced plans to move their operations overseas. And, of course, when they go, they often take good-paying jobs with them.

Our current tax code also discourages companies from reinvesting profits they earn in other countries back here in the United States. Most developed countries tax only a company's domestic profits, but we tax profits made at home and abroad. As it stands, if a company wants to bring its overseas profits back to America, then it will pay taxes twice—once in the foreign market where the money was earned, and again when they bring the profits home.

In Wisconsin, Harley-Davidson is a big employer and a source of state pride. When they send their motorcycles to Germany, they compete against several foreign competitors, like Honda. But while Honda pays the German tax on its sales and then brings the rest of the money it makes home, Harley pays the German tax and then, if they want to bring the rest of their money back to Wisconsin, they have to pay the American corporate tax as well. This gives competitors like Honda a huge advantage over American companies, like Harley.

A lot of companies facing this double taxation are holding their profits in offshore accounts rather than bringing them back to our shores. According to some estimates, $1.7 trillion in profits are now parked overseas because of the tax burden that companies face if they bring that money back to the United States. In other cases, businesses have chosen to simply reinvest their profits in other countries, giving them jobs and opportunities that we could be creating here.

My colleague Dave Camp, the chairman of the House Ways and

Means Committee, wants to reduce the corporate tax rate to 25 percent, a figure that would make us much more competitive internationally. He has also proposed exempting 95 percent of the profits made by the foreign subsidiaries of U.S. companies from taxation. That would encourage companies to bring their profits back to our shores and reinvest them here.

Taken together, these reforms would mean that no business or family would pay more than 25 percent of their income to the federal government. And by lowering rates and closing loopholes, tax reform can make the system fairer for all without increasing the deficit. In fact, this kind of reform would grow the economy and help shrink the deficit. In addition, Dave's most recent overhaul, which is similar to the kinds of reforms I've proposed, would create up to an estimated 1.8 million jobs, increase economic growth by $3.4 trillion, decrease the deficit by $700 billion, and put an extra $1,300 in the pockets of the average middle-class family of four each year. Dave's plan isn't perfect (whose is?), but it's a good start for the conversation we should be having about how to make our tax system fairer for everyone and more pro-growth.

Ending Cronyism and Corporate Welfare

> *When buying and selling are controlled by legislation, the first things to be bought and sold are legislators.*
>
> —P. J. O'ROURKE

As we reduce tax burdens and make America more friendly to investment, we must simultaneously make sure our government is not *too* friendly toward the big established players in our economy, and that we always allow room for new competitors to enter our markets and create pressure for innovation and improvement. We should be very clear about the difference between *pro-market* policies that benefit consumers and *pro-business* policies that benefit established interests.

While individuals in our country should be protected by a safety net that's there for them when times get bad, businesses should by no means be given the same protection. And we must staunchly resist the inclination toward corporatism and cronyism that has so often defined economic policy in Washington in recent years.

Favoring growth doesn't mean favoring those companies that are large and established. It means creating the conditions by which consumers can choose what is best for them and producers compete intensely and fairly for their business—giving everyone involved the incentive to push costs down and quality up.

Here again, conservatives should draw a stark and clear difference between ourselves and the Left. Cronyism is integral to the progressive approach to governing. Liberals want big government, big business, and big labor to work together to divide up the American economy. They prefer large, centralized, consolidated institutions, and they think these will be most capable of addressing large problems.

Conservatives think problems are better addressed from the bottom up, through a trial-and-error process of knowledge discovery and continuous improvement that is best embodied by an efficient market. That approach should also be the organizing principle of public policy, and that kind of process is possible only when competition is open and fair. It cannot coexist with cronyism for the wealthy and well connected.

Republicans should be staunchly opposed to corporate welfare in any form, and to the cozy relationships between big government and big business that undermine the dynamism of our economy.

House Republicans have made some efforts in this regard in recent years. Our budgets have sought, for instance, to end the bailouts of big banks that are only perpetuated in the Dodd-Frank financial-regulation law, to kill the green-energy slush fund and other corporate subsidies to the energy industry, and to eliminate $7 billion of corporate welfare in the Department of Commerce. There is much more to be done on this front, in terms of both tone and substance.

Americans need to know that their government is on their side—encouraging robust competition that will best serve their interests and grow their economy—rather than on the side of big, established corporate players. Capitalism and cronyism are not compatible, and it's time Republicans made it much clearer to voters that we are the party that stands for a competitive economy suitable for growth.

Regulatory Reform

> *Yet, the basic fact remains: every regulation represents a restriction of liberty, every regulation has a cost.*
>
> —MARGARET THATCHER

Regulatory reform is also essential for growth. Between 2009 and 2012, the Obama administration published a little over thirteen thousand rules and regulations. It also implemented 330 "major" rules, each with an economic impact of $100 million or more. Yes, that's a minimum total of $33 billion.

Many of these rules and regulations stifle innovation and serve as a drag on our economy. For example, one study estimates that the regulatory burden on manufacturers doubled between 2001 and 2011—from $80 billion to more than $164 billion. Another study found that in 2013 alone federal regulations cost $112 billion and created almost 158 million hours of extra paperwork.

These regulations range from the serious to the ridiculous. In Wisconsin, our dairy farmers were told that the Environmental

Protection Agency planned to subject them to a regulation designed to prevent and clean up oil spills. The regulation was written broadly enough to include milk, since technically it contains oils in the form of animal fat. To comply, a dairy farmer would have had to install expensive oil containment systems. Some estimates found the regulation would cost the industry $140 million annually. Ultimately the rule was eliminated, but the process took two years. This really was a case of federal bureaucrats crying over spilled milk.

Federal agencies are now issuing rules at an alarming rate—with very little oversight. What's worse is that citizens have very few ways of appealing agency regulations. Today, the vast majority of regulatory cases are handled not by a judicial court but by an administrative court tied to an agency. And Congress has very few ways to stop rules and regulations from becoming the law of the land. Our main tool is something called a joint resolution of disapproval, which can nullify a rule if the resolution is passed by the Senate and the House and signed into law by the president. However, by the time that process takes place, a rule may have already been deemed "final" and started doing damage to the economy. And then there's the invisible cost of the uncertainty for businesses, which are just trying to figure out what the rules will be so they can prepare, adapt, and comply.

One solution to this problem is the Regulations from the Executive in Need of Scrutiny (REINS) Act, which would give Congress greater oversight over the regulatory process and reestablish its primacy as the nation's lawmaker. Essentially the act says that if there is a federal rule that would cost the economy more than $100 million a year, then the House and Senate must look at it and approve it before that rule can go into effect. Giving Congress that power would stop harmful regulations in their tracks and help jump-start economic growth.

When it comes to regulation, we will need to take other steps, as well. To understand why, consider the energy industry. How we address regulatory policy will determine whether we realize our full energy potential or let this opportunity slip away.

While we've seen a boom in energy production on non-federal lands, the Obama years have also seen an aggressive resistance to domestic energy production, particularly on federal lands. In 2011 and 2012, there was a decline in total oil and natural gas production from the federal lands and waters under President Obama's control.

Instead of seeking novel ways to keep our nation's energy resources in the ground, federal bureaucrats should be making it easier for American companies to engage in responsible production. And they should start by improving the federal permitting process, which is a total mess.

According to one analysis, it took 307 days to get the federal permits needed to drill a new well in 2012, a process that is largely an exercise in getting past red tape. For proof the process can be streamlined, just look to the states. If you wanted to drill on state lands in North Dakota, you could have had permits in hand in ten days. In Colorado, you could have been up and running in as little as twenty-seven days.

The mining industry also faces significant delays. One annual report notes that, "permitting delays are the most significant risk to mining projects in the United States" often "resulting in a 7- to 10-year waiting period before mine development can begin."

Project developers need timely decisions, but the federal government all too often fails to deliver. Here, there is no more glaring example than the Keystone XL pipeline. Its developers first submitted their application to the State Department in September 2008—back when Barack Obama was still a U.S. senator. Nearly six years later, they're still waiting for a decision from the Obama administration.

Hydraulic fracturing is another potential target of regulatory overreach. Along with horizontal drilling, this production method has given us a new way to tap oil and natural gas from shale deposits located throughout the country. In 2012, it was largely responsible for the 14.4 percent increase in domestic oil production. The U.S. Chamber of Commerce estimates that advances in hydraulic fracturing have already created 1.7 million jobs—and will create a total of 3.5 million by 2035. Today, however, there are more than a dozen federal agencies and offices participating in a "working group" that President Obama created to "support" development, which likely means new ways to regulate or restrict it.

Going forward, we should ease the regulatory burden on the economy, and the best way to do that is to bring meaningful cost-benefit analysis back into the system, reconnect the law with the lawmakers, and restore the balance between the branches of government. True regulatory reform can restart economic growth—and produce the energy we need.

Immigration Reform

> *Immigration is not a* problem *for America. It's an* opportunity.
> *Immigration is a key to our American renewal.*
>   —LOS ANGELES ARCHBISHOP JOSÉ GOMEZ

The American Idea, and the American Dream, is deeply rooted in the fact that ours is a nation of immigrants—a nation that opens its arms to people from around the world who believe that if you work hard you can get ahead, and in the process can improve our country beyond measure.

Immigration is, of course, a contentious and complicated issue, as I learned about two decades ago. In the run-up to the 1994 election, Empower America got involved in a California ballot initiative known as Proposition 187. The measure aimed to curb the state's illegal immigration problem by further restricting access to state-funded services like education and health care, and it had been embraced by the state GOP.

One night on a flight home from a trip, Jack Kemp and I got to talking about Prop 187.

"If these guys in California don't watch it," he told me, "they're going to do great damage to our party. We need to be the party of immigration. Immigration is good for our country."

Jack and Bill Bennett both understood that immigration is a cornerstone of the American Idea, and they asked me to look into Prop 187. I agreed with their instincts, but the ballot measure promised to be a nasty fight and we needed to know more. I read up on the issue and met with a lot of experts, including Julian Simon, the Cato Institute's Steve Moore, and Grover Norquist.

What I learned in our work on Prop 187 went far beyond the ballot initiative. I began to appreciate the value of immigration in a new way—from an economic standpoint. I wrote a policy memo for Kemp and Bennett that concluded Prop 187 was the wrong way to go. The measure neglected to recognize that our immigration system was failing Americans and immigrants alike, and exacerbating the problem of illegal immigration. It sought to treat a symptom of the broken system, rather than advance reforms needed to address the root of the problem.

In mid-October, Jack and Bill issued a statement in opposition to Prop 187. They said it was "unconstitutional." They called it "anti-conservative," noting the "Big Brother approach" required for its enforcement. They argued that it would become "a mandate for ethnic discrimination" and that the measure would turn generations of voters—immigrant and nonimmigrant alike—away from the GOP. Instead, they advocated for commonsense reforms to ensure security along our border and enforcement of our laws, as well as to streamline the legal immigration process and reform the "bloated bureaucracy."

It was a bold stand that put Jack and Bill crosswise with much of the party, including California governor Pete Wilson, who had made the initiative a key component of his reelection campaign. One of the measure's supporters said Jack and Bill had "been sucked in by the Democratic Party line" and speculated, "[Bill] Clinton must have written their press release." Their position even earned a rebuke from the *National Review*; the magazine ran a cover story headlined "Why Kemp and Bennett Are Wrong on Immigration."

We made the announcement while Jack was traveling in California. He spent the week in appearances and interviews defending his position. I had stayed behind at our offices to work, but I saw video footage from the trip. It wasn't pretty.

When Jack came back, he walked over to my desk. "What did you get me into?" he asked in mock outrage.

"Hey, I only did what you asked me to," I replied.

"I know, I know," he said, waving me off. "It's absolutely the right thing to do."

Despite Empower America's best efforts, Prop 187 passed that November. Jack and Bill had been a little surprised by the backlash, but for the record, they were on the right side of that issue. Prop 187 ultimately died a slow death in the courts, but not before doing a lot of harm.

These days, whenever the national conversation turns to immigration, my family's roots, the teachings of my faith, and the lessons I learned during my Empower America days are at the forefront of my mind. There's no question our immigration system is broken. The evidence is overwhelming. There are around 12 million people in the United States without legal status. And we have a system of perverse incentives that encourages people to break the law and punishes those who follow it. If you play by the rules and try to come here legally, you will find yourself smothered by endless paperwork, exorbitant attorney's fees, and unconscionable waits. Our backlog for processing immigrant visas is so vast that it could take up to 60 years before you're approved for some visas. As of November 2012, more than 4.3 million people were waiting in line to get a family-sponsored green card.

A lot of people talk about the way this system harms the immigrants who try to come here. And it's true that the current system fails them in many ways. But if you ask me, it's our country that is losing out. All of America will benefit from thoughtful immigration reform—and that's why I support it.

Immigrants want to come to the United States because they share our commitment to the American Idea. They share our values, believe in our country's potential, and cherish our ideals. They want to make a better life for their families. And they have always been an important part of our story and our success—culturally and economically.

In the wake of the deepest recession since the Great Depression, we could greatly benefit from the energy and ingenuity that immigrants can bring to our economy. In 2011, one-fourth of our nation's new businesses were started by immigrants. Small businesses owned by immigrants employ 4.7 million people. And the founders of 40 percent of all Fortune 500 companies are first- or second-generation immigrants. Their successes include AT&T, Kraft, Google, Yahoo!, and eBay.

Immigration can also help us avert the collision that's coming between our demographics and our economy. Soon there will be fewer people to grow the economy. Today, the U.S. birth rate is 1.9 children for every woman. That's below the "replacement level" of 2.1, the rate needed to keep the population level steady. That means we will have fewer Americans working as the Baby Boomers are retiring and relying upon current workers to fund their entitlement benefits.

Fortunately, while the U.S. birth rate has dropped, the desire among people to immigrate to America has grown. The demand for legal immigration is there, and we need to make sure our system is wired for it.

Real reform would make the immigration system accountable, efficient, and effective. First, we must secure the border and enforce the laws we have on the books. As it stands, we don't know who's coming and going in this country. That leaves us vulnerable, and failing to address this security situation would be irresponsible.

To enhance security, we should also set up an effective visa-tracking program. Today, an estimated 40 percent of the undocumented immigrants in our country came in on a visa and then stayed after it expired. We need a system that can effectively track visitors entering and exiting the country. And we need an "e-verify" system that gives employers the ability to instantly confirm an individual's immigration status electronically.

To secure the border, we also need to set up a guest worker program that allows immigrants to take jobs that are not being filled by Americans. Such a program will help take pressure off the border, as these immigrants will enter legally with guest-worker permits. This will help the border patrol better focus their efforts on preventing illegal crossings, particularly by criminals seeking to smuggle drugs into our country or to do us harm. Furthermore, people who can contribute to our economy shouldn't have to jump the fence; they should be able to come through the front door. If an employer can't find American workers to fill open jobs, they should be able to hire immigrants on a temporary or seasonal basis.

Once an independent third party has verified that specific border security and enforcement conditions have been achieved, then we need to give those who are here illegally a chance to get right with the law. We have to deal with the world as it is, not as it should be. The simple fact is there are around 12 million undocumented immigrants currently living in the United States and we need to address that reality in a commonsense way.

We can't allow amnesty; that is unfair, corrodes the rule of law, and just creates a magnet for more illegal immigration. Nor are mass deportations a realistic solution. We need to find a way to honor the immigrant who came here lawfully and did everything right, while giving those who are here undocumented a chance to get right with the law.

The process should take the form of probation, or deferred adjudication, similar to how our legal system currently deals with some who have broken the law. Undocumented immigrants who come forward should be given an opportunity to gain a probationary legal status with specified conditions, which would include admitting to unlawful entry, paying a fine, paying back taxes, submitting to a criminal background check, learning English and civics, and staying off of any form of public assistance.

If an independent party verifies that the border and interior security reforms have been accomplished, and if the terms of probation have been satisfied, then probationary immigrants may leave probation and receive nonimmigrant work visas. After another period of time, an immigrant who wants to get a green card would go back to the end of the line and apply—just like everybody else. That means legal status must be earned. They won't be rewarded for breaking the law and they won't cut in line ahead of those who have played by the rules. This solution is fair, realistic, responsible, and enforceable.

These proposed reforms also include a specific provision aimed at helping undocumented immigrants who were brought here as children. For them, the United States is the only home they have ever known, and today, many are pursuing advanced degrees or serving in our military. These are extraordinary circumstances and should be treated as such by giving them an accelerated path to getting right with the law and earning citizenship.

The government should also provide enough visas to meet the need for highly skilled workers. If a student comes to America to receive an education in science, technology, engineering, or math, and then wants to stay, we should welcome them. Today, we are educating the world's best and brightest—and then sending them away to create jobs in China, India, or for other global competitors. American companies have long been concerned about a shortage of qualified workers for high-skilled jobs. We should help them meet the need by making it easier for them to hire foreign workers who have been trained at American universities.

We can fix our broken immigration system without creating a moral hazard that could create similar problems in the future. But how we make these reforms is important, too. All too often in Washington, we've enacted massive laws that no one has read from beginning to end and that no one truly understands. That's not the way our democracy should work. Step-by-step, commonsense reform of our immigration system will deliver the solutions we need and do it in a way that gives the public confidence and certainty for the long term. Reforms will improve our security and help jump-start our economy. They will also strengthen and renew the American Idea as we welcome immigrants who value the freedom and opportunity our country offers and want to help preserve it for generations to come.

Sound Monetary Policy

> *Since becoming a central banker, I have learned to mumble with great incoherence. If I seem unduly clear to you, you must have misunderstood what I said.*
>
> —FEDERAL RESERVE CHAIRMAN ALAN GREENSPAN, 1987

In 1913, Congress created the Federal Reserve System, our nation's central bank. The move was a response to a cycle of financial panics, the most serious of which occurred in 1907. A network of twelve regional reserve banks, its original mission was to ensure price stability and protect the value of our currency by controlling the supply of money. The system was set up so that it was cordoned off from politics and ideologies.

Over the years, Congress has expanded the Fed's mission, bringing it further into the sphere of political and legislative activity. In the 1970s, the Fed was tasked with a new mission: promoting "maximum employment." Ever since then, it has had a dual mandate, and in attempting to fulfill both duties, it has adopted risky and costly monetary policies. In recent years, the Fed has held interest rates too low for too long and pursued quantitative easing, creating money by purchasing large amounts of treasury debt and other securities.

As a result, the Fed has injected uncertainty into the economy. While this has hurt businesses, it is the senior citizen saver living on a fixed income who has been hit the hardest by these near-zero interest rate policies. Eventually, the Fed will have to withdraw the money it used to finance the purchase of all those assets, and there is great anxiety in the marketplace about its exit strategy. Move too slowly, and the value of our currency will fall and inflation will rise. Move too quickly, and the Fed will rattle investors, causing markets to drop and the economy to suffer.

This situation is all the more worrisome when one considers the global picture. Today, everything the Fed does has an impact on international markets—and international markets have a great impact on us. For years, the conditions have been building for a "currency flu" much like the one we saw in the Asian markets in 1997 and 1998. The Fed is carrying $4 trillion on its balance sheet and has just started what promises to be a difficult exit from unprecedented easing. That's going to cause consternation around the world, and it could lead to economic disruption here at home.

All these are good reasons to reform the Fed's mission to ensure our money is sound and reliable in its value. The dollar is the world's reserve currency, and we should act accordingly. Our position is a privilege and it is invaluable for our country.

In pursuing reform, a bill introduced by my friend and colleague, Congressman Kevin Brady, is a good place to start. The Sound Dollar Act does away with the dual mandate and restructures the Federal Reserve so that its sole focus is on price stability and maintaining a sound currency. We need to transition toward a rules-based monetary system anchored in certainty and predictability.

Kevin's proposal puts fiscal debates back where they belong—in the halls of Congress—and it allows the Fed to focus on sound monetary policy. Those reforms will buttress confidence in our currency, make the Fed's exit strategy more credible, and lay the foundation for a stronger economy.

A Twenty-First-Century National Defense Strategy and Foreign Policy

As far as I'm concerned, that's math—not strategy.
—SECRETARY OF DEFENSE BOB GATES

For many of the domestic problems discussed here, the last six years have been a missed opportunity. We lost ground when we could have been getting ahead. But even now, I don't see these problems as insurmountable, as long as we act soon and implement meaningful reforms.

What keeps me up at night is the real and lasting damage that is being done to our national defense and foreign policy. For years, many of us have been warning that without strong leadership backed up by a powerful military, the world will be a more chaotic place. As I write, events are, unfortunately, proving our case.

In Syria, President Obama established a "red line," warning that the use of chemical weapons would have serious consequences.

Then he stood by and proposed—in the words of his own secretary of state—an "unbelievably small" response as Bashar al-Assad launched rockets armed with chemical gas into Damascus, killing nearly fifteen hundred of his own people. More than four hundred of them were children. As I write, the administration has taken no meaningful steps to stop Assad, all while he has strengthened his grip on power.

North Korea has engaged in escalating acts of aggression, threatening to attack South Korea "mercilessly without notice," while perpetrating heinous crimes against its own people, including prison camps and forced starvation. Israel, our closest ally in the Middle East, questions our commitment to a vital partnership. As I write, Vladimir Putin has sent tanks and soldiers into Ukraine, violating its sovereignty. We are in the midst of a Middle Eastern arms race, and China thinks we're retreating and is seeking to deny us the ability to defend our friends and allies in Asia.

In part, this dangerous turmoil is a response to a lack of American leadership. Instead of taking the lead in world affairs, the Obama administration has often chosen to "lead from behind." The proof can be found in the president's fecklessness on the world stage—and in his budgets.

While spending on entitlements has exploded, our defense budget has deteriorated. And President Obama wants to further shrink spending for our military and defense. In 2011, when I attended his speech at George Washington University, the president announced that he was planning to find $400 billion in new defense cuts—a decision his own secretary of defense had been informed of only the day before. That's a reckless approach to defense spending. Our military budget must be driven by our defense strategy.

In the spring of 2014, the Obama administration doubled down and announced further plans to reduce defense spending. Its proposal would cut funding for essential equipment. Under the president's budget, the Army and Navy would shrink to pre–WWII levels and the Air Force would be reduced to its smallest size ever. But if the greater instability around the world is any indication, an even smaller capability could not match the threats to our national security.

We aren't making these choices as a matter of strategy. They are the result of misplaced priorities and economic necessity. Out-of-control spending coupled with a failure to make tough budgetary choices has put our fiscal policy and our foreign policy on a collision course. If we fail to put our budget on a sustainable path, then we are choosing decline as a world power.

* * *

Somehow, amid all of the spending increases of the Obama presidency, the only area the president seems intent on deeply cutting is our federal government's first and unique responsibility: national security.

One item in the president's most recent budget is a good illustration of the problems we face—and the president's misguided approach. The A-10 Warthog is an airplane sometimes described as a "flying cannon." The plane is designed to fly low and slow over the battlefield, providing close air support for our troops on the ground. It's also used for search-and-rescue missions when soldiers end up trapped behind enemy lines.

Other aircraft in our fleet are too fast, too fragile, or too loaded down with equipment to do what the Warthog can, so in the heat of battle it's an indispensable tool. The Warthog's unique features include its redundant systems and its ability to absorb a lot of damage and keep on flying, which is why it's so good at providing close air support. The aircraft has made a tremendous difference for our troops involved in ground operations in Iraq and Afghanistan. And with a cost of $11.8 million per plane (in 1997 dollars) and $17,564 per hour in the air, it is relatively cheap for a military aircraft.

For a few years, a plan has been in the works to replace the A-10 with the F-35 joint strike fighter. Leaving aside the debate over the differences between those planes, the simple fact is that full delivery of the F-35 has been pushed back until 2020, six years away as I write this. Despite the fact that there is no clear replacement ready, the Obama administration wants to get rid of the Warthog today—and that's because the administration is cutting indiscriminately, trying to make our defense budget fit predetermined numbers instead of a sound military strategy. While I think the approach is wrong, it's a symptom of what happens when failed budgetary policy meets misplaced priorities.

The Defense Department budget is also facing growing challenges of its own, as higher personnel costs crowd out all other defense priorities. Providing generous compensation and benefits for the troops is a solemn duty of Congress. But irresponsible politicians have made promises they can't keep, and now compensation costs are crowding out funding for training, equipment, and force structure. It is essential that we provide the resources that our troops need to accomplish their missions and to come back safely to their loved ones. But instead of confronting these problems in a strategic way, the current administration is cutting haphazardly. More to the point, they are capping and cutting compensation costs, not to shore up our military capabilities, but to funnel more money into domestic spending. They do not have a coherent, well-developed military strategy or foreign policy to guide them.

The great tragedy of this approach is how it affects our men and women in the field. When we put together our House budgets, I think of my friend who is a physician in the Army Special Forces. He has put his life on the line for our freedom more than once, earning a purple heart during multiple tours in Iraq and Afghanistan. I think about one of my childhood friends who was, until recently, a senior commander with the 101st Airborne Division and will soon be working at the Pentagon. His responsibilities are enormous, and his duty is to get the job done and bring his men and women home. I think of my parish priest, who is a chaplain in the reserves. Having served two tours in Afghanistan, the stories he has shared and the suffering he has attended to are profound. I think of my fraternity brother and former roommate who, as a Navy SEAL, has given heroic service to our nation. And I think of my chief of staff, Andy Speth, who decided to enlist not long after 9/11 and was called up for two tours in the Iraq War.

When I consider our military programs, I think about those guys and all of the men and women who are in harm's way. One of them wrote to me recently from Afghanistan about the Warthog. That morning, he had eaten breakfast in Bagram with a command sergeant major, a Delta Force operator, and a Special Forces battalion commander. All three agreed that "teams will suffer" if we retire the Warthog without delivering comparable equipment to replace it. One of his friends told him, "Three times, I thought we were all going to die, until the A-10s showed up." He explained, "Without the A-10 every soldier at the table this morning might not have been there."

As the administration puts the screws to the Pentagon in order to fit an arbitrary number in its budget, these are the lives that are being affected by those bean-counter decisions. To do right by the men and women who have sworn to protect our freedom, we need a clean break from the budget policies and feckless foreign policy of the last six years.

When it comes to reforms in this area, the overriding principle is what's simple: Providing for the national defense is the first and primary responsibility of our federal government. Our policies and budgets must serve that goal.

With that in mind, we can make our military smarter by adopting a defense budgetary policy that is strategic. First, we need to right-size the Department of Defense's civilian workforce. Today, about 800,000 civilians work for the DoD, joined by another 700,000 contractors. That means there's just about one civilian DoD employee or contractor for every active-duty soldier, sailor, airman, and marine. To scale back this workforce to a level that better suits our current needs, we should hire one worker for every three retirees with priority for new hires given to positions that are critical to national security. That policy would allow us to trim bureaucracy, and preserve funding for training and equipment for our war fighters, like the Warthog.

America must never be reduced to just one of many voices in the crowd. If we don't fulfill our role in the world, then the vacuum we leave behind will be filled by leaders who do not share our values. That will only create more violence and instability. America must be out front, protecting our interests, our allies, and our values. To do that, we need a defense strategy and foreign policy capable of leading the world in the twenty-first century—and we need the financial resources to back it up.

* * *

The reforms I've laid out here are guided by the overarching goal of making government simpler, smaller, and smarter. Such an approach can deliver more growth, more jobs, and greater opportunities. And it reflects the conservative vision of a twenty-first-century government in perfect keeping with our Constitution, the Declaration of Independence, and with the proper relationship between the citizen and the state.

Just as we seek to limit government, we are also asking our fellow citizens to take on new responsibilities. We each need to be good consumers and hold providers accountable for the cost and quality of the care they deliver. We each need to work hard and share our talents with the rest of society. The free market isn't just about competition; it's also about collaboration in the pursuit of great goals. The agenda I've outlined will foster the conditions for us to do that.

In this vision, the Republican Party has a duty, too. We have to convince the American people that our approach is the best path forward, and I believe it can be done. In my congressional races in southern Wisconsin, I have run *on* what I believe in, not *from* it. I have done my best to make my case with clarity and vigor. And the public has responded, voted, and offered their support.

That's the path the Republican Party must pursue now. We need to articulate our vision clearly and persuasively, and then let the country choose. If we lose an election that way, then, well, at least we gave it our all. But I don't think that will happen. I'm confident we'll win.

CHAPTER 7

A Virtuous, Not Vicious, Cycle

As I was sitting in a meeting about the 2015 budget, my policy director, Jonathan Burks, slid his iPad over to me. On the screen was a press release.

> My colleague Congressman Ryan's comments about "inner city" poverty are a thinly veiled racial attack and cannot be tolerated. Let's be clear, when Mr. Ryan says "inner city," when he says, "culture," these are simply code words for what he really means: "black."

My eyes were wide as I pushed the iPad back toward Jonathan.

The statement had been released a few minutes earlier by Barbara Lee, a colleague of mine in the House. I was surprised. I know Barbara. We both serve on the House Budget Committee. We've traveled together to the Middle East as part of a congressional delegation.

I sat in the meeting, mulling over the statement.

Good Lord! Does Barbara really think I'm a racist?

That day, I'd gotten up early to get a workout in, like any other morning. As I was wrapping up, I realized it was time for an interview that I had agreed to do on Bill Bennett's radio show.

I'd recently given a speech about the poverty crisis in our country. Bill asked me about the role that culture plays, about the importance of young boys learning the value of work by seeing men in their lives go to their jobs every day.

"You lost your dad at an early age," Bill noted. "Who taught you how to work?"

I explained that my mom had provided me with a strong example, and my dad's buddies had stepped in and served as mentors for me.

"But, I mean, a boy has to see a man working, doesn't he?" Bill asked.

"Absolutely," I said. "That's the tailspin or spiral that we're looking at in our communities.... We have got this tailspin of culture in our inner cities, in particular, of men not working and just generations of men not even thinking about working or learning the value and the culture of work, so there's a cultural problem that has to be dealt with. Everyone has got to get involved. So this is what we talk about when we talk about civil society—if you're driving from the suburbs to the sports arena downtown by these blighted neighborhoods, you can't just say: I'm paying my taxes and government is going to fix that. You need to get involved. You need to get involved yourself—whether through a good mentor program or some religious charity, whatever it is to make a difference. And that's how we help resuscitate our culture."

I hung up and got ready for the day, which was filled with back-to-back meetings. Up until the moment Jonathan passed me his iPad, I hadn't given that interview a second thought.

As I walked out of the meeting, I was still a bit stunned. When I returned to my office, I put a call in to Barbara. I explained that my comments had nothing to do with race. I was trying to describe some of the root causes of poverty, which run across racial lines. Barbara replied that she didn't think I was a racist, and she had actually toned the statement down.

Still, I was hurt and confused. In the days that followed, I was accused of trying to use racially coded language as a "dog whistle" to appeal to white voters. An inside-the-Beltway publication printed a story titled, "Is Paul Ryan Racist?" In the weeks that followed, several columnists and TV show hosts debated the question at length.

At the end of the day, I went back to my office and read a transcript of the interview. When I looked it over on paper, I could see how what I'd said could be misinterpreted. What disappointed me most was that it was possible to read my statement and come away thinking that I was saying the poor are lazy. I meant the opposite. What I was trying to say is that our government and our society have been careless and complacent in how we engage and help people living in low-income communities.

Multigenerational poverty is a growing crisis for our country—and a lot of what we're doing is making it worse. Instead of inviting people back into the workforce and society, we're walling them off in a massive quarantine. Our policies aren't creating opportunity or giving people the ability to climb the ladder into the middle class. Too often, they are creating barriers to work. In the process, we're isolating the poor and depriving them of the skills and resources they need to get their lives back on track.

Poverty is a complicated issue. It touches on sensitive subjects like race and culture. It taps into deep differences in political philosophy. And, as a white guy from Janesville, Wisconsin, who was born in the 1970s after the peak of the civil rights movement, I admit that I may not be the perfect spokesman.

If there's a way to talk about this issue that won't invite some level of criticism, I haven't found it yet. Sometimes my language will be clumsy or inarticulate. When it is, I'll take the heat for it, own it, and learn from it, because I believe this issue is critically important. Just consider what's at stake: the lives of millions of Americans living in poverty, and the chance for upward mobility, which has historically been a defining strength of our democracy. What I will not do is shy away from this conversation for fear of criticism.

The good news is that I'm not alone in my concern, or in thinking that culture is a contributing factor. Consider, for example, the following statement made in 2008:

> That's why if we're serious about reclaiming that dream, we have to do more in our own lives, our own families, and our own communities. That starts with providing the guidance our children need, turning off the TV, and putting away the video games; attending those parent-teacher conferences, helping our children with their homework, and setting a good example. It starts with teaching our daughters to never allow images on television to tell them what they are worth; and teaching our sons to treat women with respect, and to realize that responsibility does not end at conception; that what makes them men is not the ability to have a child but the courage to raise one. It starts by being good neighbors and good citizens who are willing to volunteer in our communities and to help our synagogues and churches and community centers feed the hungry and care for the elderly. We all have to do our part to lift up this country. That's where change begins.

That was candidate Barack Obama speaking to the NAACP's ninety-ninth annual convention, but his message is relevant to every American. And he has continued to echo these themes as president, speaking often about the importance of a culture that promotes family, responsibility, and work.

While I think the president's policies miss the mark, on this point he is right on target. And his comments lead me to believe that if we can move beyond the name-calling and recriminations, we can find common ground and work together to overcome poverty and restore upward mobility.

How can we start? By going out and talking with the people who are working to get out of poverty and the grassroots leaders who are helping them. Just by listening and observing, we can learn a lot.

* * *

Upon joining the GOP ticket in 2012, I made only two requests. I wanted to go to Boston and meet the people who were working to help Mitt and me, and I wanted to visit poor communities and the people working and living there.

I got to Boston within a week. Engaging on the poverty front took a bit longer, but by late October, the campaign found a way to accommodate the request and scheduled a visit to Cleveland, Ohio. In planning the event, we worked with my friend Bob Woodson, a seventy-six-year-old black civil rights leader who founded the Center for Neighborhood Enterprise. The center seeks to empower neighborhood organizations so they can transform their communities and help low-income people change their circumstances.

In places where despair is everywhere, Bob can find hope and good news. In Cleveland, he was eager to show us that even in a bad economy, which had hit this community particularly hard, there was cause to celebrate. He put together a list of about twenty faith-based and community leaders that he thought I should meet with and submitted it to the campaign's vetters, who were responsible for making sure everyone in attendance was cleared by the Secret Service. Not long after, a campaign staffer called Bob, very worked up because five of the people he'd recommended had criminal records.

"I'm shocked," Bob replied. "I thought *all* of them had criminal records!"

The campaign wasn't sure what to do. They were worried about the possible security risk. After some hand-wringing, the decision was made to e-mail and ask me what I thought.

"You should invite them to attend," I wrote back. "If Bob trusts them, then so do I."

A few days later, I arrived at the Waetjen Auditorium at Cleveland State University and met with the group that Bob had helped assemble. One man, Paul Grodell, shared his story of growing up in a suburb in Ohio. His parents divorced when he was twelve, and in high school he smoked marijuana, drank alcohol, and took steroids. Soon he had moved on to methamphetamine and painkillers. Then he started doing heroin.

When he turned thirty, Paul and his wife had their first child, a son. He told me, "I remember looking in his crib right after I'd got done shooting a bag of dope. I just remember looking in the crib and seeing this little baby and thinking, what kind of a father am I going to be?"

Paul checked himself into rehab. When he got out thirty days later, he learned that the doctor who had supplied his painkiller addiction had been arrested. Paul had also been indicted and was facing seven felony charges. He pled guilty to a misdemeanor and got six months' probation.

In the years that followed, Paul continued to struggle. He was able to stay sober for long periods of time, but he had a lot of rage. He told me he broke things and hurt people, emotionally and physically. Then, in 1994, a buddy invited him to church. That invitation helped Paul find his faith and his calling. In 2001 he became a children's pastor, and in 2010 he started an inner city church, Beyond the Walls. Today his ministry helps people whose lives started out a lot like his.

At the end of our gathering, Paul walked over and asked me if he could lay his hands on me to pray.

"I'm Catholic," I said, "but I'm cool with that."

Paul's head was shaved and he had tattoos up and down his arms. He'd arrived at the event on the back of a motorcycle, and he had just gotten done explaining that he'd once had a violent streak. As he approached me, I could see the Secret Service agents out of the corner of my eye; they were exchanging nervous glances.

Paul put his hands on my shoulders. He asked God to give me the strength to fulfill my mission and be a vessel for His work. When I opened my eyes, they had welled up with tears. Even the Secret Service guys seemed touched.

The moment was a testament to the power of redemption. Here was a guy who had a rough start and made some mistakes, but he got his life together and was making other people's lives better. It was a reminder that God never counts anyone out, and neither should we. Everyone has something to contribute if we can help them find their way.

After Mitt and I lost the election, I kept thinking about that day in Cleveland. I called up Bob Woodson and asked him if he could help me schedule more meetings with people in different cities. That request eventually brought me to Outcry in the Barrio, a faith-based Christian drug rehab program and outreach ministry that serves the San Antonio community. Outcry is the life's work of Freddie Garcia, a man who was once an addict. When he was twelve years old, Freddie started smoking marijuana and taking pills. By the time he turned twenty-two, he was hanging around with a gang and had graduated to heroin. Freddie tried everything to quit drugs—state-run rehab programs, group therapy, even Mexican American faith healers. Finally, his mom reached her limit and sent him to visit family living in Los Angeles.

Eager to kick heroin, Freddie tried to quit cold turkey on his trip to LA, but it didn't take. When he got there, he picked up right where he had left off. One day he was on the corner of Third and Broadway in downtown LA when he bumped into a guy he used to shoot up drugs with back home. The guy looked really put together;

he was clean-shaven and well-dressed. Freddie's first thought was, *He must be selling drugs now.*

"Hey, man," Freddie asked, "you got anything for me?"

"Yeah, I do," the man replied. "Meet me back here in a few minutes."

When they reconnected, the man handed Freddie a card with an address. "I've got Jesus," he said. "He changed my life. I haven't shot heroin in a year."

Freddie rolled his eyes. He didn't want religion. He wanted drugs. But the guy kept pointing at the card.

"This place will help you," he said. "They'll give you a place to stay while you're detoxing. They'll make sure you have three meals a day and good medical care."

Freddie made his way over to the facility on the card, and they gave him a bed. When he was sick, he liked to be alone—and when he started coming off heroin, he was sicker than he'd ever been before. The first day, a man from the facility came up to him and asked, "Freddie, do you need anything?"

"Nah, man," Freddie grumbled. "I'm sick. Just leave me alone."

At dinner, the man came back and brought him food. Freddie was feeling much worse by then. On top of the physical pain caused by the drugs leaving his system, he was edgy and impatient. He got up out of bed and pushed the guy out the door.

"I said I'm sick, and I want you to leave me alone."

Freddie got back in bed and fell asleep. When he woke up, the guy was back at his side. This time, he was praying for him. Freddie never did drugs again.

Freddie managed to stay clean and graduate from the Latin American Bible Institute in La Puente, California. But he still had friends back in San Antonio who were homeless and hooked on drugs. So Freddie and his wife, Ninfa, decided to go back to Texas and start up a program that could help addicts and the homeless there.

At first, they didn't have much to offer except basic shelter and their prayers. The Garcia family home was twenty feet long by twelve feet wide. It was a tiny space with very little privacy, but Freddie and Ninfa opened their doors to addicts, inviting them to stay and helping them get clean.

What began in their home eventually became Outcry in the Barrio. Freddie Garcia passed away in October 2009, but Outcry has helped transform the lives of tens of thousands of men who have been able to leave behind lives of drug addiction, crime, and poverty and reconnect with their family and community.

Today, Freddie's son, Pastor Jubal Garcia, is carrying on his father's work. In January 2014, I spent an evening with Jubal, meeting the people working and receiving treatment at Outcry in the Barrio. During my visit, I saw the full range of the program's stages—from intake to outcome. It was nothing short of miraculous.

At one point, Jubal walked me around the sleeping quarters, filled with row upon row of bunks. There I met Tony, who had just arrived that morning.

A Hispanic man with a calm demeanor and a quiet voice, Tony had tattoos all along his hands and arms. At one point, he showed me the ink that ran up and down the insides of his forearms. He got those tattoos, he explained, to hide the needle tracks.

Tony had been shooting tar heroin for thirty-three years. He lived on the streets, and to get money for drugs he would hustle, panhandle, pick up and recycle cans, and shoplift. He hadn't been clean since he started using—not even for a day.

This was Tony's fourth visit to Outcry. I asked him why he kept coming back.

"I believe in God," he said, "and I believe that he keeps bringing me back, trying to tell me that it's time to change. Either that, or I am going to die in the street."

If you've ever loved someone who has been addicted to drugs or alcohol, then it's easy to empathize with Tony's struggle. He's fifty-two years old—just three years younger than my dad was when he passed away. When Tony talked about his addiction as a matter of life or death, it really hit home for me.

People come to and wear addiction differently. Some end up living homeless on the city streets. For others, the struggle is less obvious; it may play out in the turmoil of a broken family life. The toll it takes can be measured in dollars spent fueling the addiction, in moments missed with loved ones, and in lost opportunities. Hitting rock bottom can mean losing a job, going to jail, getting divorced, or even overdosing and death.

And addiction is just one path people take to poverty. Some arrive there through an economic emergency like the death of a spouse or the loss of a job. Others never got the solid start they needed as children; they were sent to a failing school that didn't give them the skills they now need as adults, or they were deprived of family members and mentors who could serve as powerful examples of personal responsibility and hard work.

But whether it's in the barrio of San Antonio or along quiet rural roads—and whatever path one takes—every experience with poverty has one thing in common: It not only deprives that person of their potential and their dignity, it also deprives their family and community of their talents and gifts.

* * *

Today, more than 46 million people are living below the poverty line in our country. That's nearly one in six Americans, and the highest poverty rate in a generation. Forty-seven million of our citizens are living on food stamps. That's nearly one-sixth of the entire country.

Not long ago, many of these Americans were in the middle class. Today, they are experiencing the struggles of a family trying to make it on $23,021 or less a year. Most are between eighteen and sixty-four, the time of life when they should be working and saving, or getting ready to retire. Instead, they are falling behind. Even more troubling is the recent finding that 70 percent of children born into families in the bottom 40 percent won't make it into the middle class, meaning that in many cases these statistics signal a continuous struggle that spans generations.

The divide between the haves and have-nots is growing—not just economically, but also geographically. When I was a kid in Janesville, blue-collar and white-collar workers lived side by side. Today, as in so many communities, a lot of the wealthier citizens have moved to the tonier parts of town—or they've moved out altogether, migrating to zip codes where they are surrounded by people whose salaries and opportunities look more like their own.

There's a lot to say about the problems created by our tendency to migrate to a community of people who resemble us socioeconomically, but chief among them is the class stratification it's creating in our neighborhoods. Today, our poorest communities are poorer, and not just in terms of take-home pay. In these zip codes, children don't have access to quality schools and good jobs when they grow up. Few of them are living in two-parent families or communities with strong social networks. All of these factors mean that there are fewer opportunities to get ahead because these are the indicators of economic opportunity and social mobility.

This disparity is not a "black problem" or a "Hispanic problem" or a "white problem." It cuts across racial lines and it knows no geographical boundaries. It's true that poverty is a real problem in our inner cities. As of 2010, more than 36 percent of the people in Detroit, Michigan, were living in poverty. One of Wisconsin's major metropolitan areas, Milwaukee, was the fourth poorest city in the country with a poverty rate of 27 percent. In Racine, Wisconsin, 40 percent of children live in poverty. But it's a problem in rural areas, as well. In places like Gadsden, Alabama, and the Brownsville-Harlingen area of Texas, the poverty rate is more than 20 percent.

Statistics like these mean we're becoming more of a class-based society—and those classes increasingly seem less like permeable boundaries that can be easily transcended. We are now living in a society where people are isolated from each other economically and culturally and geographically. I believe overcoming that isolation must be our focus. If ever there was a reason for engaging in such a battle, this is it.

We need to find ways to bridge this divide and renew the spirit of hard work, family, and responsibility. A society can't be strong for long if it doesn't have a good culture underneath it—no matter how many tax credits we initiate.

In our struggle to renew the culture, we need to think about how we reinvigorate our founding values in a way that brings people together—and doesn't give insult to any person or group. Instead of pitting people against each other, we need to invite everyone in. We need to move from a state of isolation to one of participation, reintegrating our fellow citizens who live in places that haven't experienced all of the blessings of the American Idea.

Government has a role to play here. We know that in a country as blessed as ours a safety net for those facing poverty is essential. We also know that the surest way out of poverty is a job, and a big part of the problem has certainly been the lack of economic opportunity. Historically, every 1 percent increase in the unemployment rate has translated into an increase in the poverty rate of between 0.4 and 0.7 percent. So we can start to expand participation by returning to our constitutional roots, removing the yoke of the administrative state, and getting our economy growing again. In America, if any man or woman wants to work, there should be a good-paying job waiting for them.

But our poverty crisis runs much deeper, and the solution will take more than greater economic opportunities, or even federal programs or policies. It will require a new respect for American civil society.

*   *   *

Both the Left and the Right tend to split the world into two halves: the individual and the government. In different ways, they make a similar omission. They forget a key part of life—the community and all of the relationships, institutions, and connections that exist there.

Each of us understands the importance of community from our own experience. For me, the most vivid illustration occurred after my dad died, when people reached out to my mom and me. And my mom, who had always been an active volunteer, became even more involved in our community after my dad's death. She was a member of the school board, the local parish, and the garden club. She joined the bridge club, even though they never actually played bridge. Through all her joining and volunteering, she made lifelong friends. Some of them were widows who understood her loss and the new life she was trying to create. Over the years, she repaid the kindness they showed her many times over. When someone in Janesville lost her husband, my mom was the first to show up and offer a shoulder and a sympathetic ear. Together, those women took their losses and created something new. They formed a community of support.

That spirit of connection and compassion is alive and well in Janesville today. Several years ago, the Fourth Ward, where my dad came from, was overrun with drug dealers. They did deals in the light of day—even on one elderly woman's front porch. She wouldn't look out her front blinds because she was afraid she'd be shot. So a man named Burdette Erickson gathered his neighbors in his basement one night. They made a pact with one another: Either the drug dealers go—or we go. Then they formed a group to improve the neighborhood, and soon they took back the Fourth Ward. Today, young families are moving in, and the drug dealers are moving out.

In recent years, our town has rallied around neighbors facing economic adversity. A lot of guys I grew up with worked at the GM plant in Janesville, and they lost their jobs when it closed. Like so many communities in our country trying to recover from the Great Recession, our town pulled together. Our churches and charities and friends and neighbors were there for one another.

In textbooks, they call this civil society. It's that vast middle ground between the government and the individual where our families, our neighborhoods, our businesses, our groups and associations, and our places of worship reside. It's the space where we live our lives—and it's been a prominent characteristic of our culture from the very beginning.

When Alexis de Tocqueville visited the United States in 1831 to survey American life, he came away deeply impressed by all the voluntary groups and associations he found everywhere he went. In his report, which we know as *Democracy in America*, de Tocqueville wrote:

> Americans of all ages, all stations in life, and all types of dispositions are forever forming associations. There are not only commercial and industrial associations in which all take part, but others of a thousand different types—religious, moral, serious, futile, very general and very limited, immediately large and very minute. Americans combine to give fetes, found seminaries, build churches, distribute books, and send missionaries to the antipodes. Hospitals, prisons, and schools take shape that way.

De Tocqueville observed that where in other places you would find the government advancing causes and addressing concerns, in

America our people come together to promote and improve our society. That tendency to volunteer and collaborate has been one of our enduring strengths.

The formal and informal connections that make up our civil society have historically been a source of our nation's prosperity and strength. But over a decade ago, Robert Putnam, a social scientist, looked at these associations and found some disturbing trends.

Putnam studied the various ways that Americans engage civically—ranging from involvement in religious bodies and public affairs to their recreational interactions at bars and bowling leagues. These activities, Putnam argued, create what is known as "social capital."

After reviewing a lot of data, Putnam reached the conclusion that both civic engagement and social capital have been declining in America since the late 1960s. To the extent that we join organizations or associations anymore, we don't really actively participate. We're less likely to invite people into our homes or even eat dinner together as a family. And Putnam found that while people are more likely to bowl, they are less likely to do so as part of a league. We are, metaphorically, a nation of people bowling alone, which became the title of Putnam's groundbreaking work.

The decline in civic engagement is problematic for a lot of reasons. Perhaps the most worrisome is that high social capital tends to translate into lower crime rates, better schools, economic prosperity, and a stronger democracy.

There have been a lot of theories about why social capital is on the decline, and clearly it's a problem with many causes. Technological advances have changed the means of our social interactions. Powerful economic forces have imposed large-scale disruptions, as I'm reminded every time I drive past the empty GM plant near my house.

Nearly two hundred years ago, de Tocqueville identified another source. He wrote, "The more government takes the place of associations, the more will individuals lose the idea of forming associations and need the government to come to their help. That is a vicious cycle of cause and effect.... The morals and intelligence of a democratic people would be in as much danger as its commerce and industry if ever a government wholly usurped the place of private associations."

Today, the encroachment of government facilitated by liberal progressive policies weakens our bonds with one another other and drains our communities of their vitality. The progressives wanted a national community, where government stood supreme, solving our problems and tending to our needs. All of that government tends to crowd out the good work that only people freely associating and gathering in their community can do. Some of this is an unintended consequence of well-intentioned liberal progressive policies, but some of it is an inevitable and foreseeable result.

Take, for example, the impact that Obamacare is having on religiously affiliated, nonprofit groups. Today, there are some 629 Catholic hospitals in the United States, which care for over 88 million patients annually. Thousands of Catholic charities serve over 10 million people a year. In 2010, they provided food services to over 7 million people and helped almost 2.5 million people with their housing and other basic needs. And that doesn't include the immeasurable work that goes on through other Catholic groups or the more than 18,000 Catholic parishes in the United States.

Through their work, these religious people and groups help alleviate poverty and homelessness. They help the sick and the addicted get quality health care. They do this because serving their neighbors is part of how they live out their faith.

The Obamacare mandate that employers facilitate access to contraception and abortion-inducing drugs puts this good work at risk. The mandate conflicts with core Catholic teachings, forcing

Catholic groups who seek to live by these teachings to pay heavy government fines. As this mandate is implemented and those fines are imposed on Catholic organizations, we could see a significant reduction of the services provided by these groups, with many possibly forced to shut down.

Consider the Little Sisters of the Poor, an order of Catholic nuns that runs numerous nursing homes where they care for the elderly poor as part of their ministry. The Little Sisters have objected to the Obamacare requirement that they provide health insurance that covers birth control and abortion-inducing drugs to their employees, because doing so violates their Catholic beliefs.

The Obama administration's idea of a solution was to have the Little Sisters sign a form noting their objection in order to avoid the mandate. In effect, however, doing so would also violate the Little Sisters' beliefs since they would be directing a third party to provide the coverage, making them complicit in an activity that violates the teachings of their faith.

We need policies that value the Little Sisters' contributions and respect their religious beliefs, regardless of how adamant the Big Sisters of NARAL might be that they conform to its secular dogma. Otherwise, we could all lose out on the good work that they do. And "we" in this case means the poorest of the poor losing the merciful care of the Sisters—all to satisfy the stern ideological demands of Obamacare.

In 2012, the Democrats kicked off their national convention with a video that proclaimed, "Government is the only thing we all belong to." It's one of those happy-sounding liberal sayings that doesn't hold up well once you start to think about it. Do citizens really "belong" to the government? Does being the "only thing" we are all associated with give the government some kind of preemptive claim on us, regardless of what other associations we might voluntarily choose? Something about that distinctly Obama-era motto carries a false note. It was the ideological soft sell, pitching togetherness but expecting obedience.

In reality, of course, there are many other associations to which we might belong—and which, in important respects, we might consider more important than the latest social program dreamed up in Washington. And whether it's a church, a prayer group, a charity, or some philanthropic enterprise—any kind of altruistic endeavor, from the works of mercy that Doctors Without Borders performs abroad to the compassionate services that homeless shelters and humane societies provide here at home—they all have some virtues in common. They are unselfish and outward looking. They are voluntary, not mandatory, and inspired instead of compelled. Who needs mandates to serve those in need when you start with genuine compassion? Who needs coercion when you have conviction?

Academics call these various groups "mediating institutions." Really, they're just people working together, and the more work we do together—of our own free will—the stronger we become. When government tries to do too much—when it replaces cooperation with coercion—it weakens our country. It pulls us apart. It erodes civil society.

Nothing undermines the essential and honorable work of our associations quite like government overreach. The Obamacare HHS mandate is characteristic of a mindset that isn't just a threat to religious charities; it's a threat to all who turn to them in times of need. In the name of strengthening our safety net, this mandate and others will weaken it.

We need to challenge such thinking because it's destroying some of our most powerful antidotes to homelessness, addiction, poverty, and inequality of opportunity. The solution to these challenges often involves government, but in a supporting role. The people—in a robust and free civil society—should have the lead.

Robert Putnam noted that "American history carefully examined is a story of ups and downs in civic engagement, *not just downs*—a story of collapse *and* of renewal." Putnam doesn't believe that just because civic engagement is waning it will forever be receding. He thinks we can rebuild civil society and get the engines of social capital going again. Based on what I've seen during my visits to facilities that are trying to help low-income people rejoin society, I think he's right.

Traveling with Bob Woodson, I've visited a homeless shelter for alcoholics in Denver, a ministry in the barrio of San Antonio, and a residence that offers housing and counseling to people trying to get back on their feet in Washington, D.C. I witnessed 150 men—some just coming out of prison—attend a boot camp in Indianapolis, where they are learning the habits and skills they need to be good dads and husbands. I visited a mentoring program consisting of former gang members in Milwaukee that is helping young kids avoid the costly mistakes they made in life. In all of these communities, there are the foundations of a thriving civil society. I believe that these poverty-solution champions have much to teach us about how to rebuild civil society.

Anacostia is just six miles from the U.S. Capitol. A predominantly African American neighborhood, the median household income there is $34,370, and 45.6 percent of its residents live below the poverty line. In the middle of the community sit the Graceview Apartments, which provide low-income housing for individuals who are transitioning back into society.

The Graceview Apartments are part of House of Help City of Hope, a faith-based substance abuse and homelessness program that is part of Bishop Shirley Holloway's ministry. Her motto is, "We don't see the problem. We see the person." Since the ministry started in 1995, they've served over forty thousand people struggling with drug abuse, homelessness, and poverty.

The secret, of course, is the people. I've met with Bishop Holloway and the people who serve in—and who are served by—her ministry on a couple of different occasions. This fall, I met a young man and young woman who had been married just ten days earlier. They walked me through their journey. Both had lost their parents and soon after lost their way. The young woman hung with the wrong crowd and had been stabbed and shot. The man had turned to alcohol to dull his personal pain. Both were homeless when they came to Bishop Holloway. Now they were married and starting new lives. The man was back in college. He had just finished his midterms and was getting all A's.

The woman said to me, "Bishop has shown me how to be a mother and a wife, how to take care of my kids.... Bishop took me as a daughter. Everything my mother didn't do, she opened her heart up and did it for me."

That's a sentiment you hear a lot in places like the Graceview Apartments. When people talk about what a program has meant to them, they often use the language of family. That's how Bishop Holloway sees everyone who comes to House of Help City of Hope, too. She often refers to the people getting help through her ministry as her daughters and sons. It's a mindset that's a far cry from the notion that "government is the only thing we all belong to."

Bishop Holloway once said to me, "I don't believe in treating the homeless like the homeless, because when we take you into our program, you are no longer homeless. You are part of our family. And we expect you to change immediately."

That change begins the moment that someone walks in the door. They get a document that outlines what is expected of them: Take weekly drug tests. Participate in City of Hope church services. Put together a budget and stick to it. During intake, someone from the program sits down with the person coming in and goes through that document line by line, reading it aloud. The message is clear: There is love here, but there are also expectations and accountability.

Bishop Holloway explains that real compassion comes with

responsibility. "Sometimes we think love is give me some food, give me some money," she said to me, "but real love says, 'Let me show you how to survive, let me show you how to make it, let me show you how to be happy, let me show you how to do this.'"

Bishop Holloway doesn't just aim to get people off the streets and off drugs. She is interested in an individual's unfulfilled potential, and she wants to give them the skills and experiences they need to tap into that. She sets the bar high. And for thousands of people and their families, that's made all the difference.

In Denver, Colorado, I met Bob Coté, who ran a program for the addicted and homeless called Step 13. Raised in Detroit, Bob had been a boxer, but when he moved to Denver, he fell deeper into his addiction with alcohol. He was living on the streets when his wife gave him an ultimatum, "Stop drinking, or it's over."

Bob took a hard look at his life and thought, *You're killing yourself on the installment plan.* He decided to quit drinking, and once he got sober, he created Step 13, a program to help alcoholics and drug addicts get healthy and stay off the streets.

Today, one hundred men live at the Step 13 facility. They are part of a tough-love program that requires them to stay clean, work, pay their own rent, and cook their own meals. The program helps them stay sober, which allows each man to rejoin society, be a productive part of his community and his family, and hold down a job. The results are far more impressive than the comparable federal program, which has become known as "Bunks for Drunks." It costs millions of taxpayer dollars, allows the program's participants to drink on-site, and produces poor results.

The key differences are accountability and hard work. Bob Coté passed away not long after our visit, and I'll never forget something he said: "The core of Step 13 is work. Work works. Any system or program that takes responsibility from a capable person dehumanizes that person."

Before we make government policy, we should look at all the good that is being accomplished by civil society. Our job isn't to replace the Shirley Holloways or Bob Cotés; it's to help them. The federal government has a role to play, but it's a supporting role, not the commanding one. Its job is to give people the resources—and the space—to thrive.

Two principles of Catholic social teaching—subsidiarity and solidarity—can help show the way here. Subsidiarity is an idea that's echoed in our federalist system. It holds that problems should be handled at the lowest level at which it's possible to achieve a successful resolution. It's the belief that those closest to an issue know it best. If possible, government shouldn't assume tasks that can be better handled by families or communities or other civil society institutions—and responsibility for action should be left to the closest level of community or organization possible. If and when that doesn't work, an issue can then be addressed at a broader level. In practice, subsidiarity counsels that the federal government support the work of anti-poverty groups and not co-opt that work or crowd it out.

The principle of solidarity goes hand in hand with subsidiarity. It holds that we have a responsibility to stand together with our brothers and sisters—and there are social and moral goods that can only be gained only through the broader society.

Now, *solidarity* is a word that has been widely used over the years and taken on a range of connotations. What I mean here is simply that we have duties to our neighbors, duties that can be fulfilled from the local all the way up to the national, depending on the circumstances. When goals can be achieved at the local level, that should be preferred, since those closest to the problem can best address the need. However, some challenges cannot be fully resolved by a state, a locality, or citizens working together in civil society. In those cases, we have a responsibility to act together through the federal government and bring national resources to bear in order to achieve the common good. This is a premise that starts from the bottom up versus a top-down, big government approach.

The challenges of homelessness, poverty, and upward mobility demand collaboration between our citizens and our government. When local, state, and federal government as well as civil society all work together, in light of the principles of both solidarity and subsidiarity, we can best meet these challenges. Our task now is to reform our federal programs so that they shore up the work under way in our communities and provide an on-ramp to opportunity.

*   *   *

Today, we are too often isolated from each other, and that isolation cuts both ways. Many communities aren't enjoying the kind of prosperity, safety, and opportunity that should be possible in America— and other communities have lost their connection with what life is like in a neighborhood like Anacostia. As a result, a lot of our ideas about how to reverse the troubling trends in our most impoverished communities are guided more by ideology than what's actually effective on the ground. And sometimes, when imposed from on high, the best of intentions can turn into really miserable results.

For example, when President Lyndon Johnson created the Great Society, he said, "I believe that thirty years from now Americans will look back upon these 1960s as the time of the great American Breakthrough... the victory of prosperity over poverty."

We can now look back from a distance of fifty years. Are we close to winning the war? Over the years, the federal government has spent trillions of dollars and added dozens of programs in an effort to build upon Johnson's initiative. Today, there are at least ninety-two federal programs that claim to help the poor. We spent $799 billion on them in 2012 alone. And yet, the official poverty rate is the highest it has been in twenty-one years.

All of this shouldn't be completely unexpected, considering the problems that riddle our welfare system. One of the biggest issues is that the system is a product of our isolation. Think about the businesses you shop at or the private-sector services that you use. If they're successful, they're customer oriented. Good businesses don't simply ask the sales force how to improve; they talk to the people who are buying what they are selling.

Yet, too often, when it comes to our antipoverty programs, we forget to ask the poor what they want and need. We can do much better if we talk with them about what it's like to live in poverty and what it actually takes to get out. I've been doing that and I've found that there are a lot of commonsense reforms that we can—and should—make right away.

For starters, there is little to no coordination among our federal antipoverty programs, so it can be hard to figure out exactly what you qualify for. The whole system is inefficient, and for a lot of these programs we don't have any concrete evidence that they work.

What's worse is that this web of programs further isolates the poor. As in places like Outcry in the Barrio and Step 13, the best cure is connection with the broader community. Yet instead of reintegrating the poor into society, our policies wall them off.

Poverty—especially on the scale we're seeing today—obviously erodes the American Idea. Social mobility has always been at the heart of the American creed, but our current policies put hard barriers in place, making it difficult to climb the ladder into the middle class. Our welfare policies are means-tested, so families become ineligible for them as they earn more. In practice, that means the poor are subject to very high marginal tax rates—in some cases, as high as 95 percent. In a tragic example of unintended consequences, our policies are actually discouraging people from going back to work and getting ahead.

Then there's the cultural crisis underlying the economic one. Pastor Jubal Garcia explained to me that the toughest problem he confronts in helping the people in his program is not addiction or homelessness, but what he calls "character development." Others have identified something similar, explaining it in terms of virtues or beliefs. My friend Bob Woodson sums it up best, observing that "the moral characteristics inculcated in low-income citizens by grassroots leaders are precisely the characteristics that the Founding Fathers insisted would be essential for the preservation of a free republic. What may be a mere civics lesson for wealthier Americans is in fact the difference between life and death for those struggling to put their lives back together and to become responsible, self-governing citizens."

*   *   *

When Pope Francis was selected to lead the Catholic Church, he had a message for all of us. In a move befitting a twenty-first-century Pope, he tweeted, "The measure of the greatness of a society is found in the way it treats those most in need, those who have nothing apart from their poverty." Pope Francis has focused global attention on issues of poverty in a way that no other world leader has, and he has challenged all of us to stand with the poor and the vulnerable.

He has reminded us that our efforts to help the poor must involve tangible assistance to those in need, and that the government has a role to play. At the same time, real reform must go beyond this, working to engage the call to personal action at the heart of the Pope's message. I did a little research and was moved by something else the Pope had said back in 2010, when he was a less-known cardinal ministering to the people of Buenos Aires. In an interview he was asked about his work with the unemployed. He replied:

> What happens is that the unemployed, in their hours of solitude, feel miserable because they are not "earning their living." That's why it is very important that governments of all countries, through the relevant ministries and departments, cultivate a culture of work, not of charity. It's true

that in moments of crisis one must have recourse to aid.... But after that, they have to cultivate sources of work because, and I never tire of repeating this, work confers dignity.

Truly helping those in need means recapturing a sense of the dignity of work. The trouble is our current welfare system isn't sufficiently designed to encourage work and the dignity it confers. It allows people to survive, but doesn't give them the skills they need to compete and succeed. Reforming our welfare system along those lines starts with streamlining it so that it's efficient, effective, and easier to navigate.

Americans who are stuck in the cycle of poverty or who have fallen on tough times need a welfare system that can provide them with the tools and skills they need to escape the cycle and live their lives. That's why we should empower states to try a different approach to creating upward mobility for the poor. The federal government would grant states the flexibility to collapse several means-tested programs into one overall payment that would be paired with personal case management to directly benefit the recipient. Rather than running around to a series of different offices to qualify for and collect benefits, individuals will get a dedicated case manager or counselor who will help them put together a plan for getting back on their feet with measurable goals, including ultimately graduating from the program and into self-sufficiency.

Every recipient, except the disabled and the elderly, must be employed or looking for work. The counselor will help the client budget their money and find a job, and they will provide a measure of responsibility and accountability. If a client doesn't show up for class or look for a job, then the counselor will be allowed to dock their assistance—just like a boss would in the workplace. Similarly, if the client exceeds expectations, the case manager may also have the ability to provide achievement bonuses.

These counselors will be paid and evaluated on their results, meaning how successful they have been at helping people rise out of poverty. They will work quickly to find a plan for their clients, because welfare benefits are temporary, except for the disabled and the elderly. They have a time limit, which ensures that public assistance doesn't become a permanent way of life.

This approach is reminiscent of the pioneering work led most prominently by Catholic Charities USA. Together with six local Catholic Charities agencies, they have launched a series of pilot anti-poverty programs that give each client a caseworker who customizes a strategy for success to the individual's talents and needs. They also incorporate evidence-based research into their approach so that they are delivering benefits and services in a way that's proven to work. And they are doing all of this work by applying the principle of subsidiarity—that local needs are best addressed, if possible, by the people in the community who understand them.

Some of this great work is occurring right in Wisconsin, and on a visit to the Christo Rey Parish in Racine, I got a chance to see the effort up close. I met with caseworkers and clients. People told me about how the individual assistance they got from their caseworker made the difference for them, helping them move out of poverty and provide for their family.

I met a young woman whose parents had abandoned her when she was in high school. When she came to Catholic Charities USA, she was homeless and didn't have the support of a loving family to help her navigate all the responsibilities that are part of the transition to adulthood. The program at Catholic Charities provided her with a caseworker, and together they created a budget and developed a "life plan" to get her through school. Today, she's taking college courses and is newly engaged. She and her fiancé just bought a house, and she's on her way toward a better life.

The challenge now is to take what is working locally in Racine and use it as inspiration for reforming the way we deliver welfare benefits around our country. The reforms I am proposing accomplish that goal by introducing the concepts of accountability, tailored casework services, and local control. The system will be defined not by what the government can provide, but by what each individual can achieve.

We should also change the way the Earned Income Tax Credit (EITC) works. Today, it's delivered in one big check at the end of the year. The idea is to reward work, and it does. But we can deliver that message clearly and consistently if we move from an annual credit to a monthly system, so that people can see the value of their work in every paycheck they earn.

We also need to reform welfare so that it supports the family instead of eroding it. We know that on average, children who grow up in two-parent homes perform better by virtually every measure. They do better in school. They're less likely to get involved in criminal activity or do drugs. And in single-parent households, it's not just children who pay the price. Single moms have a hard job and, often, little support—and the most recent census revealed that they are nearly twice as likely to live in poverty as single dads. So it makes no sense that our federal policies dole out penalties for those who choose to make a commitment to one another and enter a loving marital relationship. Right now, our welfare programs give a couple with a child more support if they do not marry than if they do. Under Obamacare, some couples have a better chance to qualify for a federal health-care subsidy if they stay single or get divorced. We can promote marriage—and reduce poverty—by removing the penalties for getting married and taking care of our kids.

The point of reforms like these is not to suggest that government has no role in combating poverty, or that some ideal of pure volunteerism can replace the need for concrete assistance to the Americans in greatest need. The idea, rather, is to get government pulling in the same direction as the grassroots groups that our citizens run—and the way to do that is to infuse the welfare system with the same incentives, priorities, structure, and accountability that are at work in our communities. It is to make government part of the solution by using it to do what it does well rather than what it does poorly—by using it to create the space for solutions to be attempted and evaluated, for failing approaches to be left behind, and for successes to be learned from, applied, and improved upon. That is not how our government generally fights poverty today, and the results show us that we desperately need a change in direction.

*   *   *

Reforming our welfare programs is a good start, but alone it won't be enough. One of the best and earliest opportunities to get out of poverty occurs in the classroom. It is the key to upward mobility and opportunity, and so it is at the very heart of the American Dream. Economic mobility—the core promise of American life—is impossible without high-quality education, and the American Idea is in turn impossible without a firm commitment to upward mobility out of poverty, into the middle class, and beyond it.

And of course, education is not just about upward mobility; it's vital to economic growth and prosperity. No amount of tax and regulatory reform will help our economy remain strong in the future if we don't make sure that our children are getting the education and training they need to fill the jobs of tomorrow and to lead the world in scientific and technological innovation. As American workers increasingly compete with workers abroad in nearly every part of our economy, and as more and more jobs require technical competency and at least as much brains as brawn, making a great education available to every American becomes increasingly essential.

On that much, surely almost all Americans agree. And we can also agree that right now our education system has some serious problems. Internationally, the United States ranks fifth when it comes to education spending, allocating $115,000 per student. But all that spending isn't translating into better outcomes. In 2012, we ranked seventeenth out of thirty-four countries in math, with scores well below average. We placed twenty-first in science and seventeenth in reading. To put this in perspective, our mean score was just below the Slovak Republic, which spends only $53,000 to educate each child.

These figures are troubling, because they are signs that our kids are failing to reach their potential and keep pace with their global counterparts. That's reason enough to rethink our approach to education.

But even more disconcerting is this finding: In the United States, we come in below average when it comes to the number of "resilient students" in our schools. We have fewer economically disadvantaged students whose academic performance exceeds what the experts would predict based on their socioeconomic class. In plain English, that means that education is failing to give our kids an escape route out of poverty.

Too many children, and especially African American and Hispanic children, are sent into mediocre schools. African American and Hispanic children make up only 38 percent of the nation's overall students, but they are 69 percent of the students in schools identified as the lowest-performing. In the United States, one in five students won't graduate from high school. In our major cities, half of our kids don't get a high school diploma.

No one can deny the scope and importance of the problem. But again, when it comes to solutions, Republicans and Democrats diverge along familiar lines. Democrats seek to protect established, incumbent institutions from essential reforms and want to address problems by just dumping more money into the very systems that are failing. Republicans believe that this problem, like so many others, would best be solved from the bottom up by enabling new institutions to compete with existing ones and empowering the consumers of education—the parents of K–12 students, the families of college students, and those students themselves—to choose among real options. Competition improves quality and lowers cost. It does so by making providers answerable to the needs, preferences, and assessments of consumers. This would improve our education system as it improves every other system.

In K–12 education, that means allowing parents whose children attend failing schools to have the option of sending those children elsewhere, and having the money the government spends to educate those children follow them there. This seemingly simple idea—school choice—was first implemented in Wisconsin, and has shown impressive results there and elsewhere. It's no panacea, of course. But for families stuck sending children to schools that aren't offering them a shot at the American Dream, it can make all the difference.

Elementary and secondary education is, of course, largely the purview of state and local governments, and it should remain that way. But the federal government can help facilitate rather than frustrate the development of school-choice programs—for instance, by making it easier for federal dollars to follow students and by incentivizing states to give parents real options. And Washington can also help give parents more power by making more information about school quality and educational options available. To measure performance, schools should get report cards—and they should be graded on an easy-to-understand A to F scale.

We also need to start empowering educators to do what they know works. There are a lot of good teachers out there who work long hours for little pay and very few accolades. They stay up late grading papers, purchase supplies for the classroom with their own money, and volunteer their time to give kids extra help after school. It's time we started honoring their commitment and reaping the full benefit of their knowledge and experience. One way to do that is to give these teachers more control.

Along these lines, a program worth considering (again, especially at the state and local level) is the one started by Mitch Daniels when he was the governor of Indiana. Mitch required that teacher contracts be based on performance, not seniority. In turn, he gave the teachers more flexibility to tailor their lesson plans to the needs of the kids in their classroom. Reforms like that infuse our schools with meaningful accountability, much-needed flexibility, and greater local control.

And what about the adults who were simply passed on from one grade to the next even though they weren't learning? What about the grown-ups who never got a basic education because no one ever noticed—or cared—that they didn't know basic math or struggled to read? What about the people who have already dropped out or who finished school in a broken system and for whom these reforms will come too late? We can still help them get the skills they need to compete in our twenty-first-century economy and escape a life of poverty.

As I write, 3.6 million jobs remain unfilled because employers can't find workers with the skills they need. The SKILLS Act proposed by House Republicans would prepare job seekers for these positions.

The Act would take the $18 billion we spend annually on job training and put it to better use. It makes our job-training programs easier to navigate by streamlining thirty-five existing federal programs and creating a flexible Workforce Investment Fund. Some of these funds would be set aside for the specific task of helping people who have unique challenges in finding employment, including at-risk youth.

The SKILLS Act would also give states more power to tailor job-training programs to their local workforce needs, and it would make it easier for job seekers to take advantage of this training immediately so they can enter the workforce that much more quickly. It would also give employers the chance to set up training programs themselves, which assures workers actually get the skills they need to land a good job. And for those who were failed by the public school system, the SKILLS Act would help them acquire basic math and reading proficiency.

In higher education, meanwhile, the federal government has played a much more active role, and the result, not surprisingly, has been a disaster. In the last several decades, middle-class families, and those who hope to give their kids a chance to enter the middle class, have faced enormous increases in the cost of college, as tuitions have been rising at about twice the rate of inflation. Washington has responded to this explosion of growth by turning America's young people into debtors to their government—essentially nationalizing the college-loan market while, in some cases, allowing families to borrow without limit up to the full cost of tuition.

This has, of course, only further inflated tuition costs, as colleges know that students can borrow whatever schools charge, and so the cycle repeats and intensifies. What's more, because of its subsidies and control over the student-loan market, the federal Department of Education also acts as a huge barrier to entry into the higher-education market. To be eligible to admit students who use federal aid to pay for their schooling, institutions must be accredited. This makes sense, but the government's domination of the accreditation process (by insisting that institutions of higher education look and work a certain way) effectively prevents alternative forms of higher education from arising.

Here again, the key problem is public policy that stands in the way of incremental, bottom-up improvement. And the solution is to better enable a working market to form. This needs to involve a combination of student-loan reform (PLUS loans, which allow parents and graduate students to borrow unlimited amounts up to the cost of tuition, are particularly counterproductive) and accreditation reform to enable students and parents to choose from a far greater range of options and to exercise powerful consumer pressure to drive costs downward while improving the quality of American higher education. Senators Marco Rubio and Mike Lee, among others, have proposed some useful ideas along exactly these lines, which would make a huge difference for millions of American families hoping to give their children a chance to prosper.

* * *

Today, we're trapped in a vicious cycle. Too many people are stuck in the poverty trap. Our communities are isolated from one another economically and culturally. We're seeing stagnation and unemployment, little opportunity for upward mobility and low labor force participation rates. And one of our key assets for turning things around—the associations and institutions that make up our civil society—is being eroded by government overreach rather than reinforced.

The good news is that with the right agenda, we can transform that vicious cycle into a virtuous one. It starts with limiting government so we encourage a vibrant society rather than displace it. We also need to reform our welfare and education systems with an eye not toward ideology, but toward the lives and needs of the people these programs are supposed to serve.

Americans are a generous people. We care about our neighbors when they are in need. But it's time to start measuring our compassion not by how much we're spending, but by our results. We should renew the fight with a focus on giving the poor the skills and opportunity to finally break the cycle of poverty. My goal is to turn our welfare programs into a bridge instead of a trap, restoring the prospect of upward mobility. Doing so is not just the smart thing economically; it is the right course for a good-hearted country.

CHAPTER 8

The Comeback

On a cold February night in 1981, our family wrapped up dinner and my dad turned on the TV. He was excited to see President Reagan deliver his first speech before Congress since being elected to the presidency. It's one of my first political memories. I was only eleven years old, but I can still remember my father leaning forward in his chair, listening in a way that told me to save any questions for later.

Across the country, there was a sense of worry and anxiety. Interest rates were over 20 percent and climbing. The national debt was closing in on $1 trillion. Families were struggling; their paychecks kept shrinking even as the amount they paid in personal taxes kept rising. Nearly eight million Americans were unemployed and poverty was spreading.

Ronald Reagan laid out these problems, but he was not defeated or deterred. Instead, he proposed a plan to get America back on track, and when it received a standing ovation, he joked, "I should have arranged to quit right there." But he continued, smiling, and he said:

> Together we can embark on this road, not to make things easy, but to make things better. Our social, political, and cultural, as well as our economic institutions, can no

longer absorb the repeated shocks that have been dealt them over the past decades. Can we do the job? The answer is yes. But we must begin now. We're in control here. There's nothing wrong with America that together we can't fix.

And for the first time in a long time, millions of Americans believed that again.

* * *

Today, the vision that we're seeking isn't all that different from the one my parents wished for in Reagan's day. The specific challenges we face may be unique, but by applying the same timeless principles that Reagan applied to the problems of his day, we can arrive at the kinds of conservative solutions described in the previous chapters, and we can pursue them with confidence in America's prospects.

In fact, when I think about that vision, what comes to mind is the Janesville of my youth. A place where a growing economy offered opportunity and prosperity, where every life had meaning and every person had a chance to pursue happiness as they chose—whether that meant starting a business in the corner of their garage or starting a family and creating a better future for their kids.

The Janesville I remember had busy streets where commerce flowed freely, and those streets were lined with businesses and other enterprises where people gathered and collaborated, each contributing their talents and ideas. Some built the GM trucks that rolled off the line or manufactured the parts that went into those vehicles. Others followed their passion into teaching or creating. Some cooked for the crowds who came in for the lunch rush or swept the factory floor at the end of the day. Whatever their pursuit, all in their own way were helping their corner of our country, and all went home at night with the sense of dignity that comes from a hard day's work.

All of that work brought prosperity—not just money, but also wealth in the form of the things we find most meaningful. The paychecks earned covered mortgages and piano lessons and college tuitions. The neighborhoods fostered friendships among the many people who devoted their time and energy to our community in big and small ways. Some prayed together on Saturdays and Sundays, and lived their faith in good works they did every day of the week. Others volunteered for the PTA or the local Salvation Army. Still others gave of themselves in quieter ways, babysitting a neighbor's child when they had to work the night shift or bringing dinner by when they sensed time was short or money was tight.

If you passed by Janesville today, you might not think much of it at first glance. You might even wonder why this place embodies the American Idea for me.

Driving along Highway 14, you'd pass the old McArthur farm. You'd see Ryan, Inc., the company that my great-grandfather built and where I used to mow the lawn. Soon, you'd pass Schneider Funeral Home, where I washed hearses every morning for a year, then Craig High School and eventually St. John's, where my family goes to church and my kids go to school. If you stopped at the Buckhorn Supper Club for what is, in my humble opinion, the best meal on the planet and had the prime rib, you might get a chance to talk with some people that live here. They might be third- or fourth-generation Janesville. They'd show you pictures of their kids and grandkids. They'd get you up to speed on everything that's happening here.

They'd probably tell you about the shuttered GM plant and how we've seen our fair share of adversity. But they'd also tell you about how we're rebuilding. We're not letting our challenges get us down, because we have something special in Janesville. It's a comfort that comes with belonging to a community, of being part of something that is bigger than yourself.

That spirit of community makes Janesville a place that is second to none when it comes to raising a family. It's why generation upon generation has stayed in our town—and why so many people who leave for the big cities of New York and LA eventually move back. It's why people come from around the country and the world for a job and stay and plant roots here. The absolute warmth and hospitality, the sense of community, and the we-are-in-it-together spirit are what make our town great. It's why so many people call it home. And we aren't leaving. Instead, we are rebuilding the American Idea one job, one family, one block at a time.

As in Reagan's day, our community is a work in progress. Our vision for what it can become is a destination that we are constantly striving to reach. Over the last several years, fewer opportunities and hard fiscal realities have made the journey harder. The struggle has been compounded by the fact that rather than leading us toward our vision of revival and improvement, Washington, D.C., has been pulling us further away.

One of most harmful habits people in our nation's capital can fall into is the tendency to speak and think as if Washington is the center of Americans' lives, hopes, and dreams. You hear that sentiment a lot in executive agencies and federal reports and during debates on the floor of the U.S. Senate and the House of Representatives. But our nation's capital is not the center of our lives. It's not where all of the dreaming and working and innovating and risk taking happens—and it's not where the great renewal of the American Idea will begin.

In many communities, the great American turnaround is starting. That's where the real change is happening. That's where hope actually lives.

You can see it in Janesville. You can see it even in places like Detroit, where failed leadership and bad policies have left devastation in their wake. If you know where to look, it's clear that the hard work of restoring the American Idea is already under way. And often it's our people who are doing the heavy lifting, not our government or our politicians.

* * *

After Detroit declared bankruptcy in late 2013, its new emergency manager got right down to work, trying to save the city from ruin by getting a handle on its liabilities and balancing the books. It will take months before that task is complete—and possibly years before we know if it was a success. That's when the real work will start.

Once the emergency manager hands power back over to Detroit's elected officials, they will begin to take on the full range of responsibilities of governing again. Their duties will include delivering basic services like picking up the trash and keeping the streetlights on. They will have to take back entire blocks by rehabilitating or demolishing vacant buildings, and put enough cops on the beat to make neighborhoods safe again. They will have to convince people to move back into Detroit so they can expand the tax base, and enforce policy changes that break the cycle of borrowing and spending.

Those are just a few of their tasks, and when one considers how many things went wrong in that once-great city, it's tempting to doubt whether Detroit can ever come back. But there are signs of hope.

Philanthropists, entrepreneurs, and concerned citizens aren't waiting around. They've been out there working and volunteering, getting their city up and running again.

A network of local and national charitable foundations has donated hundreds of millions of dollars to worthy and promising ventures, including public-safety initiatives, groups that give parents information about educational options for their kids, and efforts that try to get private-sector job growth going again.

The New Economy Initiative, funded by $70 million from ten

charitable foundations, has helped bring 423 new businesses to the region. Those businesses alone have generated $22 million in annual revenue and created 6,898 new jobs. And when the city was confronted with the prospect of either selling its art collection or making drastic cuts in pensioners' benefits, local and national foundations stepped up again and pledged $365 million to the city's pension fund.

Little by little, shoots of opportunity are springing up through the rubble and cement. The M@dison Block is now an incubator for technology companies; there are twenty-four start-ups on-site. Twitter opened an office there, and Google has named it one of seven North American hubs for its "Google for Entrepreneurs" program.

Rock Ventures, an entity that owns several companies including Quicken Loans, has placed a big bet on Detroit. Quicken Loans moved its headquarters downtown; in total, Rock Ventures has over twelve thousand employees located there.

Organizations are starting to see Detroit as a good destination for conferences and meetings. The Detroit Metro Convention and Visitors Bureau has twelve major conventions scheduled for 2014 and eleven booked for the following year. Already the area's hotels have booked up 236,000 room nights in 2014, almost doubling the number of nights booked the year before.

In several neighborhoods, residents have opted against fleeing to the suburbs or other cities, deciding instead to stay and fight for their community. They have formed neighborhood watches and partnered with police to stop vandals and criminals from defacing property. In some neighborhoods, volunteers have adopted vacant homes, cutting the grass so it doesn't get too high and patching up roofs before the weather causes entire buildings to cave in. Their hard work is keeping property values from slipping even further and ensuring their areas will be ready if and when people start moving back in.

In places where maintenance and rehabilitation isn't possible because blight has set in, the people of Detroit are attacking the problem with new energy and innovative thinking. There are about seventy-eight thousand abandoned buildings in Detroit, and the city pays between $8,500 and $10,000 to demolish a single home. It simply doesn't have the money to topple all these vacant buildings, which attract criminal activity, drive down real-estate prices, and pose a grave fire risk.

Where the government has failed, the community is stepping up. The Save Detroit Project has approached this problem with twenty-first-century ingenuity. Using the power of the Internet, the organization is engaged in a crowd-funding campaign to raise $250,000 in sixty days so it can demolish fifty houses. The Detroit Blight Authority, a nonprofit, public-private partnership, is also on the front lines. The effort is led by Bill Pulte, whose grandfather created a national real estate development business on the east side of town. While Bill's grandfather used his expertise to build homes, Bill is using his knowledge to tear down dilapidated ones so Detroit can start again.

After reading about a girl in Detroit who was afraid to walk through blighted neighborhoods on her way to school, Bill decided to figure out how to reverse engineer home construction so that demolition could be faster and cheaper. Today, he has partnered with several public and private entities to apply what he learned, including the mayor's office, the Michigan State Housing Development Authority, Michigan Caterpillar, DTE Energy, and a number of charities.

To truly appreciate the Blight Authority's work, it helps to compare their results to the city's own track record. In 2010, Detroit's mayor launched a program that promised to tear down ten thousand structures. By 2013, the city had spent $72 million and demolished about half of the vacant buildings. In contrast, in a little over a year, the Blight Authority has demolished 218 lots over ten blocks and has plans in the works to clear thirty-five more blocks and at least 117 more blighted buildings. It is doing its work for less than $5,000 a building, about half of what the city government pays.

Then there is the work that's going on at places like the Cornerstone School. Rather than wait for city officials to fix a public school system that's failing their kids, parents and teachers and community leaders are building new schools that can educate them. This year, Cornerstone will graduate another class of highly capable young people ready to fulfill their potential.

A lot has been said about Detroit's failures, but we should take some time to appreciate the good things that are happening there, too. Countless individual acts are turning around that city and bringing hope back again. Their efforts are proof that Detroit is more than a cautionary tale of what happens when poor leadership avoids the tough choices, choosing only to tax, spend, and borrow. It is also a reminder that the big challenges of our moment are small matters compared to the spirit and resolve of our citizens. And that gives me hope for the future of Detroit—and for the future of the American Idea.

* * *

What I have found since 2012 is that the good things under way in Detroit aren't an anomaly; they're happening throughout our country. Losing a national election isn't an experience I would recommend, but the silver lining is discovering friends you never knew you had.

These days, people stop me in airports, restaurants, and convenience stores. They tell me about the kind of future they want for themselves and for their kids. A lot of them are Republicans, but some of them are Democrats and independents. The thing they have in common is that they are all concerned citizens who are passionate about our country and pulling for the American Idea. They are ready for our comeback to finally begin.

I've seen a new political coalition forming—one that isn't limited by old labels or organized into tidy groups of red or blue. This new coalition of Americans is looking for leadership that can finally bring our country together again. They are tired of politicians who divide us by race or class or creed. They want leaders who unite us by appealing to the hopes, values, and beliefs we share as Americans. They want candidates who engage in the battle of ideas fully and honestly, giving us meaningful choices when it comes to public policy. And they want leaders who govern prudently, moving us closer to that vision out on the horizon by advancing our principles as the circumstances allow—sometimes quickly and broadly, sometimes incrementally.

*   *   *

By October 2013, the federal government had reached a new low. Congress wasn't fulfilling its appropriations and oversight duties. Instead, it was budgeting from crisis to crisis, using stopgap spending bills to keep us afloat. We'd just lived through one government shutdown, and we were looking at the possibility of two more in 2014. We had spent three years waiting for one party to blink on its core principles, and we were getting nowhere.

That was the state of affairs when Senator Patty Murray and I met in her office in the U.S. Capitol and began the seemingly impossible task of hashing out a budget agreement.

Patty and I are the chairs of the Senate and House budget committees. We are about as different as two people can get. When we stand next to each other, we look like the odd couple; she's petite with a small frame and I'm a lanky Irish guy. I root for Green Bay, and she's a Seattle Seahawks fan. And ideologically, we're at opposite ends of the spectrum. What we did have in common was a determination to start doing the business of Congress in a different way. We both wanted to stop the shutdowns, make Congress work, and restore some sense of financial stability.

At first there were just four of us—Patty, me, and our staff directors. It's not the way we ought to be governing, but these days nobody trusts each other and everybody leaks to the press. We kept the group small so we could be really honest with each other right from the get-go.

Then we set some ground rules. We weren't going to force each other to violate a core principle; our negotiations would be guided by a search for common ground. We weren't going to swing for the fences and miss. We were going to take a step—even if it was a modest one—in the right direction. We knew at the end of the day everybody would have to give a little, but nobody had to lose.

Over the next few meetings, we started building trust with each other. We'd share our ideas and priorities, and when they didn't end up in the *Wall Street Journal* or the *New York Times*, we knew we were both serious. That was when the real deliberations began.

Finding common ground wasn't easy to do. Senator Murray wanted a big tax increase, and I wanted entitlement reform. Soon, it became clear that neither one of us was bluffing on those issues. If we wanted to get something done, we would have to focus on the areas where we could agree.

So we started looking at our lists of priorities and trading policies, just throwing ideas at one another. Patty and I are both football fans, and we spoke of having to scale back our ambitions: from trying to score a touchdown, to getting a first down, to just getting positive yardage. When we tried to go big, we realized we were on different teams with different end zones. But there was in fact common ground. We both wanted to reduce the deficit. We both wanted to avoid further shutdowns. We both thought mandatory spending reforms were smarter than arbitrary discretionary cuts. And while this wasn't much to unite us, it was a start. Most important, it put us on the same team. It allowed us to think about what steps we could take together—albeit modest steps—that would result in positive yardage for both of us.

So we whittled down our lists and knocked some stuff off. We set up a process that let us achieve the most good for the country in the circumstances we were in.

The deal ended up being small in substance but big in symbolism. It reduced the deficit by $16 billion without raising taxes. It provided $63 billion in sequester relief, replacing arbitrary cuts with targeted reforms. It gave the power of the purse back to Congress. And it set the precedent that when fiscal pressure is high, we should look first to entitlement spending so that we can cut the deficit without raising taxes.

For it to have been the deal I wanted, we would have needed to tack a couple of more zeroes onto the end, in terms of deficit reduction, but we moved in the right direction, and the deal lined up with conservative principles.

The most significant thing about the deal is that it got us governing again. Right now, Washington, D.C., is set to divide and conquer. Negotiations are dead before they ever get going. Everybody goes into their corners and starts attacking before the details are even put to paper. That's the tone that has been set.

Making policy is always going to be somewhat partisan, but it doesn't have to be this divisive and unproductive. Senators and congressmen from opposite sides of the aisle don't have to see each other as enemies—and there doesn't have to be a sense of complete distrust among Republicans.

It's not too late to solve our problems, but we need a new approach in Washington, D.C.—and it's more than just a change in political philosophy or public policy; we also need a new approach to politics, campaigning, and governing.

One thing is for certain: There is no silver bullet in politics. When our country gets off course, we can't change things overnight. We can't twist arms and force a solution.

When it comes to campaigning, we have to offer voters a meaningful choice. We have to explain how limited government, constitutional principles, and conservative policies can improve people's lives. We have to explain how our solutions can deliver health and retirement security to seniors, create jobs and opportunity, restore upward mobility at every rung of the ladder, and give our kids a future that is secure and debt-free. And we have to take our message to every corner of our country, opening up a dialogue with Americans of all walks of life about what we believe. Our plans and policies shouldn't be secret. We have to run on them so we have a mandate to implement them when we win.

We must be clear about our principles and our path. Only in light of those can we see—and explain—how to get there. That means we must also practice prudence, which is good judgment in the art of governing. Not for the sake of compromise, but for the sake of a better future.

The prudent leader is like the captain of a ship. He doesn't curse the wind; he uses it to reach his destination. Our elected leaders have to be able to see our destination out there on the horizon and then tack their way to it accordingly. The important thing is where we are going, not the stops we make along the way.

This isn't a new idea. In fact, it's how our Founders created the framework for the greatest country that the world has ever known.

Take James Madison. Today he's known as the Father of the Constitution, but at the Constitutional Convention, he lost some key arguments. At first, he wanted to give Congress the power to veto state laws, and he opposed adding a bill of rights.

In both cases, Madison argued vigorously for his side, and in both cases he lost. But when it came time to ratify the Constitution, there was no greater advocate than Madison. He helped write editorials in support—*The Federalist Papers*—and he led the charge for approval at Virginia's state convention.

Madison paid a price for his support. When he ran for Congress, his political adversaries drafted James Monroe to run against him. This was the eighteenth-century equivalent of "getting primaried." But Madison decided that for all its imperfections, he would support the Constitution because it was the best framework for building a more perfect union. And during the First Congress, Representative Madison wrote the Bill of Rights and was its chief sponsor. We became the country we are because James Madison was a prudent man.

Like the Founders and like Lincoln, we must stay true to our principles but, like them, we must make practical decisions to advance our principles under the circumstances in which we find ourselves. Sometimes we must be bold, and at other times we must be careful and bide our time. Sometimes, we'll have to reject certain proposals. At other times, we'll work to make them better. But our answer can't be simply to oppose—or support—every proposal based on partisan tactics.

Going forward, the key is to lay out our priorities so that people understand the moves we make—however big or small they may be. A common vision allows us to move forward together in service to our shared goals. In the end, we seek the same objective: We want a leaner, smarter government. We want to recover our founding principles. We want to restore prosperity, opportunity, and security. We want to free the engines of moral reform and heal our culture. We want to ensure that our nation remains a symbol of all of the blessings that can be secured only through a commitment to liberty and the rule of law. We want to renew the American Idea.

* * *

That night in 1981 when I sat on the floor watching TV and listened to a new president speak, I didn't know that what I was hearing was the beginning of something. I was too young. But looking back, I remember the moment because of what followed.

Nearly eight years later, Ronald Reagan addressed the nation for the last time as our president. From a quiet Oval Office, he took stock of his achievement, and the nation's. Our country was "more prosperous, more secure, and happier," Reagan said. "It still stands strong and true on the granite ridge, and her glow has held steady no matter what storm. And she's still a beacon, still a magnet for all who must have freedom, for all the pilgrims from all the lost places who are hurtling through the darkness, toward home."

My dad was gone by the time Reagan said good-bye, but I remember thinking that if he had been alive, he would have been proud. I was about to turn nineteen—old enough to understand and appreciate that his generation had done the hard work of bringing America back from a dark period marked by pessimism and malaise.

That night Reagan said, "We've done our part," and he didn't just mean himself. He meant a whole generation—people in every city and small community—that had come together to make life better for everyone, including my brothers, my sister, and me.

That is what inspires and motivates me now. When I'm on the other side of life and my grandchildren ask me about this moment, I don't want to tell them how America lost its way. I don't want to say, "Don't blame me. I didn't vote for any of it." I don't want to complain about the opportunities we missed or the chances we squandered.

I want to tell them the great story of how America came back. I want to tell them about the courage it took to make the tough choices and the noble vision that saw us through. I want to pass to them a country made stronger by the struggle, a future that's brighter, and a world that's safer and more secure.

This will not be easy. At times, it will certainly be messy. But when all is said and done, I want to be able to say, "It was tough, but we did our part. It's what my parents did for me, and when our moment came, it's what my generation did for you. And that's why the American Idea lives on."

Acknowledgments

This book was made possible by the support and friendship of many individuals.

I would like to thank Bob Barnett for his advice and assistance. Bob was the first person to suggest that the ideas contained within these pages could become something more, and his wise counsel made this book possible.

I am deeply grateful to my editor at Twelve, Sean Desmond, who helped transform several pages of thoughts into a full manuscript that became the perfect expression of my vision for this project. His encouragement, his edits, and his guidance were invaluable. I would also like to thank the entire team at Twelve—Deb Futter, Brian McLendon, Paul Samuelson, Libby Burton, and Mari C. Okuda—for their dedication to this project.

The biggest thanks of all go out to Lindsay Hayes, who, because of her immeasurable patience, hard work, and great talent, helped keep me focused and on task. She helped make the whole experience a real pleasure.

At various stages of the drafting process, I have benefitted from the generosity of several people who provided suggestions, advice, and edits. I am deeply grateful for the contributions of Yuval Levin, Matthew Scully, Matthew Spalding, Pete Wehner, Mitt Romney, Bob Woodson, Lanhee Chen, Bill Bennett, Dan Senor, John McConnell, Kim Daniels, and James W. Ceaser.

For reading and commenting on the manuscript, I am grateful to Andy Speth, Tim Kronquist, Jonathan Burks, Conor Sweeney, Brian Bolduc, Jake Kastan, Dennis Teti, Donald Schneider, Kevin Seifert, Ted McCann, Stephanie Parks, Matt Hoffmann, and Casey Christine Higgins.

Ted Newton helped track down critical facts and important pieces of research, and I appreciate his tireless efforts. I would also like to thank Sarah Peer, Vanessa Day, Clare Burns, Terence Mathis, Jubal Garcia, Paul Grodell, and Shirley Holloway for their assistance.

The support I have received from countless colleagues in Congress all along the way has been invaluable. Too often, people look to Congress with cynicism. Yet that is not the full picture. To the many hardworking, principled men and women with whom I serve, I simply want to say thanks for the friendship, the lessons, and memories.

My family was not only very supportive of sharing the Ryan-Little story, but also read this book and provided suggestions to improve passages and refresh my own memory of events. I would like to thank my brother Tobin and his wife, Oakleigh; my brother Stan; my sister, Janet; and my mom, Betty. I would also like to thank Dan Little and Dana Little Jackson.

Above all, I am grateful to my wife, Janna, and our three children, Liza, Charlie, and Sam, for their support, patience, and understanding as I worked on this book. As with everything I do, they made this endeavor possible and enjoyable.

Finally, I would like to thank my friends and neighbors in Janesville—and all of the residents of the First District of Wisconsin—for reminding me daily that the American Idea is worth fighting for. It is an honor to serve them.

Notes

Chapter 1: A Tale of Two Cities

Much of the material that covers Janesville and the 2012 campaign is based upon my own recollections. However, I also relied upon the following published sources to refresh my memory about the campaign: Philip Rucker, "Romney Predicting Victory in Wisconsin GOP Primary," *Washington Post*, March 31, 2012, http://www.washingtonpost.com/blogs/post-politics/post/romney-predicting-victory-in-wisconsin-gop-primary/2012/03/31/gIQARqawnS_blog.html; and Garrett Haake and Alex Moe, "How Did They Do It? Romney Campaign Explains How It Kept the Biggest Secret in Politics," *NBC News First Read*, August 12, 2012, http://firstread.nbcnews.com/_news/2012/08/11/13239042-how-did-they-do-it-romney-campaign-explains-how-it-kept-the-biggest-secret-in-politics?lite.

The following sources were consulted in drafting the sections about Janesville: Mike Dupre, "GM Has Long, Rich History in Janesville," *Janesville Gazette*, June 3, 2008, http://www.gazettextra.com/news/2008/jun/03/gm-has-long-rich-history-janesville/; Al Hulick, "Population Statistics of Janesville, Wisconsin," Hedberg Public Library, http://hedbergpubliclibrary.org/pdfs/Janesville%20Population%20Statistics.pdf; Matthew DeLuca, "Paul Ryan Used Government Funds and Power to Try and Save GM Plant in His District," *Daily Beast*, August 17, 2012, http://www.thedailybeast.com/articles/2012/08/17/paul-ryan-used-government-funds-and-power-to-try-and-save-gm-plant-in-his-district.html; Frank Schultz, "Local Delegation Meets with GM Execs," *Janesville Gazette*, September 13, 2008, http://

www.gazettextra.com/news/2008/sep/13/local-delegation-meets-gm-execs/; Neal Boudette, "The History of the Janesville GM Plant," *Wall Street Journal*, August 30, 2012, http://blogs.wsj.com/drivers-seat/2012/08/30/the-history-of-the-janesville-gm-plant/; Rick Popely, "Janesville Facing Future Without GM, *Chicago Tribune*, June 4, 2008, http://articles.chicagotribune.com/2008-06-04/business/0806030571_1_gm-plants-chevrolet-tahoe-and-suburban-gmc-yukon; and "Lear Closing Janesville Plant," *WMTV*, October 17, 2008, http://www.nbc15.com/news/headlines/31178899.html.

For material about the crisis in Detroit, Nathan Bomey and John Gallagher's detailed investigative report on the city's fiscal problems was an invaluable resource. I relied upon it heavily to construct the historical narrative included in chapter 1. See Nathan Bomey and John Gallagher, "How Detroit Went Broke," *Detroit Free Press*, September 15, 2013, http://www.freep.com/interactive/article/20130915/NEWS01/130801004/Detroit-Bankruptcy-history-1950-debt-pension-revenue.

In drafting the section about Detroit, I also drew from and relied upon the following published sources: Arthur Herman, "The Arsenal of Democracy," *Detroit News*, January 3, 2013, http://www.detroitnews.com/article/20130103/OPINION01/301030336; "Automobiles," History Channel, 2010, http://www.history.com/topics/automobiles, from Eric Foner and John A. Garraty, eds., *The Reader's Companion to American History* (Boston: Houghton Mifflin Harcourt, 1991); Daniel Okrent, "Detroit: The Death—and Possible Life—of a Great City," *Time*, September 24, 2009, http://content.time.com/time/magazine/article/0,9171,1926017,00.html?artId=1926017?contType=article?chn=us; Katharine Q. Seelye, "Detroit Census Confirms a Desertion Like No Other," *New York Times*, March 22, 2011, http://www.nytimes.com/2011/03/23/us/23detroit.html?_r=0; Steven Church and Steven Raphael, "Detroit Retirees Put on Notice in Bankruptcy Ruling," *Bloomberg BusinessWeek*, December 3, 2013, http://www.businessweek.com/news/2013-12-03/detroit-to-stay-under-bankruptcy-protection-judge-says-1; Lauren Knapp, "Detroit's Population Decline: 1 Person Departed Every 22 Minutes," *PBS NewsHour*, March 23, 2011, http://www.pbs.org/newshour/rundown/-sarah-hulett-of-michigan/; Marilisa Sachteleben, "Detroit Emergency

Manager Orr Enters Loan Repayment Negotiations," *Yahoo! News*, June 14, 2013, http://news.yahoo.com/detroit-emergency-manager-orr-enters -loan-repayment-negotiations-190300771.html; "Editorial: For Decades, Detroit Leadership Was Blind to City's Mounting Problems," *Detroit Free Press*, September 15, 2013, http://www.freep.com/article/20130915/ OPINION01/309150049/; Peter Hayes and James Schwartz, *Distress in Detroit: A BlackRock Analysis* (New York: BlackRock, 2013), https:// www.blackrock.com/cash/literature/whitepaper/distress-in-detroit -a-blackrock-analysis.pdf; Josh Barro, "11 Charts That Show Why Detroit Is Falling Apart and Heading for Bankruptcy," *Business Insider*, June 14, 2013, http://www.businessinsider.com/11-charts-that-show -why-detroit-is-falling-apart-and-heading-for-bankruptcy-2013-6# -and-detroit-police-mismanaged-and-under; Elisha Anderson, "Safety Concerns Prompt Detroit Fire Department to Place Restrictions on Use of Aerial Ladders," *Detroit Free Press*, February 3, 2013, http://www .freep.com/article/20130203/NEWS01/130203029/Safety-concerns -prompt-Detroit-Fire-Department-to-place-restrictions-on-use-of-aerial -ladders; Harriet Alexander, "'Motor City' Detroit Files for Bankruptcy with 100,000 Creditors," *Telegraph*, July 19, 2013, http://www.telegraph.co .uk/news/worldnews/northamerica/usa/10190640/Motor-City-Detroit -files-for-bankruptcy-with-100000-creditors.html; George Hunter, Mike Wilkinson, and Holly Fournier, "Police Cuts Loom as Detroit Struggles to Curb Violence," *Detroit News*, June 8, 2012, http://www.detroitnews .com/article/20120608/METRO01/206080362; Matthew Dolan, "Record Bankruptcy for Detroit," *Wall Street Journal*, July 19, 2013, http:// online.wsj.com/news/articles/SB10001424127887323993804578614144173709204; Derek Melot, "Report Details Surge in Child Poverty in Detroit," *Bridge Magazine*, January 24, 2013, http://bridgemi .com/2013/01/report-details-surge-in-child-poverty-in-detroit/; Ryan Beene, "Detroit's Public Schools Post Worst Scores on Record in National Assessment," *Crain's Detroit Business*, December 8, 2009, http://www .crainsdetroit.com/article/20091208/FREE/912089997/detroits-public -schools-post-worst-scores-on-record-in-national; "Ed Trust-Midwest Statement on the 2011 NAEP TUDA Reading and Math Results," Education

Trust—Midwest, press release, December 7, 2011, http://www.edtrust .org/midwest/press-room/press-release/ed-trust-midwest-statement-on-the -2011-naep-tuda-reading-and-math-r; Data Driven Detroit, *State of the Detroit Child, 2012 Report* (Detroit: The Skillman Foundation, 2012), http://www.datadrivendetroit.org/publications/D3_2012_SDCReport .pdf; Kristi Tanner, "Raw Data: Detroit's Unemployment Rate over the Last Decade," *Detroit Free Press,* July 21, 2013, http://www.freep.com/ article/20130721/OPINION05/307210033/; "Interactive Map: Major Crimes in Detroit," *Detroit News,* http://www.detroitnews.com/article/ 99999999/SPECIAL01/120606001; and Steven Yaccino, "Kwame M. Kilpatrick, Former Detroit Mayor, Sentenced to 28 Years in Corruption Case," *New York Times,* October 10, 2013, http://www.nytimes .com/2013/10/11/us/former-detroit-mayor-kwame-kilpatrick-sentencing .html?_r=0.

Chapter 2: Sink or Swim

Chapter 2 draws upon the following published materials: Robert Costa, "My Brother, Paul Ryan," *National Review Online,* August 20, 2012, http://www.nationalreview.com/articles/314426/my-brother-paul-ryan -robert-costa; William J. Bennett, *The De-Valuing of America: The Fight for Our Culture and Our Children* (New York: Simon & Schuster, 1992), 34; and Nia J. Stanley, "What Is Sam Brownback's Religion?" *Politics Daily,* October 27, 2010, http://www.politicsdaily.com/2010/10/27/what -is-sam-brownbacks-religion/.

Chapter 3: Lesser of Two Evils

To help fill out the narrative regarding my years in Congress, I consulted and drew from the following sources: Michael Crowley, "Newt the Impeacher: Will 2012 See Gingrich's Role in the Clinton Scandal Relitigated?" *Time,* December 19, 2011, http://swampland.time.com/2011/12/ 19/newt-the-impeacher-will-2012-see-gingrichs-role-in-the-clinton -scandal-relitigated/; Stuart Rothenberg, "Analysis: A Small But Historic Shift for the Democrats," CNN, November 3, 1998, http://www.cnn.com/ ALLPOLITICS/stories/1998/11/03/election/house/roundup/; Guy Gugliotta and Juliet Eilperin, "Gingrich Steps Down in Face of Rebellion," *Washington Post*, November 7, 1998, http://www.washingtonpost.com/wp-srv/politics/govt/leadership/stories/gingrich110798.htm; Ann Curley, David Ensor, Bob Franken, and John King, "Gingrich Calls It Quits," CNN, November 6, 1998, http://www.cnn.com/ALLPOLITICS/stories/1998/11/06/gingrich/; "Freshmen Confront Maelstrom in House," *Lubbock Avalanche-Journal*, November 14, 1998, http://lubbockonline.com/stories/111498/LA0699.shtml; Catharine Richert, "Axelrod Claims Bush Saddled Obama with a Big Deficit," *Tampa Bay Times*, January 15, 2010, http://www.politifact.com/truth-o-meter/statements/2010/jan/15/david-axelrod/axelrod-claims-bush-saddled-obama-big-deficit/; "Text of President Bush's 2001 Address to Congress," *Washington Post*, February 27, 2001, http://www.washingtonpost.com/wp-srv/onpolitics/transcripts/bushtext022701.htm; Thomas R. Oliver, Philip R. Lee, and Helene L. Lipton, "A Political History of Medicare and Prescription Drug Coverage," *Milbank Quarterly* 82, no. 2 (2004): 309, http://www.amcp.org/WorkArea/DownloadAsset.aspx?id=11196; Jonathan Weisman and Jim VandeHei, "Road Bill Reflects the Power of Pork," *Washington Post*, August 11, 2005, http://www.washingtonpost.com/wp-dyn/content/article/2005/08/10/AR2005081000223.html; and Stephen Hayes, "Man with a Plan," *Weekly Standard*, July 23, 2012, http://www.weeklystandard.com/articles/man-plan_648570.html?nopager=1.

The following government sources were also consulted and incorporated: Clerk of the House, "Election Statistics," U.S. House of Representatives, http://history.house.gov/Institution/Election-Statistics/Election-Statistics/; "Social Security History: Frequently Asked Questions," Social Security Administration, http://www.ssa.gov/history/hfaq.html; "Remarks by the President in Social Security Announcement—May 2, 2001," Presidential Statements, George W. Bush—2001, Social Security Administration, http://www.ssa.gov/history/gwbushstmts.html#05022001; and Office of Management and Budget, *Budget of the United States Government: Fiscal Year 2003*, February 4, 2002, http://georgewbush-whitehouse.archives.gov/omb/budget/fy2003/budget.html.

This chapter also includes material adapted from an op-ed that I drafted, which appeared in the *Wall Street Journal*: Paul D. Ryan, "How to

Tackle the Entitlement Crisis," *Wall Street Journal*, May 21, 2008, http://online.wsj.com/news/articles/SB121132850555608905.

Chapter 4: The Battle of Ideas

Chapter 4 makes use of the following sources to help fill in the narrative account covering the Obama administration's first term in office: "Camp-Cantor Plan Provides Fast-Acting Tax Relief, Not Slow-Moving and Wasteful Government Spending," Speaker of the House John Boehner, January 27, 2009, http://www.speaker.gov/general/house-gop -economic-recovery-alternative-will-create-62-million-new-american-jobs; Mark Knoller, "TV Coverage Limits Success of Health Care Summit," *CBS News*, February 24, 2010, http://www.cbsnews.com/news/tv-coverage-limits -success-of-health-care-summit/; Herman Schwartz, "Democrats: It's the States, Stupid!" *Reuters*, July 14, 2013, http://blogs.reuters.com/great -debate/2013/07/14/democrats-its-the-states-stupid/; and "About: Young Guns," Young Guns, http://www.gopyoungguns.com/about/.

This chapter also includes material adapted from an op-ed that I authored for the *Wall Street Journal*: Paul D. Ryan, "The GOP Path to Prosperity," *Wall Street Journal*, April 5, 2011, http://online.wsj.com/news/articles/SB10001424052748703806304576242612172357504.

Chapter 5: Beyond Makers and Takers

The following sources were referenced and incorporated in chapter 5: Scott A. Hodge, *Accounting for What Families Pay in Taxes and What They Receive in Government Spending* (Washington, DC: Tax Foundation, 2009), available at http://taxfoundation.org/article/accounting-what-families-pay -taxes-and-what-they-receive-government-spending-0; Tom Coburn, "The 10 Most Outrageous Government Boondoggles I Ever Saw," *Politico Magazine*, February 5, 2014, http://www.politico.com/magazine/story/2014/02/ government-spending-tom-coburn-103189.html#.Uv5zc_3OVg1; Harry V. Jaffa, *A New Birth of Freedom: Abraham Lincoln and the Coming of the Civil War* (Lanham, MD: Rowman & Littlefield, 2000): 395; Ronald J. Pestritto and William J. Atto, "Introduction to American Progressivism," in *American Progressivism: A Reader*, eds. Ronald J. Pestritto and William

J. Atto (Lanham, MD: Rowman & Littlefield, 2008); Matthew Spalding, *We Still Hold These Truths: Rediscovering Our Principles, Reclaiming Our Future* (Wilmington: Intercollegiate Studies Institute, 2009); Woodrow Wilson, "Address to the Jefferson Club of Los Angeles, May 12, 1911," in *Papers of Woodrow Wilson*, ed. Arthur Link (Princeton: Princeton University Press, 1977), 23:33–34; "Woodrow Wilson Asks, 'What is Progress?'" Heritage Foundation, http://www.heritage.org/initiatives/first-principles/primary-sources/woodrow-wilson-asks-what-is-progress; David Remnick, "Going the Distance: On and Off the Road with Barack Obama," *New Yorker*, January 27, 2014, http://www.newyorker.com/reporting/2014/01/27/140127fa_fact_remnick?currentPage=all; James L. Gattuso and Diane Katz, "Red Tape Rising: Regulation in Obama's First Term," Heritage Foundation, May 1, 2013, http://www.heritage.org/research/reports/2013/05/red-tape-rising-regulation-in-obamas-first-term; Charles Krauthammer, "Obama's Campaign for Class Resentment," *Washington Post*, December 8, 2011, http://www.washingtonpost.com/opinions/obamas-campaign-for-class-resentment/2011/12/08/gIQApYDagO_story.html; "Discontinued Projects," Loan Programs Office, U.S. Department of Energy, http://lpo.energy.gov/our-projects/discontinued-projects/; Jack Kemp, *An American Renaissance: A Strategy for the 1980s* (Lake Wylie, SC: Robert E. Hopper and Associates, 1980), 3; Doug Mataconis, "Demographic Trends Not Looking Good for Republicans," *Outside the Beltway*, May 11, 2013, http://www.outsidethebeltway.com/demographic-trends-not-looking-good-for-republicans/; and "Revitalizing America's Cities," C-SPAN, aired May 10, 1992, http://www.c-span.org/video/?25997-1/revitalizing-americas-cities.

Chapter 6: Simpler, Smaller, Smarter

Chapter 6 covers several policy areas, and the following sources were consulted and incorporated in the drafting the section on health care and entitlement reform: William Safire, "Third Rail," On Language, *New York Times*, February 18, 2007, http://www.nytimes.com/2007/02/18/magazine/18wwlnsafire.t.html?_r=0; Alison Acosta Fraser, "Federal Spending by the Numbers—2012," Heritage Foundation, October 16. 2012,

http://www.heritage.org/research/reports/2012/10/federal-spending-by-the
-numbers-2012; Congressional Budget Office, "The 2013 Long-Term Budget Outlook," September 13, 2013, http://www.cbo.gov/publication/44521; "Medicare Will Be Exhausted in 2026, Social Security in 2033," *CNBC*, May 31, 2013, http://www.cnbc.com/id/100780248; Congressional Budget Office, "April 2014 Medicare Baseline," April 14, 2014, http://www.cbo.gov/sites/default/files/cbofiles/attachments/44205-2014-04-Medicare.pdf; The Boards of Trustees, Federal Hospital Insurance and Federal Supplementary Medical Insurance Trust Funds, "2013 Annual Report of the Boards of Trustees of the Federal Hospital Insurance and Federal Supplementary Medical Insurance Trust Funds," May 31, 2013, http://www.cms.gov/Research-Statistics-Data-and-Systems/Statistics-Trends-and-Reports/ReportsTrustFunds/Downloads/TR2013.pdf; Congressional Budget Office, "Detail of Spending and Enrollment for Medicaid for CBO's April 2014 Baseline," April 2014, http://www.cbo.gov/sites/default/files/cbofiles/attachments/44204-2014-04-Medicaid.pdf; Congressional Budget Office, "The Budget and Economic Outlook: 2014 to 2024," February 4, 2014, http://www.cbo.gov/publication/45010; National Association of State Budget Officers, *State Expenditure Report: Examining Fiscal 2011–2013 State Spending* (Washington, DC: National Association of State Budget Officers, 2013), http://www.nasbo.org/sites/default/files/State%20Expenditure%20Report%20%28Fiscal%202011-2013%20Data%29.pdf; Avik Roy, "Oregon Study: Medicaid 'Had No Significant Effect' on Health Outcomes vs. Being Uninsured," *Forbes*, May 2, 2013, http://www.forbes.com/sites/theapothecary/2013/05/02/oregon-study-medicaid-had-no-significant-effect-on-health-outcomes-vs-being-uninsured/; Grace-Marie Turner, "The Real Tragedy of ObamaCare Has Yet to be Felt by the Poor," *Forbes*, August 21, 2012, http://www.forbes.com/sites/gracemarieturner/2012/08/21/the-real-tragedy-of-obamacare-has-yet-to-be-felt-by-the-poor/; "Patient's Choice Act," Office of U.S. Congressman Paul Ryan, May 2009, http://paulryan.house.gov/uploadedfiles/pcasummary2p.pdf; "Medicare Advantage Fact Sheet," Henry J. Kaiser Foundation, May 1, 2014, http://kff.org/medicare/fact-sheet/medicare-advantage-fact-sheet/; and Elise Viebeck, "Insurers: Nearly All Seniors Happy with Medicare Advantage," *Hill*, February 28,

2013, http://thehill.com/blogs/healthwatch/medicare/285543-insurers-nearly
-all-seniors-happy-with-medicare-advantage.

The following sources were consulted and incorporated when drafting
the section on economic growth: Mark Knoller, "National Debt Up $6
Trillion Since Obama Took Office," *CBS News*, March 1, 2013, http://www
.cbsnews.com/news/national-debt-up-6-trillion-since-obama-took-office/;
"Ryan: CBO Report Is a Call to Action," Committee on the Budget, U.S.
House of Representatives, press release, February 4, 2014, http://budget
.house.gov/news/documentsingle.aspx?DocumentID=368741; Tom Feran,
"Rob Portman Says Buffett Rule Would Raise Just Enough to Cover
1 Week's Interest on National Debt," PolitiFact Ohio, April 23, 2012,
http://www.politifact.com/ohio/statements/2012/apr/23/rob-portman/
rob-portman-says-buffett-rule-would-raise-just-eno/; "Obama's Top 10
Broken Promises," GOP.com, April 6, 2011, http://www.gop.com/news/
research/obamas-top-10-broken-promises/; Bureau of Labor Statistics,
"Labor Force Statistics from the Current Population Survey," U.S.
Department of Labor, February 27, 2014, http://data.bls.gov/timeseries/
LNS14000000; and Eric Morath, "What's to Blame for Slower Potential
Growth in U.S.?" *Wall Street Journal*, February 24, 2014, http://on.wsj
.com/1hqn6H3.

The section on tax reform drew upon the following materials: "National
Taxpayer Advocate Delivers Annual Report to Congress; Focuses on Tax
Reform, IRS Funding and Identity Theft," Internal Revenue Service,
press release, January 9, 2013, http://www.irs.gov/uac/Newsroom/
National-Taxpayer-Advocate-Delivers-2012-Annual-Report-to-Congress;
Kelly Phillips Erb, "Tax Code Hits Nearly 4 Million Words, Taxpayer
Advocate Calls It Too Complicated," *Forbes*, January 10, 2013, http://
www.forbes.com/sites/kellyphillipserb/2013/01/10/tax-code-hits
-nearly-4-million-words-taxpayer-advocate-calls-it-too-complicated/; Louis
Jacobson, "Hatch Says Senate Health Care Bill Is Longer Than 'War and
Peace,'" PolitiFact.com, November 20, 2009, http://www.politifact.com/
truth-o-meter/statements/2009/nov/20/orrin-hatch/hatch-senate-health
-care-bill-longer-war-peace/; Nina E. Olson, *National Taxpayer Advocate
2012 Annual Report to Congress: Executive Summary*, (Washington, DC:

Internal Revenue Service, 2012), vii, http://www.taxpayeradvocate.irs.gov/
userfiles/file/2012-Annual-Report-to-Congress-Executive-Summary.pdf;
Dave Camp, "How to Fix Our Appalling Tax Code," *Wall Street Journal*, February 25, 2014, http://online.wsj.com/news/articles/SB10001424
052702303426304579403252458098042; Kyle Pomerleau and Andrew
Lundeen, "The U.S. Has the Highest Corporate Income Tax Rate in the
OECD," Tax Foundation, January 27, 2014, http://taxfoundation.org/blog/
us-has-highest-corporate-income-tax-rate-oecd; John D. McKinnon and
Scott Thurm, "U.S. Firms Move Abroad to Cut Taxes," *Wall Street Journal*, August 28, 2012, http://online.wsj.com/news/articles/SB1000087239
6390444230504577615232602107536; Mike Obel, "Paul Ryan, Leading
Republican Fiscal Conservative, Endorses Call by Apple CEO Tim Cook
to Repatriate Foreign Earnings, Provided the Tax on Such Earnings Is
Cut," *International Business Times*, May 29, 2013, http://www.ibtimes.com/
paul-ryan-leading-republican-fiscal-conservative-endorses-call-apple
-ceo-tim-cook-repatriate-foreign; and Dan Dzombak, "The Highest Corporate Tax Rates in the World," *Motley Fool*, March 1, 2014, http://www.fool
.com/investing/general/2014/03/01/the-highest-corporate-tax-rates-in
-the-world.aspx.

In writing about regulatory reform, I drew from and consulted the following sources: Margaret Thatcher, *Statecraft: Strategies for a Changing World* (New York: HarperCollins Publishers, 2002), 423; Benjamin Goad, "Government Report Finds Regulations Have Spiked Under Obama," *Hill*, May 15, 2013, http://thehill.com/blogs/regwatch/administration/299617
-government-report-shows-spike-in-regulations-under-obama; Maeve P.
Carey, "Counting Regulations: An Overview of Rulemaking, Types of Federal Regulations, and Pages in the *Federal Register*," Congressional Research Service, May 1, 2013, http://www.fas.org/sgp/crs/misc/R43056.pdf; Peter Whoriskey, "Regulations a Rising Economic Burden to Manufacturers, Report Says," *Washington Post*, August 21, 2012, http://www.washingtonpost
.com/business/economy/regulations-an-economic-burden-to-manufacturers
-report-says/2012/08/20/3aa4501a-eb01-11e1-9ddc-340d5efb1e9c_story
.html; Sam Batkins, "A Regulatory Flurry: The Year in Regulation, 2013,"
American Action Forum, January 8, 2014, http://americanactionforum.org/

research/a-regulatory-flurry-the-year-in-regulation-2013; Molly Moorhead, "Barack Obama Says He Eliminated EPA Rule Treating Spilled Milk Like It Was Oil," PolitiFact.com. January 24, 2012, http://www.politifact .com/truth-o-meter/statements/2012/jan/24/barack-obama/barack -obama-says-he-eliminated-epa-rule-treating-/; Jonathan Turley, "The Rise of the Fourth Branch of Government," *Washington Post*, May 24, 2013, http://www.washingtonpost.com/opinions/the-rise-of-the-fourth -branch-of-government/2013/05/24/c7faaad0-c2ed-11e2-9fe2-6ee52d0eb7c1 _story.html; Marc Humphries, "U.S. Crude Oil and Natural Gas Production in Federal and Non-Federal Areas," Congressional Research Service, March 7, 2013, http://energycommerce.house.gov/sites/republicans.energy commerce.house.gov/files/20130228CRSreport.pdf; "U.S. Oil Production Up, But On Whose Lands?" Institute for Energy Research, September 24, 2012, http://www.instituteforenergyresearch.org/2012/09/24/u-s-oil -production-up-but-on-whose-lands-2/; Chris Wyatt and Taylor McCurdy, eds., "2013 Ranking of Countries for Mining Investment: 'Where Not to Invest,'" Behre Dolbear, available at http://www.dolbear.com/news -resources/documents; Charley Blaine, "Can the U.S. Frack Its Way to Freedom?" MSN Money, June 28, 2013, http://money.msn.com/investing/ can-the-us-frack-its-way-to-freedom; Kari Lydersen, "U.S. Chamber's Fracking Job Boom: Behind the Numbers," *Midwest Energy News*, January 10, 2013, http://www.midwestenergynews.com/2013/01/10/u-s-chambers -fracking-job-boom-behind-the-numbers/; and "Executive Order—Supporting Safe and Responsible Development of Unconventional Domestic Natural Gas Resources," Office of the Press Secretary, White House, press release, April 13, 2012, http://www.whitehouse.gov/the-press-office/2012/04/13/executive -order-supporting-safe-and-responsible-development-unconvention.

The section on immigration reform draws from the following material: Ronald Brownstein and Patrick J. McDonnell, "Kemp, Bennett and INS Chief Decry Prop. 187: Campaign: Statements by GOP Leaders, Clinton Administration Official Broaden Opposition on Two Fronts," *Los Angeles Times*, October 19, 1994, http://articles.latimes.com/1994-10-19/news/ mn-52096_1_illegal-immigrants; Roberto Suro, "Kemp Says Battle over Immigration Policy May Rend Republicans," *Washington Post*, November

22, 1994; Richard Nadler, "One, Eight, Seven, Hike!" The Corner, *National Review Online*, May 4, 2009, http://www.nationalreview.com/ corner/181314/one-eight-seven-hike/richard-nadler; Immigration Research Initiative, *Immigrant Small Business Owners: A Significant and Growing Part of the Economy* (New York: Fiscal Policy Institute, 2012), available at http://fiscalpolicy.org/wp-content/uploads/2012/06/immigrant-small -business-owners-FPI-20120614.pdf; Archbishop José H. Gomez, "Immigration and the 'Next America': Perspectives from Our History," *National Catholic Register*, August 1, 2011, http://www.ncregister.com/daily-news/ immigration-and-the-next-america-perspectives-from-our-history/; "The 'New American' Fortune 500," Partnership for a New American Economy, June 2011, http://www.renewoureconomy.org/sites/all/themes/pnae/ img/new-american-fortune-500-june-2011.pdf; "As U.S. Birth Rate Drops, Concern for the Future Mounts," *USA Today*, February 13, 2013, http:// www.usatoday.com/story/news/nation/2013/02/12/us-births-decline/ 1880231/; Jonathan V. Last, *What to Expect When No One's Expecting: America's Coming Demographic Disaster* (New York: Encounter Books, 2013), 3; and Julia Preston, "Number of Illegal Immigrants in U.S. May Be on Rise Again, Estimates Say," *New York Times*, September 23, 2013, http://www.nytimes.com/2013/09/24/us/immigrant-population-shows -signs-of-growth-estimates-show.html.

In drafting the section about sound monetary policy, the following sources were consulted and incorporated: Binyamin Applebaum, "A Fed Focused on the Value of Clarity," *New York Times*, December 13, 2012, http://www.nytimes.com/2012/12/14/business/economy/a-federal-reserve -that-is-focused-on-the-value-of-clarity.html; and Martin Crutsinger, "Federal Reserve Turns 100 with a Mission Quite Different Than Envisioned," *San Jose Mercury News*, December 23, 2013, http://www .mercurynews.com/business/ci_24781649/federal-reserve-turns-100 -mission-quite-different-than.

When drafting the section on foreign policy and national defense strategy, I reviewed and incorporated the following works: Joby Warrick, "More Than 1,400 Killed in Syrian Chemical Weapons Attack, U.S. Says," *Washington Post*, August 30, 2013, http://www.washingtonpost.com/

world/national-security/nearly-1500-killed-in-syrian-chemical-weapons
-attack-us-says/2013/08/30/b2864662-1196-11e3-85b6-d27422650fd5
_story.html; Stew Magnuson, "Fight to Keep A-10 Warthog in Air Force
Inventory Reaches End Game," *National Defense Magazine*, September
2013, http://www.nationaldefensemagazine.org/archive/2013/September/
Pages/FighttoKeepA-10WarthoginAirForceInventoryReachesEndGame
.aspx; U.S. General Accounting Office, "Operation Desert Storm: Evalua-
tion of the Air Campaign," Appendix IV, Air University, June 1997, http://
www.au.af.mil/au/awc/awcgate/gao/nsiad97134/app_04.htm; Brian Ever-
stine, "Future of A-10s Uncertain," *Air Force Times*, September 23, 2013,
http://www.airforcetimes.com/article/20130923/NEWS04/309230002/
Future-10s-uncertain; and "Human Capital: Additional Steps Needed to
Help Determine the Right Size and Composition of DOD's Total Workforce," U.S. Government Accountability Office, May 29, 2013, http://
www.gao.gov/products/gao-13-470.

This chapter also adapts content from an op-ed I coauthored for *Investor's
Business Daily*: John B. Taylor and Paul D. Ryan, "Refocus the Fed on Price
Stability Instead of Bailing Out Fiscal Policy," *Investor's Business Daily*, November 30, 2010, http://news.investors.com/ibd-editorials-perspective/113010
-555234-refocus-the-fed-on-price-stability-instead-of-bailing-out-fiscal
-policy.htm?p=1.

It also incorporates material adapted from a speech delivered before
the Hamilton Society. See Michael Warren, "Paul Ryan Embraces American Exceptionalism, Rejects Isolationism in Foreign Policy Speech,"
Weekly Standard, June 2, 2011, http://www.weeklystandard.com/blogs/
ryan-embraces-exceptionalism-rejects-isolationism-foreign-policy
-speech_573194.html?nopager=1.

Chapter 7: A Virtuous, Not Vicious, Cycle

When assembling the narrative account about my experiences with
colleagues and the media, I consulted and incorporated material from
the following sources: "Congresswoman Lee Responds to Ryan's Racially
Charged Comments," Office of U.S. Congresswoman Barbara Lee, press
release, March 12, 2014, http://lee.house.gov/newsroom/press-releases/

congresswoman-lee-responds-to-ryan-s-racially-charged-comments; John McCormack, "Paul Ryan: Suburbanites Need to Volunteer in Blighted Inner Cities Where There's a Culture of Fatherlessness and Unemployment," *Weekly Standard*, March 13, 2014, http://www.weeklystandard.com/blogs/paul-ryan-suburbanites-need-volunteer-blighted-inner-cities -where-theres-culture-fatherlessness-and-unemploymentdemocrats-?page=2; Ian Haney López, "Is Paul Ryan Racist?" *Politico Magazine*, March 14, 2014, http://www.politico.com/magazine/story/2014/03/is-paul-ryan-racist -104687.html#.UzcMbtxh4ds; and Barack Obama, "Address at the 99th Annual NAACP Convention," Presidential Rhetoric, July 14, 2008, http:// www.presidentialrhetoric.com/campaign2008/obama/07.14.08.html.

I consulted and drew from the following works when drafting material about my experiences with antipoverty grassroots leaders, civil society, and proposed reforms for poverty programs and education policy: Guillermo X. Garcia and J. Michael Parker, "Victory Outreach Minister Garcia Dies," *San Antonio Express-News*, October 16, 2009, http://www .mysanantonio.com/news/local_news/article/Victory-Outreach-minister -Garcia-dies-847161.php; Diane Davis, "Heritage Mourns Loss of Pastor Freddie Garcia," *Foundry*, Heritage Foundation, October 23, 2009, http:// blog.heritage.org/2009/10/23/heritage-mourns-loss-of-pastor-freddie -garcia/; United States Census, "About Poverty: Highlights," U.S. Census Bureau, https://www.census.gov/hhes/www/poverty/about/overview/; "U.S. Sees Highest Poverty Spike Since the 1960s, Leaving 50 Million Americans Poor As Government Cuts Billions in Spending...So Does That Mean There's No Way Out?" *Daily Mail*, April 2, 2013, http://www .dailymail.co.uk/news/article-2302997/U-S-sees-highest-poverty-spike -1960s-leaving-50-million-Americans-poor-government-cuts-billions -spending.html; Brad Plumer, "Why Are 47 Million Americans on Food Stamps? It's the Recession—Mostly," *Washington Post*, September 23, 2013, http://www.washingtonpost.com/blogs/wonkblog/wp/2013/09/23/why -are-47-million-americans-on-food-stamps-its-the-recession-mostly/; Aparna Mathur and Abby McCloskey, *Fostering Upward Economic Mobility in the United States* (Washington, DC: American Enterprise Institute,

2014), available at http://www.aei.org/files/2014/03/19/-fostering-upward
-economic-mobility-in-the-united-states_165153222749.pdf; Bill Glauber
and Ben Poston, "Milwaukee Now Fourth Poorest City in Nation,"
Milwaukee Journal-Sentinel, September 28, 2010, http://www.jsonline
.com/news/wisconsin/103929588.html; Mark Schaaf, "Ryan Seeks Fix for
Fed Programs on Poverty," *Journal Times,* March 11, 2014, http://journaltimes
.com/news/local/ryan-seeks-fix-for-fed-programs-on-poverty/article
_a2f80aea-a90e-11e3-9281-001a4bcf887a.html; "Richest and Poorest Cities
in America," *Los Angeles Times,* October 25, 2013, http://www.latimes.com/
business/money/la-fi-mo-american-cities-rich-poor-20131025,0,4446084
.photogallery?index=la-fi-mo-american-cities-rich-poor-20131025-005;
Alexis de Tocqueville, *Democracy in America,* vol. 2, trans. George Law-
rence, ed. J. P. Mayer (New York: Anchor, 1969), 513–515.

I also consulted: Robert Putnam, *Bowling Alone* (New York:
Simon & Schuster, 2000); "Catholic Health Care and Social Services,"
United States Conference of Catholic Bishops, http://www.usccb
.org/about/media-relations/statistics/health-care-social-service.cfm;
Louis Jacobson, "Does the Catholic Church Provide Half of Social Services in the U.S.?" PolitiFact.com, March 19, 2013, http://www.politifact
.com/truth-o-meter/statements/2013/mar/19/frank-keating/does-catholic
-church-provide-half-social-services-/; "Laity and Parishes," United States
Conference of Catholic Bishops, http://www.usccb.org/about/media
-relations/statistics/laity-parishes.cfm; "CNE Bids Farewell to Bob Coté,
a Brother in Arms," Center for Neighborhood Enterprise, http://www
.cneonline.org/cote-tribute/; Step 13 and Contrast Media, "A Fighter's
Heart" (video), directed by Rob Stennet, posted September 27, 2013, http://
youtu.be/mb5CAsdDxxU; Congressional Budget Office, "Effective Marginal Tax Rates for Low- and Moderate-Income Workers," Congressional
Budget Office, U.S. Congress, November 2012, http://www.cbo.gov/
sites/default/files/cbofiles/attachments/11-15-2012-MarginalTaxRates
.pdf; Francesca Ambrogetti and Sergio Rubin, *Conversations with Jorge
Bergoglio* (New York: G. P. Putnam's Sons, 2013), 18; Robert D. Putnam,
Carl B. Frederick, and Kaisa Snellman, "Growing Class Gaps in Social

Connectedness Among American Youth," (Cambridge: Harvard University Kennedy School of Government, 2012), available at http://www.hks.harvard.edu/var/ezp_site/storage/fckeditor/file/SaguaroReport_Diverging SocialConnectedness_20120808.pdf; Amanda Hess, "30 Percent of Single American Moms Are Living in Poverty," *Slate*, September 19, 2013, http://www.slate.com/blogs/xx_factor/2013/09/19/census_poverty_data _not_good_for_women_particularly_single_women.html; Darrell Issa, "The Truth About Obamacare's Tax Subsidies and Marriage Penalty," *National Review Online*, December 6, 2011, http://www.nationalreview .com/critical-condition/285966/truth-about-obamacare-s-tax-subsidies -and-marriage-penalty-darrell-issa; Julia Ryan, "American Schools vs. the World: Expensive, Unequal, Bad at Math," *Atlantic*, December 3, 2013, http://www.theatlantic.com/education/archive/2013/12/american -schools-vs-the-world-expensive-unequal-bad-at-math/281983/; Marie C. Stetser and Robert Stillwell, *Public High School Four-Year On-Time Graduation Rates and Event Dropout Rates: School Years 2010–11 and 2011–12*, National Center for Education Statistics, U.S. Department of Education, April 2014, http://nces.ed.gov/pubs2014/2014391.pdf; Lyndsey Layton, "High School Graduation Rates at Historic High," *Washington Post*, April 28, 2014, http://www.washingtonpost.com/local/education/ high-school-graduation-rates-at-historic-high/2014/04/28/84eb0122 -cee0-11e3-937f-d3026234b51c_story.html; Education & the Workforce Committee, "Bill Summary: The Supporting Knowledge and Investing in Lifelong Skills (SKILLS) Act (H.R. 803)," U.S. House of Representatives, http://edworkforce.house.gov/uploadedfiles/short_bill_summary _-_skills_act_final.pdf.

Chapter 8: The Comeback

When drafting material about President Reagan, I consulted the following works: Peter Ferrara, "Reaganomics vs. Obamanomics: Facts and Figures," *Forbes*, May 5, 2011, http://www.forbes.com/sites/peterferrara/2011/05/05/ reaganomics-vs-obamanomics-facts-and-figures/; Ronald Reagan, "Address Before a Joint Session of the Congress on the Program for Economic Recovery," American Presidency Project, February 18, 1981, http://www

.presidency.ucsb.edu/ws/?pid=43425; and Ronald Reagan, "Farewell Address to the Nation," American Presidency Project, January 11, 1989, http://www.presidency.ucsb.edu/ws/?pid=29650.

In drafting the material about Detroit, I consulted and drew from the following sources: Liz Essley Whyte, "Philanthropy Keeps the Lights On in Detroit," *Philanthropy Magazine*, Winter 2014, http://www.philanthropyroundtable.org/topic/excellence_in_philanthropy/philanthropy_keeps_the_lights_on_in_detroit; Mike Boehm, "Foundations Pledge $330 Million to Prevent Sale of Detroit Museum Art," *Los Angeles Times*, January 14, 2014, http://www.latimes.com/entertainment/arts/culture/la-et-cm-detroit-institute-of-arts-foundation-bailout-20140113,0,6040697.story#axzz2w4XTXpmb; Mark Stryker, "DIA Grand Bargain Could Prove to be a Work of Art, But Not a Done Deal," *Detroit Free Press*, March 9, 2014, http://www.freep.com/article/20140309/OPINION05/303090057/Detroit-Institute-of-Arts-Bankruptcy-Kevyn-Orr-DIA; Kate Abbey-Lambertz, "Twitter Opens Detroit Office in Downtown Madison Building," *Huffington Post*, April 4, 2012, http://www.huffingtonpost.com/2012/04/04/twitter-opens-detroit-office-madison-building_n_1402644.html; Michael Martinez, "Detroit Startups Will Compete to Pitch Business Plan to Google," *Detroit News*, February 3, 2014; Tim Alberta, "Is Dan Gilbert Detroit's New Superhero?" *National Journal*, February 27, 2014, http://www.nationaljournal.com/next-economy/america-360/is-dan-gilbert-detroit-s-new-superhero-20140227; Corey Williams, "Detroit Seeing Uptick in Conventions, Visitors," *Washington Times*, January 29, 2014, http://www.washingtontimes.com/news/2014/jan/29/visitors-bureau-reports-uptick-in-conventions/; Nick Carey, "Detroit Blight Fought By Resident Volunteers in Grandmont Rosedale Neighborhood," *Huffington Post*, July 2, 2013, http://www.huffingtonpost.com/2013/07/03/detroit-blight-grandmont-rosedale_n_3537270.html; Eric Lacy, "Detroit's New Challenge: Tear Down 50 Blighted Homes with 60-Day Crowdfunding Campaign Dollars," *Michigan Live*, March 15, 2014, http://www.mlive.com/news/detroit/index.ssf/2014/03/detroits_new_challenge_tear_do.html; David Muller, "Detroit Blight Authority's Bill Pulte Named to Forbes '30 Under

30,'" *Michigan Live*, January 7, 2014, http://www.mlive.com/business/ detroit/index.ssf/2014/01/detroit_blight_authoritys_bill.html; Jillian Kay Melchior, "Battling Blight in Detroit," *National Review Online*, March 6, 2013, http://www.nationalreview.com/articles/342267/battling-blight-detroit -jillian-kay-melchior/page/0/3; Joann Muller, "Bill Pulte: From Home Builder to Detroit's Unlikely Blight Buster," *Forbes*, October 9, 2013, http://www.forbes.com/sites/joannmuller/2013/10/09/bill-pulte-detroits -unlikely-blight-buster/; and Kirk Pinho, "Blight Authority Targets Additional 21-Block Area of Brightmoor," *Crain's Detroit Business*, January 20, 2014, http://www.crainsdetroit.com/article/20140120/NEWS/140129996/ blight-authority-targets-additional-21-block-area-of-brightmoor.

Index

About the Author

PAUL RYAN is the United States Representative for Wisconsin's 1st Congressional District and current chairman of the Ways and Means Committee. He was the Republican Party nominee for Vice President of the United States in the 2012 election.

ABOUT TWELVE

TWELVE was established in August 2005 with the objective of publishing no more than twelve books each year. We strive to publish the singular book, by authors who have a unique perspective and compelling authority. Works that explain our culture; that illuminate, inspire, provoke, and entertain. We seek to establish communities of conversation surrounding our books. Talented authors deserve attention not only from publishers, but from readers as well. To sell the book is only the beginning of our mission. To build avid audiences of readers who are enriched by these works—that is our ultimate purpose.

For more information about forthcoming TWELVE books, please go to www.twelvebooks.com.